WITHDRAWN

Conversations with Reynolds Price

Literary Conversations Series

Peggy Whitman Prenshaw
General Editor

Conversations
with Reynolds Price

Edited by
Jefferson Humphries

University Press of Mississippi
Jackson and London

Books by Reynolds Price

A Long and Happy Life. New York: Atheneum, 1962. Novel.
The Names and Faces of Heroes. New York: Atheneum, 1963. Stories.
A Generous Man. New York: Atheneum, 1966. Novel.
Love and Work. New York: Atheneum, 1968. Novel.
Permanent Errors. New York: Atheneum, 1970. Stories.
Things Themselves. New York: Atheneum, 1972. Essays, Sketches, and Scenes.
The Surface of Earth. New York: Atheneum, 1975. Novel.
Early Dark. New York: Atheneum, 1977. Play.
A Palpable God. New York: Atheneum, 1978. Essay and Translations.
The Source of Light. New York: Atheneum, 1981. Novel.
Vital Provisions. New York: Atheneum, 1982. Poems.
Mustian. New York: Atheneum, 1983. Two Novels and a Story.
Private Contentment. New York: Atheneum, 1984. Play.
Kate Vaiden. New York: Atheneum, 1986. Novel.
The Laws of Ice. New York: Atheneum, 1986. Poems.
A Common Room: Essays 1954–1987. New York: Atheneum, 1987.
Good Hearts. New York: Atheneum, 1988. Novel.
Clear Pictures. New York: Atheneum, 1989. Memoir.
The Tongues of Angels. New York: Atheneum, 1990. Novel.
New Music. New York: Theatre Communications Group, 1990. Plays.
The Use of Fire. New York: Atheneum, 1990. Poems.
The Foreseeable Future. New York: Atheneum, 1991. Stories.

Copyright © 1991 by the University Press of Mississippi
Reynolds Price's text copyright © 1991 by Reynolds Price
All rights reserved
Manufactured in the United States of America
94 93 92 91 4 3 2 1
The paper in this book meets the guidelines for permanence and durability of the Committee on Production Guidelines for Book Longevity of the Council on Library Resources.

Library of Congress Cataloging-in-Publication Data

Price, Reynolds, 1933–
    Conversations with Reynolds Price / edited by Jefferson Humphries.
        p.   cm.—(Literary conversations series)
    Includes index.
    ISBN 0-87805-482-0 (alk. paper).—ISBN 0-87805-483-9 (pbk. : alk. paper)
    1. Price, Reynolds, 1933–   —Interviews. 2. Novelists, American—20th century—Interviews. I. Humphries, Jefferson, 1955–
        II. Title. III. Series.
PS3566.R54Z466   1991
813'.54—dc20
                                                          90-49284
                                                            CIP

British Library Cataloguing-in-Publication data available

Contents

v

Contents

Introduction

In the interview which I did with him, Reynolds Price compares writing (anything, not just fiction) to singing opera, quoting his friend, the soprano Leontyne Price, as having said of a particularly difficult aria, "Shoot, either you can sing it or you can't; if you can you just get up and do it." So much for writers who excuse nonproduction as a case of high standards. He might have said the same of *speaking*, for Reynolds Price is as meticulous, and as comfortable, with the spoken word as he is with the written. This fact will be apparent in every one of the interviews in this book.

Price has shown himself, through the various stages of his career, ready to discuss the sources (real and literary) of any work, its evolution, the way in which it was written—to Phyllis Meras, for example, of *A Generous Man*: "It was late in 1963. Lying in bed one night, in the sleepless, wasteful wake of John Kennedy's death, I suddenly remembered two separate anecdotes I had known for some time and thought were funny," or to Daniel Voll, about the character Rosacoke Mustian, invented before *A Long and Happy Life* for the story "A Chain of Love": "On a Sunday afternoon when I was a senior, I went with a Brazilian friend to Howard Johnson's for lunch . . . I was sitting there, and suddenly this lovely girl walked in with her boyfriend and sat at the ice-cream counter. She was in her church dress, and she just immediately threw me back into my own adolescence in rural North Carolina. I instantly knew a whole story about her and who she was." Price has been willing to speak his mind about virtually anything, including his critics (to John Baker): "I don't like to see reviewers and writers getting so seriously involved"; (to Wallace Kaufman) "What critics usually mean in calling a writer's prose 'mannered' is that the manner is not their manner"); his "second" occupation, that of teacher: "I think, on balance, teaching has been very important to me, and I consider it part of my work"; writers he admires and those whose influence he has felt, "from

Stephen Spender to W. H. Auden to Eudora Welty to John Updike, Bernard Malamud, Toni Morrison"; and the state of American and southern political and literary culture: "I know that some southern writers slightly older than I have a vested interest in denying that there is anything new or interesting or certainly anything that matches the unquestioned high quality of Faulkner or Welty . . . I disagree" (Humphries interview).

He seems extraordinarily and copiously frank, though the reader looking for any detailed disclosure of Price's private life will not find it. Anyone interested in a sense of the writer as a man, or more precisely as a living *voice,* with the inevitable high and low moments, will find that. Price expressed in his interview with me a certain anxiety that he might have been too glib in some of these pages: "I would hate to be faced with a heavenly record of everything I've ever done or said, especially in interviews which are so frequently given when one's exhausted or angry or bored by the interviewer or appalled by one's own ignorance in the face of a given question . . ." This isn't an exhaustive record, much less a heavenly one, but it does present a large portion of Price's transcribed voice, mostly unedited.

His interviews, like his work, may be said to fall into three categories: the "Mustian" years (1962–1966), when *A Long and Happy Life, The Names and Faces of Heroes,* and *A Generous Man* were published; the "stoic" period, 1968–1981, during which *Permanent Errors, Love and Work, The Surface of Earth* and its companion volume, *The Source of Light,* appeared (the last is a transitional work, pointing to the next stage); and finally the most recent years, since Price's 1984 bout with a spinal tumor (a malignant but non-metastasizing astrocytoma) which left him confined to a wheelchair. Lately he has produced what many critics judge to be his finest and most accessible work: *Kate Vaiden* and *Good Hearts.* By far the bulk of these interviews come from the latter two periods of Price's career, though during both he frequently looks back to the earliest work. I might best frame the interviews in a useful context by relating them, in terms of these stages, to Price's work. Often here discussion of a particular work takes place during a period subsequent to that in which the work was written and published; this is less true of works after *A Generous Man* than of those before. Until the most recent period, Price's interviews deal exclusively with literary concerns, or closely related issues; except for the often repeated description of his writing habits, anecdotal reminiscences of childhood family life or experiences as a college student, and discussion of his career as a university teacher, his personal life only becomes a subject of discussion after his illness and surgery in 1984. This book might best be read as an autobiography of Price's literary persona, until the most recent interviews, since about 1986, when he began to be asked a good deal about the illness, and more purely personal information emerges.

By the time he had begun to be interviewed seriously, he was finishing up the "Mustian" period; there are only a couple of interviews here from this early phase, and they come from the end of it, the time of the publication of *A Generous Man*. Of *A Long and Happy Life*, he says in his interview with the student literary magazine *Ariel*: "I think *A Long and Happy Life* was popular for a while for a lot of the wrong reasons—because people thought it was a nice love story; they failed to see that it was a bitterer pill than that." He has long been thought, by many who know him well and many who don't, to have identified with the novel's heroine. This he has both admitted ("Rosacoke, c'est moi . . .") and strenuously denied, insisting that it is Rosacoke Mustian's overwhelming desire to pin down the hapless Wesley Beavers that closes their youth prematurely, putting an end which Wesley neither deserved nor wanted to his simple and freewheeling pleasures and plunging the both of them into the narrow strictures of rural conjugal existence. In the interview with Constance Rooke he says: "Wesley is just in the process of sowing the last of his rather sparse wild oats, and Rosacoke is doing that common thing women do—trying to slow a man down faster than the man himself wants to slow." One can't help feeling, however, that Price's often rather harsh statements about Rosacoke, and his at times surprising defense of Wesley, are sentiments which the writer did not have to such an extent at the time their story was written. What can be said about his first published book is that it reflects a preoccupation with love, with the difficult vagaries of desire between two humans, that runs through all of Price's work, and all of these interviews. But the early work is always seen from the vantage point of the later, and this means that Price usually discusses the first

books (implicitly or explicitly) at a distance from his thoughts while
writing them, sometimes in terms of their relation to later work, and
the fact that critics have often misunderstood that relation, or anecdo-
tally, in terms of the circumstances in which they were initially conceived or executed. They are never an immediate concern.

In *The Names and Faces of Heroes,* Price published a number of
stories which had actually been written before *A Long and Happy
Life,* with one exception, that of the title story of the collection. He
alludes in the interview with Daniel Voll, from the late middle period
of his career, to the genesis of one of the stories ("A Chain of Love")
which was written during his last year as a student at Duke, and in
the interview with me, from the most recent period, he talks about
how Elizabeth Bowen, while visiting a writing class at Duke, told him
how to revise "Michael Egerton," the only one of the stories he
says he completed before his stint at Oxford. "It was at Oxford," he
tells John Baker late in the middle or "stoic" period, "that I did my
first good stories"—by which he apparently includes rewriting earlier
ones—"and where I first began to be taken seriously as a writer." *A
Long and Happy Life* was originally included in the book of stories
that would become *The Names and Faces of Heroes*; it was Hiram
Haydn, Price's editor at Atheneum, which had just been started up,
who decided that it ought to be published as a separate book first.
Haydn had read Price's first story, published by Stephen Spender in
Encounter, and signed him to a contract for a first book of stories
while Haydn was still at Random House. By the time the manuscript
came in, Haydn had left Random, and Jason Epstein rejected the
manuscript of stories—which included *A Long and Happy Life*—
vehemently, according to Haydn in his memoirs. So the book went
to Haydn at Atheneum. "Hiram and Pat [Knopf, with Haydn and
Simon Michael Bessie one of the founding editors of Atheneum] kept
postponing it until the astrological moons were right," Price tells
Baker. "It was fortunate they did, because eventually John Fischer
heard about it and published it in *Harper's.*" Some of these early
stories are as much sketches as stories (which I do not intend as a
criticism): "Uncle Grant" and "The Warrior Princess Ozimba" read
like loosely fictionalized, autobiographical vignettes; the title story,
even, seems highly autobiographical—William Ray says as much, in
his middle-period interviews with Price, and RP does not contradict

him, though he is usually quick to insist, as to Wallace Kaufman, that "more than 99 percent" of all his characters "were invented from the ground up."

Price's third book, A Generous Man, is one of the most revealing of all, and the first one about which he talks in this book as a more or less immediate concern, as the one most recently written and published. It narrates three short days in the life of Rosacoke's brother, Milo, who is older than she so that the action of the book is situated earlier than that of A Long and Happy Life. The narration is rather grandly and evidently allegorical, described by Price to Kaufman as not a novel so much as a romance, like Nathaniel Hawthorne's fictions, resembling "only—in kind, understand—the late plays of Shakespeare (The Tempest, The Winter's Tale, Cymbeline), certain operas (say, The Magic Flute of Mozart) in that it does negotiate with the 'real world' . . . but a real world which is capable of swelling at moments of intensity to a mysterious, transfigured world, a world in which all manner of 'unrealistic' events can and will occur—the return of the dead, outrageous coincidence, great rushes of communication between people, great avowals of love or hate—events which I suspect, almost know to lie only slightly beneath the surface of the world of most men." This quality of the novel, what Price calls here its unrealism or surrealism (in the sense of more real than the real), makes it one of the best places to start reading him, because that quality is present in everything he has ever written. Price discusses with Kaufman, Ray, and me his recurring use of the supernatural; he may in fact have introduced "magic realism" to American fiction before Marquez and company were translated into English.

Some of the same critics who saw A Long and Happy Life as a simple and simply charming love story were upset by what appeared to them as a turn toward pessimism, toward a bleaker vision, in Love and Work and Permanent Errors. This was a concern to Price at the beginning of the middle period, when these books were written and published, the time of the last part of his interview with Wallace Kaufman. He tells Kaufman that "Love and Work did constitute a violent break with a number of the procedures of my earlier work—at least, a number of readers found it a very baffling change of signal." But note the word he uses: "procedures." Price insisted that if anything had changed, it was not the vision so much as the style, the "procedures"—the writing and the way he presented his characters and his settings. That change had to do with two stylistic influences which Price talked about a little later to William Ray: Milton and, particularly, the Bible. "Just in the last two or three years I've been returning to the Bible in a way which I think has really been important in the fiction that I'm writing now. I've been doing a series of translations into very literal, very plain twentieth-century English prose of short narrative passages from the Old and New Testaments—really attempting to learn, or relearn, something about the bare bones of narrative."

The difficulty of *Permanent Errors,* really of all Price's work, but more evidently of *PE* and what follows, is not a difficulty of understanding. The writing is clear, if dense. What is hard is the unyielding reality transcribed, the sense that the smallest, the most apparently inconsequential human act, pursued without reflection, has consequences which may be immense and in any case are irreversible. This vision, so central to all Price's work, and so evident in these interviews, is as biblical and Miltonic as the language in which it is expressed: "At times he [God] is absent or stands, face averted. Creatures are left at the mercy of creatures; they die in agony, no hint of reward." Also: "Some wounds, though made by mere creatures, never heal: we are dreadfully free." The kind and subtle ambiguity of *A Long and Happy Life,* which made it possible for some readers to understand the title as benediction rather than ominous irony, is no longer available.

The latter two citations are from Price's essay in *A Palpable God,* and they make clear his own, essentially spiritual justification for stories that don't end happily, that are essentially tragic. "Only the story which declares our total incurable abandonment is repugnant and will not be heard for long." To the question why this should be so, Price replies, "Because such claims are literally intolerable for long." His narratives, if they never deliver the quick fix, the happy resolution—the happy resolution, that is, without ambiguous clouds hovering on the horizon—never tell us that we are abandoned. We are far less alone than we know or see. Price says in his interview with me that "I couldn't imagine being a writer or an artist of any sort if I weren't also a person whose bedrock beliefs are founded upon a powerful and traditionally Christian sense of the structure of reality."

As for the most recent period, what we get in Price's work is perhaps a mellower, less stern enactment of the same vision. The interviews of this period—post-1984—are in some ways the best: they show a voice which has fought great battles personal and physical, and which has achieved a firm, calm peace with its own gifts and limitations. Price's bout with cancer could have embittered and stymied him, but it did the opposite: "I am approaching," he said to me in 1986, "the second anniversary of the discovery of that condition and of the surgery and treatment to combat it. I have done, however—once I recovered from the initial shock and depression—more writing in the past two years than I've done in any other two-year period of my life." After 1984, there is a gentleness, I would almost say a humility, in what Price says about certain subjects, that was not there before. His opinions may not change in any essential way, but his manner of expressing them does, and this seems to alter the content. In Constance Rooke's interview, after the publication of *The Surface of Earth,* there is a virtual testiness, a near sarcasm in some of the answers Price gives, as for instance in this exchange: "I think in fact that *The Surface of Earth* ought to become a kind of feminist textbook." Rooke asks why, and he continues: "Because, to be utterly modest about it, I can't think of a novel written for years that says more about women than *The Surface of Earth.*" Contrast this with what he said to me, almost ten years later, on a similar subject: "I think our [men's and women's] knowledge of one another is simply there, waiting. It's a common room which we inhabit, and it's waiting to be used by each of the genders." Or contrast, in the same two interviews, how Price expresses similar opinions about the institution of marriage: to me in 1986 he said "I think marriage is one of the most difficult of balancing acts to bring off." To Rooke he had said "married love in the American middle- and upper-middle classes is becoming a near impossibility." The difference is subtle, but striking, the fine but crucial line between "difficult" and "impossible." That sort of difference exists between all the interviews of the second period and the most recent one, and I would say there is the same subtle difference between the work of those two periods. It is why *The Surface of Earth* (1975), while perhaps his grandest, most ambitious work, and one in which all his technical literary resources are at full power, may not be as appealing or as successful as *Kate Vaiden* or *Good Hearts*.

It is often true of the interviews of this last period that Price is not much interested in commenting on his earliest work, even though he might be better situated to do so than ever. He says in my interview that "For me to stand up now and read pages from *A Long and Happy Life* is about as exciting as reading you an excerpt from my high-school yearbook. I like the book but I certainly don't feel any longer like the man who wrote it; I don't have any specially proprietary sense about it. I'm always far more interested in what I'm doing now or have just done."

Since the appearance in 1986 of *Kate Vaiden,* which won the National Book Critics Circle Award, Price has become something of a media darling, written up in *Vanity Fair* and *People* and turning up on network television. The media, and many of the interviewers of this time, often seem more fascinated by the story of Price's illness than by specifically literary issues or questions, and he obliges them by talking frankly about the experience.

Also since 1984, Price has worked more in other genres than fiction: plays, poetry, even a memoir, a sort of writing which he had indicated in earlier interviews he would or could not write. The interviews from these recent years reflect the increasing eclecticism of the work. As he began to work on the memoir in the late eighties—it would be published in 1989—he also talks a little more about the private aspects of his early life which is that work's subject, but in fact, allusions to persons and events that would turn up in the memoir are scattered throughout these interviews.

In the interviews as in the books, throughout Price's life and work, between the life and work, despite the nuances of evolution, there is a remarkable consistency. His own routine as a writer, described to William Ray, despite many other circumstantial changes, including being confined to a wheelchair, has never varied much: "I sleep eight hours every night. . . . I have breakfast and then I sort of putter around the house for half an hour . . . warming up, and then I go into the study and just begin to write; with brief pauses for cups of coffee and listening to the news on the radio or something, I will work from perhaps nine or ten o'clock until noon. And then I will shave and dress, then drive into campus, where I have my mailbox, and get the mail and eat lunch . . . I always take Sundays completely off . . . Boring as it is, that's the way I do it." He also said to Ray, as he would undoubtedly say now, that the concerns of his fiction have remained much the same, despite outward appearances of difference: "I think in many ways there's a combination in *The Surface of the Earth* of the kinds of materials and the kinds of relations to those materials which were visible in the books before, say, *Love and Work* . . . In fact, . . . as you know, I never saw a sharp break in the work. . . ." There is no sharp break in the work or the interviews, despite the evolution I have described above in both, which Price says he "didn't see . . . because I was very conscious of having been *me* the whole time . . ." What runs through all his interviews, fiction, poetry and plays is what RP professed to me and my classmates at Duke some fourteen years ago, as much by example as by eloquence, a lesson which he says he got from reading Hemingway: "the lessons of one master, diffidently but desperately offered— Prepare, strip, divest for life that awaits you; learn solitude and work; see how little is lovely but love that."

As with the other books in the Literary Conversations series, the interviews are reprinted as they originally appeared. They come from the pages of literary quarterlies, student literary journals, newspapers and magazines. The one I conducted has never appeared before, and the ones with William Ray were published in one volume, now out of print, as a number of the *Mississippi Valley Collection Bulletin* (Memphis State University). I have tried to include every interview of any substance, excluding only those which are not really interviews but brief newspaper articles based loosely on interviews and those which seemed too insubstantial or too purely repetitious of other interviews. But since Price's preoccupations and opinions vary little throughout the thirty year span of his writing career, the considerable repetition is inevitable. Still, no two interviews are exactly alike, and each one adds to the portrait of Price that emerges.

I would like to thank Reynolds Price for his active cooperation and assistance with work on this book; special thanks are due Seetha Srinivasan and Ginger Tucker for their patience and help in the editing process, and Hunter Cole for bringing together this project

and the University Press of Mississippi. Harriet Wasserman, RP's
agent, was also helpful with many different aspects of the book.

JH
May 1990

Chronology

1933   William Solomon Price and Elizabeth Rodwell Price have their first child, Edward Reynolds, on February 1, in Macon, North Carolina.

1947   The family moves to Raleigh, North Carolina. RP attends Needham Broughton High School in Raleigh.

1951   RP graduates from Broughton High and enters Duke University as an A.B. Duke Scholar. While at Duke, RP meets Eudora Welty and serves as editor of the student literary magazine, *The Archive*.

1955   RP graduates from Duke Phi Beta Kappa, summa cum laude. Wins a Rhodes scholarship and enters Merton College, Oxford University.

1958   RP receives B.Litt. degree from Oxford, and his story, "A Chain of Love" is published by Stephen Spender in *Encounter*. He is appointed to an instructorship at Duke University. Hiram Haydn, then an editor at Random House, signs Price to a contract for a first book.

1958–60   RP works on *A Long and Happy Life*. Jason Epstein rejects the manuscript of stories which includes *ALHL*. Hiram Haydn, now one of the founding editors at Atheneum, accepts the manuscript and advises Price to publish *ALHL* separately, as a novel.

1961–62   Price returns to England to write and travel.

1962   *A Long and Happy Life* is first published in a special
            issue of *Harper's* through the efforts of Hiram Haydn,
            and then by Atheneum. The novel is greeted by
            effusive critical praise.

1963   RP receives the William Faulkner Foundation Award
            for *A Long and Happy Life*. His first collection of
            stories, *The Names and Faces of Heroes,* is published.

1964   RP receives a fellowship from the Guggenheim
            Foundation.

1965   RP is named writer-in-residence at University of North
            Carolina.

1966   *A Generous Man* is published.

1967   RP receives a fellowship from the National Endow-
            ment for the Arts and is writer-in-residence at the
            University of Kansas.

1968   *Love and Work* is published.

1969   Price is again writer-in-residence at the University of
            Kansas.

1970   RP's second collection of stories, *Permanent Errors,* is
            published.

1971   RP is writer-in-residence at University of North Caro-
            lina at Greensboro and Glasgow Professor at Wash-
            ington and Lee University.

1972   Price is promoted to full professor at Duke. *Things
            Themselves,* a collection of "essays, sketches, and
            scenes," is published.

1975   *The Surface of Earth* is published.

1977   *Early Dark,* a play based on *A Long and Happy Life,*
            is published. RP is named James B. Duke Professor
            of English.

1978   RP receives an honorary doctorate from St. Andrew's
            Presbyterian College. *A Palpable God,* a long essay
            and translations from the Bible, is published.

1979   RP receives an honorary doctorate from Wake Forest
            University.

1981   *The Source of Light,* a sequel to *The Surface of
            Earth,* is published.

1982   *Vital Provisions,* a collection of poems, is published.

1983   Atheneum publishes *Mustian,* a volume containing
            the story "A Chain of Love," *A Long and Happy
            Life,* and *A Generous Man.*

1984   *Private Contentment,* a play commissioned by PBS
            for the American Playhouse series, is published by
            Atheneum. Price is stricken by a spinal astrocytoma, a
            malignant tumor on his spinal cord, treatment for
            which is successful but results in paraplegia. Hendrix
            College commissions RP to write a play for its drama
            students.

1985   *August Snow* is completed in January and produced
            at Hendrix College in the fall. Price completes drafts
            of two more plays, *Night Dance* and *Better Days,*
            which with *August Snow* make the dramatic trilogy
            New Music.

1986   *Kate Vaiden,* Price's most critically acclaimed book
            since *A Long and Happy Life,* is published. It receives
            the National Book Critics Circle Award for Fiction.
            The Laws of Ice, a second volume of poems, appears.

1987   *A Common Room,* RP's collected essays, is pub-
            lished.

1988   *Good Hearts,* a novel of Rosacoke Mustian and
            Wesley Beavers in middle age, is published.

1989   *Clear Pictures,* a memoir, is published. Price's trilogy
            of plays, *New Music,* is produced by the Cleveland
            Play House with significant support from the Fund for
            New American Plays.

1990   *The Tongues of Angels,* a novel, *The Use of Fire,*
            poems, and *New Music,* a trilogy of plays, are pub-
            lished.

1991   *The Foreseeable Future,* a collection of long stories, is
            published.

Conversations with Reynolds Price

Talk with Reynolds Price
Phyllis Meras/1966

From *The New York Times Book Review*, 27 March 1966, 44.
Copyright © 1966 by New York Times Company. Reprinted by
permission of *The New York Times* and Reynolds Price.

The author of the newly published *A Generous Man* lives alone in a
recently purchased nine-room brick and timber house on a beech-
wooded hill between Durham and Chapel Hill, N.C., teaches English
for a semester each year at Duke University, and writes novels with
themes that come to him in such disparate environments as the art
museum in The Hague and restless nights in his own bed in Durham.
It was on one such night, he said recently, that he first had the idea
for *A Generous Man*.

"It was late in 1963. Lying in bed one night, in the sleepless,
wasteful wake of John Kennedy's death, I suddenly remembered two
separate anecdotes I had known for some time and thought were
funny. I think I even laughed aloud, and suddenly I saw a way of
joining the two anecdotes by telling them through the Mustians, the
fictional family I had invented in an early short story, "A Chain of
Love," and used again in my earlier novel, *A Long and Happy Life*.

"As I thought more about the new story, and began planning it,
it seemed to me that it would be quite short—perhaps 70 pages—
and basically a rural farce. It was, I thought at first, going to be simply
a sort of cheering up of myself and a close friend in the face of that
awful time."

But as Mr. Price recalls it, the story rapidly took its own head.
Soon, it was writing itself in a way that no previous work of his had.

"I have never been one of those 'writing is fun' people. Writing has
never been a pleasure for me, but this time I was writing with great
delight—accepting the tumult of story and characters as they came.
But it was by no means automatic writing." Indeed, for all its beginning as a farce, Mr. Price soon discovered that his book was intensely
concerned with "perpetually urgent matters—youth and joy and the
relation of age to youth."

"It really seemed to me as I worked that this was a new kind of novel," he said, brushing a hand through dark, wavy hair, "that it was a novel which took as its premise situations that were patently absurd—escaped snakes and mad dogs and impotent sheriffs—but that, as it grew, it became a deadly serious book, not a farce at all. The farce proved to be—as farce often does in life—gravely revealing. If I had to describe the book in one phrase, I guess I'd call it—today, at least—a 'somber comedy.' "

Mr. Price's first short stories grew out of the death of his father, which occurred while he himself was a student at Duke, but he denies that his writing is autobiographical.

"It's agonizingly difficult to write both autobiographically and truthfully, you know, because then you must encounter yourself directly and entirely. It's far more possible to encounter only 20 per cent of you than all of you. Only very occasionally and fragmentarily do I write autobiographically. My ideas come from all sorts of places, generally an exterior fact or object will precipitate an interior crystallization—like those anecdotes that started A Generous Man or the Vermeer painting in The Hague that began A Long and Happy Life. It's a picture of a pregnant girl in blue, at a window reading a letter, and with a map behind her."

He writes slowly. "If I veer wrong and take the story or a character up to a dead end for more than three pages, it's almost impossible to reverse and steer it aright. So I proceed very warily, testing the ground every inch of the way. But, of course, there are dangers in writing slowly. The chief danger for me is that since I, myself, change as time passes, I may begin with one book and end two years later with another. All the same, I can't accelerate any more than I can permanently accelerate my heart, and I've stopped trying. I rewrite very little—not at all in the sense of separate drafts of a whole work. Maybe because I grew up in the Depression and the war and was constantly told to wear out my clothes and eat up my food.

"How do I write? I do page one, and then when that's right—after a day or a week or a month—I do page two. The danger to this, of course, is overcooking. But there are possible virtues, too—a gaze so steady and entire and broad and deep as to leave nothing unconsidered, even if not comprehended."

Notice, I'm Still Smiling: Reynolds Price

Wallace Kaufman/1966

From *Shenandoah*, 17:4 (Summer 1966), 70–95. Reprinted
by permission of *Shenandoah* and Reynolds Price.

Reynolds Price was born in 1933 and educated at Duke University and
Merton College, Oxford, where he was a Rhodes Scholar. He now lives in
Durham, North Carolina, and teaches at Duke.

His novels have attracted high praise and have been widely reprinted and
translated into several languages. His first novel, *A Long and Happy Life*,
appeared in 1962. The next year *The Names and Faces of Heroes* appeared. *A Generous Man* was published in 1966 and *Love and Work* in
1968. *Late Warning* (poems) came out in 1968 also. *Permanent Errors*
(stories) appeared in 1970 and *Things Themselves* (essays) in 1972. His
short stories have been published in *Shenandoah*, *Red Clay Reader*, the
Southern Review, *Esquire*, and other magazines.

The best interview is a conversation, and the best conversation is one that
does not end but lives on as its participants live on, finding new ideas and
changing old ones. This is also the kind of conversation that cannot be fully
recorded. What follows, therefore, is not so much a thing in itself but
evidence of something—evidence of the nature of one writer's mind.

The first part of this conversation was recorded in May, 1966. I begin it by
looking back to even earlier conversations. The second part is from January,
1970. These pages added up are samples of eleven years of conversation.

I

From a grove of gray beech trees Reynolds Price's house looks over
a small pond. In mid-January five years ago when Reynolds lived in a
trailer on the other side of the pond, I was out on the new ice,
skating figures. Reynolds sat on the hard-crusted snow, watching
because he had never in his life lived outside North Carolina (except
for three years as a Rhodes Scholar in England) and had a Southerner's fear of ice. But when coming down from a miscalculated leap I
fell and struck my head so hard the ice cracked, he jumped up to
rescue me. He slipped on the snow crust, went down on his back and

5

threw his shoulder out of joint. So when I came to and looked through the blood from my forehead, he was lying on the snow, his arm bent behind him as if no longer attached. I pulled his arm back in place, he cleaned and bound my wound and for five minutes we laughed like lunatics.

Literally and figuratively we have been doing that for seven years, kind of a Laurel and Hardy friendship. Price was born in Macon, North Carolina, brought up in Asheboro, rural Warren County, and Raleigh—a lonely kid who was never an athlete but whose earliest hero was Tarzan. I met him at Duke his second year of teaching, my second as a student. Brought up in New York City and on Long Island, I had come down to Duke to get nearer a girl in Alabama, for a good scholarship, to play soccer and wrestle. And to write poetry, which had been my hidden work since sixth grade.

So now, in May, 1966, I am pulling up his driveway with a tape recorder on the engine box of the van, coming with a batch of questions I am going to ask and thinking I know what kind of answers I'll get. I began getting the answers when Reynolds, advising student writers, said he thought I should work more on my visualized writing, images which were hard and clear and blunt. He was not far from his own real beginnings as a writer. It was just the year before, 1958, that the English magazine *Encounter* gave him his first publication by printing the long story, "A Chain of Love." The advising session was seven years ago, Reynolds was talking about poetry, and I was a stranger.

I have to shift into first to get up the first slope of the drive. The rain has washed away much of the bluestone dumped last month. The drive crosses a small brook, turns in front of the low dark brick house and turns again to pass under the side carport into a gravel parking area. I park beside the Mercedes sedan which is disguised by a coating of red dust and oil from the dirt roads near the house. I haul out the recorder and go to the back door.

"You almost hit my car," Reynolds yells coming out. (He has had two wrecks in the past year, both in his own yard.) He is standing on a brick patio I engineered for him last summer. Behind him are the big plate-glass windows which make one wall of the living room and look out on the beech grove behind the house and the pasture beyond that.

Inside, the first thing I do is see what is new. I was here last week but there has to be a new picture, a Noh mask, a fossil, book, or lamp. Today it is a sun-bleached cow vertebra hung on the brick chimney wall. So before I even plug in the recorder I'm asking, "Where did the cow come from?"

"Let me finish the coffee before you start the interview, Buster," Reynolds says from the kitchen.

I go to the birch-paneled wall opposite the windows. There are twenty or thirty nicely framed pictures on this wall—the "new" things Reynolds has been collecting item by item since he was a student at Oxford in the mid-fifties. He spends almost everything he makes, even in today's relative affluence, buying what he likes. These pictures I'm looking at are mostly etchings—a series of three from Blake's *Job*, two of Rembrandt's Abraham and Isaac etchings, two Malliol nudes; then a drawing by Graham Sutherland, two Sidney Nolan illustrations from Price's story "Uncle Grant," a small oil by Philip Sutton, a large Picasso aquatint of a satyr unblanketing a sleeping nymph. I suppose it is a conservative collection—no pop art, no abstract expressionism. But it is not for the sake of prestige, for there are also the unknowns—an English girl's pencil drawing of an apple sprig, a small rather conventional eighteenth-century English landscape in oil, a watercolor of a sick child in bed (by Arthur Severn, son of Keats's Severn). There is nothing you could call topical or timely, only the television in one corner of the room, and this, I know, is well used—every night for news, often for documentaries and sometimes for the latest serial.

Reynolds comes in with the coffee tray and unloads the cups, sugar, cream, and a coffee cake while I get the recorder wired up.

When we sit down and I start the reels, we are laughing so hard I have to turn the machine off and drink some coffee. Then we start.

Interviewer: When we first met in 1959 I was writing poetry and you were working on a short story that became your first novel. But you started in high school and college by writing poems, didn't you?

Price: To be accurate, the first things I wrote were plays. When I was in the eighth grade, I wrote a Christmas play about the Magi; and at some point I wrote a play called *The Jewels of Isabella* about Columbus and Queen Isabella of Spain and then a screenplay for an

eight millimeter neighborhood version of the life of Bernadette
Soubirous (never produced; funds unavailable). But yes, the first
things that I wrote, thinking of myself as a writer, were poems, in the
third year of high school in Raleigh, in the class of Phyllis Peacock.
Looking back on those poems now—which I don't do nightly—the
interesting thing about them—bad as they were—is that they were,
almost all, poems about *people*; poems proceeding from my relations
with people who held large places in my life—a girl named Jane
Savage, another girl dying of leukemia, my parents, Marian Ander-
son, who first excited my interest in music. A great many novelists
have tried to begin as poets; but if one looks back at those early
poems, one generally finds tired Swinburnean lyrics.

Interviewer: What made you give up writing poetry? Can you see
some basic difference between the way you think and see now that
makes you write prose instead of poetry?

Price: The chief reason was that I knew the poems weren't any
good, as poems. I wrote poems on into the middle of my college
career; but by that time I had read enough good poetry in classes in
Elizabethan and seventeenth-century poetry, in Milton, Shakespeare,
and in a most important class in modern poetry taught by Helen
Bevington—Yeats and Eliot and Hopkins—to see very clearly that my
own verses were pale and loose. Only when I began to write narrative prose—to order, on class assignment—and had written a quantity of prose, did I begin to feel that this was my *intended* work, this
was my vocation; that verse could not be for me a means of examining my experience and controlling my experience, of understanding
and controlling my life in the way that prose has become. I don't
know why verse failed me—or I failed it. I often wonder; still try an
occasional poem for a friend's birthday, say; and I've done a good
deal of translation—Michelangelo, Hölderlin, Rimbaud. Perhaps
because a novelist's gift is for structural and visual stamina, not verbal
intensity.

Interviewer: And there was that poem we wrote together one
evening while you were doing *A Long and Happy Life*, the poem for
Rosacoke's unborn child?

Price: That's right. It's on the shelf here.

Interviewer: Read it. We might as well give it a first publication in
this interview.

Price: Reborn to light this day in late July
When blinded fields send up their cries for rain
As silent waves which break against the sky
Bleached blank of hope but what hope you may bring
(Who shuddered from your father's lonely joy
That autumn night when like a funeral ship
He shed you nameless to your mother's sea,
Which, opening, gave you passage through the dark
To where you were encrusted with her life
And stole the print and purpose of her years,
The beauty of her surface and, beneath,
The strength and movement of her secret tides).
We are the waves that break against your life,
In hope against the terror that we know.
The hope is that your living will be rain;
The terror, that your life is only blood
To dry like thousands under blinded fields.
But hope is like the love that caused your birth
And harbors in its heart the seed of death.
No life has yet achieved our general aim,
The circular continuance of rain.

Interviewer: It's not as good as the book; but going back to your change from poetry to prose, did you deliberately turn to prose when poetry failed or was prose something that *came* and then you discovered you were good at it?

Price: I don't think there was any deliberate turning. The first story I wrote was in my freshman year of college at Duke University in the class of the late Philip Williams. It was an advanced class of freshman composition, and we were allowed to write anything we wanted for our weekly themes. Almost all my themes were narratives—little episodes (mostly invented) from the lives of people my own age at the time, eighteen or so, or of children—which obviously was that time of life I knew best. The first piece of any consequence that I wrote was written in that class, a story which eventually was revised and became "Michael Egerton." At the same time I was writing those early prose pieces, I was continuing to write inadequate verses. But I didn't look upon the prose as an escape

route from the bad verse. I don't think at that time I'd realized quite
how bad the verse was because intelligent people were still telling me
that the verse was good. I suppose on looking back at it now, one
sees—hopes—that they weren't totally misled, that there was a
certain fascination with language visible through all the echoes, ar-
chaisms, and general metaphoric fatigue. Auden said once that if
a young man came to him and said he wished to be a poet and that
if Auden read his verses and felt they were empty of thought but
brilliant in language, he would feel that the man stood a chance of
becoming a poet but that if the verse were tired and unimaginative in
language but interesting in thought, there would be little chance of
that man's maturing as a poet.

Interviewer: So you began writing stories. Most reviewers now
consider you as a Southern writer. What do you think your relationship is to the first generation of modern Southern novelists? People
like Faulkner, Carson McCullers, Robert Penn Warren, Katherine
Anne Porter, and Eudora Welty?

Price: I would say that my relation to all those names, except
Eudora Welty, is a relationship of varied admiration and respect. But
a distant relation. Those were not the people I was reading when I
was young and formable. Those were not, and have not become, the
people I have returned to and read continually at moments of curiosity and leisure in my life. Faulkner, of course, is a special and
enormous case. All Southern writers who have written in the last
twenty years have had to bear the burden of being called Faulknerian. But the truth, if anyone is interested, is this, certainly and simply:
they write about the South, which is their home as well as Faulkner's.
Reviewers who lament the "influence" of Faulkner are really only
asking that all other Southern writers arrange to be born outside the
South. It is a curse, of a sort, to be born a writer in the same region
and at the same time as a great regional novelist. Imagine being born
in southwest England in the lifetime of Thomas Hardy and trying to
write your own novels about Wessex, the world that you also know.
You would have been cursed with being "influenced by Hardy" for
the rest of your life, called that at least. I am serious in speaking of "a
curse" only to the extent that the cry of Faulknerian influence has
become a conditioned reflex among literary journalists, even serious
critics; the application of influence labels being—as any college

English major knows—the easiest way to (a) write your 3,000 words and (b) avoid at all costs *facing* a work of art, its new vision, its new and necessarily terrible way of stating the injunction of Rilke's Apollo: "You must change your life!" I can say, quite accurately, that Faulkner has been no influence, technical or otherwise, on my work. I admire the work of Faulkner that I know—by no means all—but with a cold, distant admiration for a genius whom I know to be grand but who has proved irrelevant to my own obsessions, my own ambitions. The writer in your list who did affect me greatly, and continues to do so, is Eudora Welty. I had read a few of her stories in high school. I remember especially that "A Worm Path" was in one of our high school anthologies, but it was in my senior year in college that I read her stories in quantity. They were an instantaneous revelation and a revelation about my life, not about literature nor the methods and techniques of fiction. They revealed to me what is most essential for any beginning novelist—which is that his world, the world he has known from birth, the world that has not seemed to him in any way extraordinary is, in fact, a perfectly possible world, base, subject for serious fiction. I recognized in those stories of Eudora Welty's which I read as a senior in college a great many of the features of the world I had known as a child in rural eastern North Carolina, and so I felt confirmed by her example in the validity of my own experience as a source of art. That was her great service to me, and I shall always be grateful to her for that service she rendered me unknowingly, but most deeply grateful for the fact that she came to Duke to give a lecture—"Place in Fiction"—in the second semester of my senior year and kindly asked to see some student writing. One of my stories (the only serious story that I had written, "Michael Egerton") was given to her by William Blackburn. She read it, encouraged me, offered to send the story to her agent, Diarmuid Russell, who has since been my agent, and championed my work in the early years when no one in America was interested in publishing it. What she offered me was what any young writer demands in varying ways at various times in his career—adequate judgment. I knew that she was a sound judge; and I knew it because she was judging my work as *art*, not as the product of a favorite student or a friend. Her mind was filled with the example of her own work and all the work she had seen and read in her life, and she was still able to say to me what was utterly valuable, utterly meaningful at that time—that my story was a good story. Not "This is the best story by a college senior which I have read in the past five years," but "This is an excellent story. Let me see the rest of your stories." I said truthfully that there were no other stories because to that time I had only written eight pages of fiction; but at her request I very rapidly went to work and began writing another story—"A Chain of Love." And in the next three years, the years of my study at Oxford, I produced about a hundred pages of short stories, all of which were later published in a volume called *The Names and Faces of Heroes*.

Interviewer: What about the new Southern writers, your contemporaries like William Styron and Walker Percy, Fred Chappell and Shirley Ann Grau? Do you read these people conscientiously? Are you conscious of them as Southern writers?

Price: I read them because I think they are serious writers but very different writers. I feel no duty to read them because they are in any sense "fellow Southern novelists." I have never felt myself a "Southern novelist." I am a novelist—who was reared and has lived most of his life in the South. Insofar as the South is a unique world, my work reflects that uniqueness; but my work is not, has never been *about* the South. Some of the agrarians in the 20's, early 30's may have thought of themselves briefly as "Southern"; but I don't think it's been the feeling of anyone in the last twenty years, not any serious writer certainly. No, I read the writers you mentioned and two or three of them are friends of mine; but I don't feel that their work has any special relationship with my work. I don't feel any dialogue between my work and theirs, except that dialogue which exists between all honest artistry—a relationship not of imitation but of emulation. One reads good work and that good work invites not imitation but a parallel effort of quality.

Interviewer: Why do you still live in the South? You often make trips away from it. What does the South offer you as a writer? Does it offer you something culturally or something more intangible?

Price: Because the South is my home. It is where I was born. It is where I spent the first twenty-two years of my life and where I've spent the rest of my life with the exception of four years in Europe. The South is a place; and that place has been the scene of most of the crucial events of my life, both external and internal. Therefore I remain in that part of the world which has been—and seems likely to be—the site of my life.

Interviewer: Both your novels and the stories take place in the South, mainly in the area where you grew up. How close does the material in your fiction come to real people and real events? I guess what I'm asking is—to what degree are you a chronicler?

Price: Every character in the novels is invented; and even the stories which appear to be autobiographical are really a kind of historical fiction, a drastic arrangement, reinvention of memory. No, I have no sense of being a conscious chronicler—either of Southern life or of human life as I've known it in my lifetime, which has after all been an enormous time in human history (I was born in 1933). What I've chronicled is my own world, that world which has seemed to me (since I began to see at all) to exist *beneath* the world perceived by other people, that world which seems to me to impinge upon, to color, to shape, the daily world we inhabit.

Interviewer: Are the events and people in *A Generous Man* the events and people of a real world? A lot of reviewers have called it a myth and some of them suggest that many of the characters, especially Milo, are more in the nature of symbol than people.

Price: *A Generous Man* is about a very real world, yes; but it is not a realistic novel. If I must catalogue it, perhaps I'd call it a romance. If *A Generous Man* has literary ancestors, those ancestors are not really to be found in the novel but in other forms. I was not conscious of this when I began *A Generous Man* nor, in fact, until I had completed the novel; but in all the literature known to me, *A Generous Man* resembles only—in kind, understand—the late plays of Shakespeare (*The Tempest, The Winter's Tale, Cymbeline*), certain operas (say, *The Magic Flute* of Mozart) in that it does negotiate with the "real world" which all human beings perceive, however dull, however bored, however fogged by routine, but a real world which is capable of swelling at moments of intensity to a mysterious, transfigured world, a world in which all manner of "unrealistic" events can and will occur—the return of the dead, outrageous coincidence, great rushes of communication between people, great avowals of love or hate—events of a sort that do not occur in any world which I've experienced with my own eyes and ears but which I suspect, almost *know* to lie only slightly beneath the surface of the world of most men.

Interviewer: I'm not trying to push this symbol business; but I can see why a lot of people find them, especially in *A Generous Man*. Because it's not a realistic novel, people feel free to translate its images and events as they wish. The other night a man told me it was difficult to talk to women about the book because of "the all-pervasive phallic symbol of the snake." Of course symbols do exist, in writing and nature. To what extent, if any, are you ever conscious of symbols in your work?

Price: I am never conscious of symbols when I am planning a story nor when I am writing it. Any sense that certain objects have become symbolic—such as the python in *A Generous Man*, or, say, the deer in *A Long and Happy Life*—comes to me, if at all, only after the story is done and the whole can be seen. Python and deer were, for me, first—and indeed finally—python and deer, *things* grander in their own mysterious life than I or my characters could ever make them by meditation. More nonsense—criminal nonsense because it is generally inflicted by teachers on their innocent trusting students—is talked about symbols now than about any other single aspect of fiction, even "influence." And most of the nonsense can be attributed to two causes: first, as with "influence," it is far easier to take a little greased-rail side-track round the edges of a work, felling a harmless symbol or two, than to plunge through rock to its terrible core—that small clearing in the jungle which may be empty of all but a polished mirror; and second, that there is now a great deal of confusion about what a symbol is, how a thing becomes a symbol and—perhaps most important—*when* a thing becomes a symbol, so much confusion that I almost never use the word myself, least of all when I teach, and would be much happier if it could be retired for ten years, say, and replaced by "emblem." It seems to me that this many true things should be said—and distributed to every college freshman upon arrival: a symbol is a thing (though occasionally an intangible thing—fire, air) which one or more men make immanent with emotional, even spiritual significance. There are two kinds of symbols, private and public. Public symbols have traditional agreed significance for large numbers of people—the cross, the sword, blind justice. A private symbol is a thing containing significance for one person, at most two or three—my father's gold watch there (on the desk) with the blackened dents which are in fact my own toothprints (he allowed me to use it for teething, thirty years ago). Public symbols have variant private meanings for most of us—the dove means more to me now than to you because my brother is in Vietnam. But anyone—artist or critic—who attempts to make a private symbol into a public symbol is almost always doomed to a failure of communication, occasionally ludicrous failure as in Wordsworth's famous address to Wilkinson's spade. Wilkinson was a friend of Wordsworth's, and Wilkinson's spade became for Wordsworth imbued with private power to symbolize both Wilkinson's rural virtues and Wordsworth's love of a loyal friend. The failure results from Wordsworth's inability to convey to an unknown reader the processes—visual and chronological—by which the spade (not suddenly but over a long period of time) became symbolic for the poet. Literature is strewn with nobler but equally incommunicative private symbols—Yeats's tower, Virginia Woolf's lighthouse; even Moby Dick for nine-tenths of the novel, until the whale *appears* and we ourselves see him at last as Melville and Ahab have seen him from the first. All the failures of symbolism—artistic and critical—spring from one great sin: failure to take the world seriously, to respect and revere the singular dignity of each created thing.

Interviewer: It's this then that transfigures your characters, that makes them something more than the surface people we see on the street, in a bus queue, or in a supermarket?

Price: Yes. The characters of *A Generous Man*—of all my work—are men and women transfigured by possibility, by the intensity of their own passion, the intensity of their own need for destruction, for communication, order, for contact with the past and with the future.

Interviewer: Does this transfiguration take place in your mind or is it external? That is to say, do you, the novelist, make it happen—transfiguring the characters for a purpose—or are you looking at the character and seeing him transfigured?

Price: I look at the character and see him become transfigured—as I look at you now and see you transfigured by our seven years' friendship, by all that I know of your gifts and needs and chances. This is always a difficult thing for a novelist to discuss—the degree to which characters create themselves—but in *A Generous Man* especially, I did feel the characters very much creating themselves as the story created itself from day to day; the characters demanding those actions—however outrageous, incredible, coincidental—which would express their passions, needs, potentials. Just as characters in *The Tempest* or in *The Winter's Tale*, as characters in *The Magic Flute*, as characters in Japanese Noh plays behave quite unrealistically and yet with a hyperrealism, with a truth which is beyond question. If one comes to *A Generous Man* expecting it to be a novel like *A Long and Happy Life*—or *Studs Lonigan* or *A Farewell to Arms*—to be in that basically lyrical, realistic tone, then he's going to be baffled, disappointed, and angered. He's going to feel that I've consciously constructed a very artificial myth and an outrageous deck of inhuman symbols. But if he will consider *A Generous Man* as an independent work (though it does concern the same family as *A Long and Happy Life*), as an unrealistic work, which it in fact announces that it is on every page, then he can approach it as it must be approached before it will yield. That sounds forbidding, doesn't it?—and ridiculous. The book is first—and finally, perhaps—an entertainment. So is all art— the B-Minor Mass, the Sistine ceiling. No, I'm only hoping that *A Generous Man* can be seen for what I know it to be—a unique vision of certain valid, even urgent kinds of human experience, known till now by no one but me (because no one but me has lived my life).

Interviewer: In *A Generous Man*, you have a ghost, Tommy Ryden. Is he supposed to exist only in Milo's head in the novel or is he an actual ghost?

Price: The book says quite clearly that what returns is a ghost, on page 200: "What came after, came in two places—in the room itself (bare of all but prone Milo and the kneeling man) and behind shut eyes in Milo's bloody head, a sleeping vision." So the curious stranger had both physical and spiritual reality, objective and subjective. What has interested me always about ghost stories—respectable, well-authenticated ghost stories—is that ghosts almost always appear in unexceptional corporeal form. That is, they do not appear as filmy, vaporous, emanations of light but have simply—and terribly—the opaque reality of a live person walking through a room or sitting in a chair. That is how Tom Ryden, who's been dead for years, appears to Milo; and like so many ghosts, seems not to know that he is indeed dead, useless, unwanted.

Interviewer: You also introduce the supernatural into *The Names and Faces of Heroes*. Do you believe in the supernatural? And how can you create it if you don't really understand what it is?

Price: There are a great many things in the universe which we don't understand but make constant use of—electricity, the energy of the atom. We make use of our bodies every moment of our lives; and we certainly don't understand a tenth that there is to know about our eyes, our hearts, our kidneys. I suppose what you're referring to in *The Names and Faces of Heroes* would be that in the end of the title story, the child has a vision of the twelve years which wait between now and his father's death. And in *A Generous Man* there is the appearance to Milo of someone who has been dead for years, whom Milo had never seen in that person's earthly life. It's obviously difficult to discuss one's own relation to what you call the supernatural without sounding fishy in the extreme. I'd rather say this much and then pass on: that I do strongly suspect, even avow the existence and presence of forms of reality quite beyond those forms which we encounter in our daily routines. And whether or not those forms do manifest themselves—ever, in observable, sensually perceptible ways—certainly there can be no question that the dead linger, most powerfully, in our lives; the meaningful dead, those people who by the time most men have reached the age of twenty-one stand as one's ancestors on the black side of death in relation to our present continuing lives. That's all.

Interviewer: Where do you think all this strange stuff belongs in the larger context of literature? You mentioned Shakespeare's *Tempest*, *The Winter's Tale*, and *Cymbeline*; and you mentioned Noh plays. What about your contemporaries and other twentieth-century writers? Where do you think the supernatural or at least the extranatural fits in?

Price: There's a long and continuing tradition of the supernatural, not only in the epic, the lyric, and poetic drama but in the novel itself. Very obviously, the novel before the late nineteenth century was not committed to realism. The novels of eighteenth-century England, the great Victorian novels—the Brontës, Dickens—are highly "unrealistic" visions of human existence. Dickens makes as profound and revealing and convincing use of the supernatural as Kafka. His coincidences alone are acts of God. And to mention Kafka is to mention the great modern student of the supernatural. I wouldn't claim that there are many serious novelists who are presently employing ghosts in their novels—there is a credible and necessary ghost in Agee's *A Death in the Family*, and there are the ghosts and demons in Isaac Singer—but I do claim that the supernatural in the form of ghosts is still a possible, occasionally a necessary component of a serious novelist's vision.

Interviewer: Most of your work is quite serious fiction, yet in all of it there's a great deal of comedy. In fact, I believe *A Generous Man* started as an attempt at a comic novel. What role do you see comedy playing in your work?

Price: All my work is comic—not by conscious choice but because in attempting to embody the world that I've known, I have portrayed a comic world. Comedy is almost always a function of experience, a function of life. Even in the intensest moments of despair, pain, grief, wild bursts of laughter will insist upon rising and asserting themselves. And any literary form which abolishes or ignores the laughter at the heart of human life—even the laughter on the edges of human life— does so at the expense of its own truthfulness. Certain very large and important kinds of literary art have eliminated comedy, at least so far as we can see. For instance, with the possible exception of two or three scenes, there seem to be no elements of the comic in Greek tragedy. Laughter was simply postponed for plays which were comedies or for the satyr plays which were performed in cycle with the tragedies. But the fullest, therefore truest, most useful picture of human life is a picture which will necessarily and gladly contain much that is hilarious, mocking, and satyric—satyric in the oldest sense: a picture of satyrs, grinning, hairy, ithyphallic dancers, cruel (no, indifferent) witnesses of man's only—partially—relevant existence.

Interviewer: What about Pop Art and the Theater of the Absurd? A lot of people say that these forms reflect, more than other present forms, the absurdity of our time, its confusion and the extremes of modern life. Some reviewers seem to have this in mind when they imply that you, in writing about rural life in the South—in your part of the South—are out of touch or at least out of date.

Price: I know very little about Pop Art and the Theater of the Absurd. I strongly suspect that as terms they are meaningless. They are mere descriptions of fashions created by journalists, and like all such fashions are irrelevant, not only to the time but to whatever the history of that particular art may be. Pop Art and the Theater of the Absurd seem to me—on slim acquaintance—reflections of a pursuit of, an acceptance of chaos in life. I can think of no art of the past which has made such acceptance, which has collaborated willingly, almost hysterically with the chaos at the center of life; and I cannot imagine any future art, any enduring art which will make such collaboration. I don't think that my art does, my fiction. This perhaps is a reason why some of my work may be unfashionable, seem out of date. I hope though—in fact, I *know*—that there's something more important, more enduring, than fashion and the fads of journalists; and that is the attempt to seize territory from chaos, to clear and tend and fortify a circle in the forest, then to stage games there.

What I really think you're broaching is the matter of rural versus urban art. Rural art is unpopular in America because the centers of book reviewing in this country are urban. Most of the journals of book reviewing are manned by committed urbanites, large numbers of whom have a loudly declared aversion to non-urban life. But this again is simply an irrelevant taste, a peeve, a pet on the part of such reviewers. It has no relation whatever to matters of artistic importance, to the fact that there's a very serious question as to whether or not a totally urban novel is a possible literary form. It's fascinating, for instance, that the novels of Kafka—and at that perhaps only *The Trial*—are the only successful urban novels, novels which occur entirely within the confines of a city. And in many ways Kafka's city is a city of the mind, not a city on the map—not Prague, not Vienna. The great novels of the eighteenth and nineteenth centuries turned on the poles of city and country. One only has to mention Fielding, Dickens, Tolstoy, Turgenev, even Dostoevski, Proust to realize that their novels oscillate between visits to the city, visits to the country, visits which are not mere changes of backdrop for the sake of variety but which reflect profound needs of character and, in turn, shape character profoundly. It's a central dilemma of the novel now—the possibility of an entirely urban novel—and it's going to be fascinating to see what happens to the novel as novelists more and more originate in, live in and write about an entirely urban world, where every tree chokes beneath coats of soot. The possibility of producing anything other than a nightmare—about twentieth-century American cities, at least—is a dim possibility at best.

Interviewer: Aren't you taking the view that rural life is intrinsically better than city life? If human beings are, in fact, social animals, then why can't we have great writing about city life? Especially modern city life in which technology has created ways of living together in great masses?

Price: Well, to answer very briefly an enormously complex question, I would say that the danger for the novelist in a forced preoccupation, an obsession, with city life is not that city life isn't a form of social activity which is obviously here for a good while yet but that city life is, by definition in an age of potential nuclear destruction, impermanent. It is literally easier to destroy the city of New York—to vaporize every brick—than to destroy any single human being within that city, for the simple reason that the human being with fair warning can take shelter but the city cannot. Therefore cities have acquired this *added* nightmarish quality of impermanence, of threat—not of threat to destroy but to *be destroyed*, of threat to fail the inhabitants. The countryside, however, has at least the advantage for the artist of permanence. It can provide for him the objects of meditation, in the presence of which the literally human qualities of his life can be understood, calmed, controlled, and shaped. The profoundest examination of this dilemma is Wordsworth's preface to the *Lyrical Ballads*, in which he has already sketched the entire problem and, more than sketched, developed it in great detail (a development which has survived Coleridge's famous but frail objections).

Interviewer: This is going way out on a limb; but would you say that assuming an almost complete urbanization of society in the future, this urbanization could be the death of literature as we know it?

Price: It could be the death of the *novel* as we have known it—the urbanization of man combined with the mobility of man, the fact that man is becoming almost infinitely mobile, that even now one can travel from North Carolina to London in seven hours or less (which time will decrease rapidly with each decade). This fact surely means a lessening value in human life of roots, of literal rootedness in place, in land—or in asphalt—in an intimately known and long-experienced atmosphere. What the effect is going to be on the novelist is clearly incalculable. It's conceivable that we might again have a great upsurge of the poem at the expense of the more sustained novel; but this again is to play a fool's game, the game of speculation in matters of art—because art is made, all arts are made, by endlessly devious, resourceful individuals, not by groups of guessers. And it's hard to believe that a time will come when there will not be individual human beings who will need and wish to make from their own visions of their lives—and surrounding life—works of understanding and defense and control.

Interviewer: Let me cover one more objection people have to your work. In reviewing all three books, some reviewers call you a gifted stylist and others say the prose is mannered or contorted. What's your side of it?

Price: What critics usually mean in calling a writer's prose "mannered" is that the manner is not their manner. The simplest reply is this: there is no law that forbids to my prose—or anyone else's—the degrees of rhythmic and syntactical complexity which go unchallenged in the verse of Pindar, Shakespeare, Milton, Hopkins. But the fullest reply would be an old one that has gone unbelieved: that the style is the *man*. If *style* means "consciously achieved beauty of diction" or "decoration," then I have never given a moment's attention to style. To be sure, I know that the language of most of my fiction is often complex and occasionally difficult; but the complexity and density are not appliqué, not conscious "effects." They are functions of the vision of one attentive man. They are my literally reflexive responses to a given moment in a story, a character's life. The voice of a story is the vision of a story. I never pause to think, "This is a Price story, therefore must sound like a Price story." I wouldn't want to suggest, though, that I never take conscious care of my language. Of course I do—enormous care but a care which is directed towards fidelity, not "beauty" or "manner"; fidelity to the complexity of experience, to the mystery and dignity of objects. I wouldn't suggest either that some prose (and verse) isn't too complex, too difficult (serious prose, I mean—not rapt purple ranting). There are obviously passages in *Lear* and *Samson Agonistes,* in the late sonnets of Hopkins, in Joyce and Faulkner and Virginia Woolf in which language buckles under the burden it strains to assume. Such failures can be richly instructive—they show us that certain forms of experience have so far not yielded to art; but they certainly do not warn us to shun the attempt. If anything, they urge us on. They affirm and promise that the *whole* truth will at least not yield to copybook sentences, to the clear-water flow of subject-predicate-direct object.

Interviewer: It seems that throughout history, or in terms of our perspective today, when so many people are writing *about* literature, almost every writer can be shown to be intimately connected with his time, perhaps only in the way that you say—that he's making his literature out of his own life—but what about popular culture in your life? By popular culture, I mean things like comic books, hamburgers, automobiles, the fights, advertising, television, movies. How has all this influenced you as a person and as a writer, in a particularly twentieth-century sense?

Price: The popular culture that you're talking about is, again, pop culture, isn't it?—a phenomenon of the late 50's and the 60's. I shouldn't have thought that had influenced me at all, either as a human being or as an artist. All the manifestations you mention are simply things I drive past on the way to my work, occasionally stopping for a hamburger. I did, as a child in the 40's, read comic books, play war games, listen to the radio. I was a pretelevision child entirely, never seeing television until I was a college student; but the phenomenon of American culture, American *history* which influenced me most profoundly was all that we mean by the Depression. I was born at the very pit of the Depression, in the winter of 1933, to parents who had suffered great financial deprivation and therefore humiliation at the hands of the economy. I was an only child until I was eight years old, which is tantamount to being an only child; and I was therefore the sharer of my parents' lives, the confidant (whether they liked it or not) of all their fears and shames. So the Depression was for me, as it must have been for most children born in its shadow, the great initial terror, the great vision of possible tragedy and ruin. My fears and fantasies as a child were the fears and fantasies of David Copperfield or Oliver Twist—utter poverty, desolation, separation from one's parents, from one's home, from one's familiar surroundings because of the faceless interference of some quite uncontrollable force. *Destitution*. Not that we ever for a moment went hungry or went without adequate food and shelter but that as a child, reading the whispered worries and concerns of my parents in my own desperately hopeless child's way, I suspected the power of the nonhuman forces in life to deprive one of one's life. Last summer after my mother's death, for example, I was sorting out forty years of family papers and found cold confirmation of my darkest childhood suspicions—checkbooks with balances of eight dollars on payday, letters showing that in 1942 my father lost the only house we ever built because he could not borrow fifty dollars. *Fifty dollars.* Grayest shame, and I saw him wear it most of his life. The Depression was my generation's Civil War, the force which shaped and confirmed my earliest fears, demanded the building of my earliest defenses against the anonymous forces of ruin, humiliation before one's kin, in one's love. These, I suspect, are not the terrors of children born since, those whom I teach year after year in college. Their fears, and therefore their defenses, are quite different, as I suppose their art will be when they come to produce those defenses, statements, celebrations which will be their art.

Interviewer: We've talked about popular culture, about Pop Art, Theater of the Absurd. What about modern music and art, excluding the most recent movements and the most recent fashions? Who moves you in music and art and theater today?

Price: Living artists, you mean?

Interviewer: Well, say artists since the 20's or 30's. I suppose what I'm trying to say is, what modernists do you find interesting?

Price: I can't say honestly that I'm profoundly moved by any music written since 1920, since *Wozzek* and the early work of Stravinsky. I'm not a student of contemporary music, however. There might be a great deal which moved me if I only knew of it. The music which I listen to continually—for at least an hour each day, if not longer—is essentially eighteenth and nineteenth century. The operas of Mozart and Verdi and Wagner, the symphonies and quartets of Beethoven, *Fidelio*. In painting, I'm deeply moved by—and I know that my own work has had a continuing, growing, and deepening relationship with—the work of Picasso. I have spent more time looking at Picasso drawings and etchings than in reading Hemingway and Faulkner. But again I feel the profoundest admiration for and communication with older painters—Vermeer, Rembrandt, Michelangelo.

Interviewer: Isn't there part of *A Long and Happy Life* which can be said to be like a Vermeer? I think you compared it to a Vermeer at one time.

Price: One of the impetuses to my beginning *A Long and Happy Life*—or beginning to create the book in my head long before I began to write it—was my first sight of a particular Vermeer in the summer of 1956 in The Hague. The painting permanently resides in the Rijksmuseum, but it was in The Hague that summer for a special Vermeer exhibition. It's a picture of a young woman in her early 20s, in a blue smock before that window of Vermeer's. She's reading a letter against the light. Behind her on the wall is a map, presumably of some distant place; and the woman appears to be, beneath the smock, pregnant. No comment, no explanation, only a picture. But I remember circling that picture in the gallery for long minutes, not at all sure why it held me so, and buying a reproduction of it and propping it on my work table when I returned to Oxford later that summer to work. It was almost two years before I began to think of and plan in great detail the novel which would be about a girl reading letters from a lover at a distant place and that girl pregnant with that lover's child. I'm sure, though, that Vermeer's image had worked in my mind for those two years upon questions and needs and knowledge of my own to produce the story which later became *A Long and Happy Life*. There are other pictures deeply embedded in *A Long and Happy Life*. One of them is the portrait of a young man by Botticelli which hangs in the National Gallery in London, a full embodiment of the sort of man I imagined Wesley to be in *A Long and Happy Life*.

Interviewer: You have a lot of personal pictures around the house; in fact, in almost every room—in bedrooms, in the hallways, even in the bathrooms. Who are the people and why are they so ever-present? What part do they play in your life or in your work even?

Price: The pictures or the people?

Interviewer: Both.

Price: The pictures are images of household gods, I suppose. Images of what I have loved and love and worship—worship in the sense of offering my life and work to them. The pictures are of members of my family—some of whom I never knew, who died before I was born—and of friends who have caused my life and my work. They are here, and here in such numbers, for the sake of my present and future work, not for the sake of nostalgia, not as souvenirs of a lifeless past. That is an aspect of my own work, as it is of almost every artist's work, which is little understood by people who are not themselves artists—the extent to which any work of art, especially verbal art, is a private communication between the artist and a small audience, often as small as one. If others look on with interest and pleasure—and curiously, artists must almost always make public their most private communications—then one is glad enough, one's ego is stroked, one purrs for a moment; but the others *are* others, not the cause, not the subject, not the object of the labor, the final gift.

And with this last answer as if to imitate a film or a story, the tape pulls loose from the starting reel, wraps itself on the other side. (It actually does!) The last answer has supplied a unifying vision of the relationship between a writer and his surroundings, at least here. You can look around this house at the pictures, the records, the furniture, the views and feel that what is here in the house is there in the work. If you will pardon the kitchen images, Price is like a funnel through which all memory and these material things travel; a funnel which is not only a straight-through narrowing tube but one which is also a blender, which transforms vast quantities of raw material into goblets of clear wine, filled to the brim and a fraction over the brim.
    "Did you ever think of yourself as a wine-making funnel?" I ask.
    "Enamel or tin?" he says.

II

This ought to be a bad time to continue an interview. Of Reynolds' last two books, *A Generous Man* is remaindered in first edition at the local store and *Love and Work* got a lot of hostile reviews. Reynolds, however, is satisfied with the work he did on those books, and that ability to survive on his own satisfaction is probably what keeps him working steadily and steering a course that has great integrity. Writers

who dry up or who pause to write the formula best seller probably
cannot sustain their work on the strength of their own judgments.

So here we go again: same house and setting, only four more
years' collection of pictures and objects. The basement now has a
wall full of American Indians. On end tables and coffee tables are
new technological toys—a kaleidoscope, a magic egg of steel, and
moulage for making life masks (Reynolds calls them death masks).

Interviewer: *Love and Work* has appeared since the first part of this
conversation. There were no Mustians in it, and some readers said
that this was you launching into an entirely new kind of writing while
some said it was you examining yourself via a main character who is
also a writer and a teacher. To what degree is either of these proposi-
tions valid?

Price: Both are valid and invalid. *Love and Work* did constitute a
violent break with a number of the procedures of my earlier work—at
least, a number of readers found it a very baffling change of signal.
But the closing down of one's parental family and home (by death) *is*
a violent break with the past: the only possible death of childhood.
That implies autobiography, right? Well, the novel was begun about a
year after my mother's death and the closing of our family home (in
which I hadn't lived for fifteen years) and it does contain some of the
actual materials of that experience; but I'm being accurate, not coy,
in saying that, though I could confabulate, I couldn't *truthfully* tell
you what "happened" and what didn't. You probably know better
than I. But it isn't anyone else's legitimate concern, not while I'm
alive anyhow. I've offered the book as an organism quite independent of my life, perfectly ambulatory. If anyone wants to deal with
the *book*, it exists, and seems to me the strongest thing I'd done till
then. One more word though—while *Love and Work* may at first
look radically disconnected from my earlier work, it isn't. It isn't set in
the South, admitted (the places in it are houses, literal real estate,
not towns or counties), and the central figure is a reasonably well-
informed novelist and university teacher; but the central obsessions
of the book are continuous with the early books, though—I hope—in
changed and developed forms. Which is to say that I hope *I'm*
changed and have developed—toward what? Lucidity, of sight and
statement.

Interviewer: How much of all that did you know when you set out to write *Love and Work?*

Price: Impossible to say (in any truthful or usable form), impossible to retrack any impulse to its extremely multiplex—and always mysterious—beginnings. I'm sorry if that sounds oracular. But it's accurate.

Interviewer: I don't mean to try to box you in with a hot new genre, but—returning to *Love and Work*—would you say that it was in any way a nonfiction novel? Or maybe I ought to ask if you think the nonfiction novel exists or maybe if it has always existed?

Price: Yes, in a way it is. But so were *A Long and Happy Life* and *A Generous Man* though in all three cases more than 99 percent of the characters were invented from the ground up. So are most good novels surely—*Bovary, c'est moi*. In that sense, surely, serious *fiction* doesn't exist.

Interviewer: You don't like grand schemes and you're not overtly ambitious in any material sense, but you are also the kind of man who makes sure you have insurance and a solid savings account; so have you in any way thought about the direction of your career; have you stored up any kind of literary or creative savings account?

Price: Oh I do like grand schemes (the writers I admire most are the grandest available—Tolstoy, Milton). And of course I do think a great deal about the course of my work, because it is to a large extent the course of my life. In another month I should, with any luck, have finished a second volume of short stories—this one called, I think, *Permanent Errors* (because they are all concerned with that—mistakes that cannot be rectified). And these stories again seem to me a break with, or advance on, past work (*Love and Work* included), though there are a number of different kinds of pieces in the volume—from what, for want of a satisfactory name, I call personal elegies to recognizable "short stories" to, for me, a new kind of hectic first-person narrative (in no case is the first person "me"). After that, if I live intact and work goes on surfacing in my head, I hope to begin a fourth novel. I have clear ideas for it; I can feel it, in the night, cohering, coalescing—it has been for years now. And it begins to feel—to use your word—"grand"; but nothing would be worse than to talk about it now.

Interviewer: It makes me feel good, thinking you are six years older and grayer than me; so let me put one of the "old man" questions to you. Looking back, do you think now that you would be writing anything you haven't written if you could do it over?

Price: Well, works of blinding genius. No, lucid genius. But maybe they are that. Nice to think so, one day a year at least. My birthday's this Sunday, age thirty-seven—I'll try to think it then. No, without meaning to sound sleek and self-adoring, I can't think of anything I've published since 1958 that I wouldn't stand by today (which is not to say that I would write it, in that way, today). And there are no great wrecked ambitions back there either, beyond the universal ones—that one wants to be better, as a man, more useful, funnier, wiser, happier. Also as a writer. But mightn't that follow? No— Beethoven, Wagner. Though I think a lot of Milton—old, blind, all but bankrupt, every political hope defeated, his work by no means popular—dependent on a third wife—swinging in his garden and singing in his gout-fits: a better man and a better poet. *Samson Agonistes.* Give me time, though. The Prices have been short-lived enough as it is.

Interviewer: Since the first part of our conversation, I've occasionally thought about your insistence that writers need to see man in the presence of the natural world. Do you think there is going to be any really new sense of relationship between man and nature in the next ten, fifty, or a hundred years? I'm asking this, knowing you've been reading men like Konrad Lorenz and a lot of astronomy and following the astronauts to the moon.

Price: Just in the four years since we talked this out before, conservation's hour has struck, hasn't it? Just *this* year, in fact. So maybe "man and nature" will be getting along a little better ten years, twenty years from now—though if man doesn't rapidly stop making other little men, reclamation of nature is going to be literally impossible. When will population's hour strike? I look around at my university colleagues: station wagon-loads of babies. Lovely babies, some of them, but intended essentially as toys, something-to-do for tired couples. Hasn't it *ever* crossed their minds that the population explosion means *them?* Well, rant, rant—no, to return to your question, I can't imagine any better or closer relations between man and the natural world, the planet, in the next fifty years, say. Only deeper, longer nightmares—filth, crammed space, *all* waters fouled. There are whole moments when one wonders if some sort of nuclear Armageddon isn't positively desirable—or won't be within the next twenty years. I mean, really, how else do you rectify an error like New York City? And wouldn't it be healthy to have a good poet around saying things like that?—a better Robinson Jeffers; is there one? So far as I understand anything, the two major hopes seem very long-term indeed—first, some sort of genetic reengineering of human folly and secondly, space. The out-there. Both very scary but at least *serious* hopes. It's appalling—isn't it?—that schoolchildren aren't given some basic grounding in elementary astronomy, cosmology. I've taught dozens of university seniors who hadn't the vaguest notion of what a galaxy was or that we belong to one. We should all have the image of Andromeda, say, tattooed on our retinas. For cheer, if not hope—that there's something that lovely. Unreachable, no doubt (or is it?) but *there* and free and eminently usable—for contemplation, calm, exercises in proportion. I'm using it now.

Interviewer: How?

Price: Well, I point out that I'm *smiling*. Name three others who are.

A Glimpse into the Very Private World of a Novelist
Rod Cockshutt/1971

From *The Raleigh News and Observer*, 24 January 1971, sec. 4, 3. Reprinted by permission of *The Raleigh News and Observer*, Rod Cockshutt, and Reynolds Price.

The long and winding road to Reynolds Price's comfortable home in the quiet countryside near the Durham-Orange County line was unpaved and difficult to negotiate, the red clay at its base like congealed tomato soup in the wake of a heavy morning rain.

The long and winding road to an understanding of Reynolds Price's personality seems equally difficult to negotiate. For Price is a very private person. Another interviewer put it this way several years ago: "Talking to him is like talking to an articulate brick wall—a high facade which conceals the mysteries and secrets of the craft from curious passers by."

None of this is to suggest that the 37-year old novelist is coy or hostile or insufferably self-important in his demeanor.

On the contrary, Price projects a combined aura of quiet congeniality and tentative self-confidence, pleasingly flavored with flashes of an acerbic wit, which he frequently turns on himself.

He is, by his own admission and by his own choice, basically a solitary person; by no means a recluse or an exile, but more a careful spectator than a team player in most of life's ephemeral games.

He lives alone in the modern brick cottage, which sits at the top of a gentle rise overlooking a small pond. The living room is cozy, heterogeneously busy with antiques, Oriental pieces and comfortably functional modern and traditional furniture. A picture window takes up almost an entire wall. Comingled with the literary classics in the bookcases are copies of Price's own successes: *A Long and Happy Life,* which was published in 1962 to wide acclaim and which won the prestigious William Faulkner Foundation Award that year, *The Names and Faces of Heroes,* a collection of short stories which

30

followed in 1963. Later came *A Generous Man* and *Love and Work,* and then, last fall, *Permanent Errors.*

During the interview, which took up the better part of a recent afternoon, the author was dressed casually in a Navy blue shirt, khaki trousers and worn moccasins. He is a "fidgety" (his word) type, and during almost the entire conversation some part of his body was in motion, suggesting an endless supply of nervous energy simmering inside. His voice is deep and resonant, carrying an accent which seems to blend two parts Warren County to one part Oxford (England).

Q. Can you tell a little bit about your family background? Was it a writing or reading family you came from? How did you get to where you are now?

A. Both my parents were from Warren County. My father from Warrenton and my mother from Macon. There's no previous writer in either family, but I think like most Southern families, they were definitely pre-literary in the sense that there was always a lot of talk going on—the kind of retrospective narrative talk about the past.

The past was constantly redramatized, relived. And it was celebrated in a sacred sense, with a body of family anecdotes, which were endlessly retold, and which I loved to hear. I much preferred to listen to my parents and aunts and uncles than to my contemporaries.

So in that sense I think it was a helpful set of families to me.

I was born in Warren County, at my mother's family home at Macon, during the depth of the Depression in 1933. I spent the early years of my childhood living in several places—Henderson, Roxboro, then for about nine years in Asheboro. Then we moved back to Warrenton and then to Raleigh. I went to high school at Needham Broughton in Raleigh when we moved there in 1947.

Q. When did you first begin to think of yourself as a writer?

A. From the time that I can first remember—pre-first grade, I thought of myself as some kind of artist. The thing that I most wanted to be up until the time I was in junior high school was a painter. I spent the largest part of my childhood painting and drawing, when I wasn't reading.

Like most people who ultimately wind up in the arts, I was a lonely

child, sort of solitary. I was an only child until I was eight, then my
brother was born, and that's tantamount to being an only child.

Then when I got to high school, I think two things happened. First,
I began to realize that none of my painting was ever going to be good
enough. Secondly, I happened to have a teacher at Broughton,
Phyllis Peacock, who very much encouraged my writing. I think it
was from about the 11th grade on that I thought: This is it; I'm going
to be a writer.

Q. So that encouragement was kind of crucial?

A. The encouragement was very important. Then I came to Duke,
and received more encouragement, from numerous people. Finally,
then, and most importantly, my senior year at Duke, Eudora Welty
happened to come through to give a reading, and William Blackburn
showed her a story I had written—at that time, the only story I had
written—and she liked it and offered to send it to her agent, which
she did.

I think it was her encouragement coming at that point in my
career, when I was just getting ready to graduate and somehow the
sense that a writer whom I knew to be about as good as writers get
thought this was good seemed to be very convincing. So I moved off
from there to Oxford (on a Rhodes scholarship) in September of
1955.

I stayed three years and did an awful lot of writing while I was
there—probably three-fourths of *The Names and Faces of Heroes*,
my first volume of short stories. And also, the last year I was there, I
made a lot of notes for my first novel, *A Long and Happy Life*,
although I didn't actually begin writing until I got back here to begin
teaching at Duke.

Q. Getting back to your early background in rural North Carolina,
could you discuss a little bit how that background affected your
development as a writer?

A. Well, I think it certainly deepened that natural tendency I'd had
from the beginning to be a very solitary, contemplative, observing
person. It gave me enormous amounts of time to sit down and read
or draw and even write. I wasn't constantly bopping out to ball
games and parties.

Q. What have you read that has had an impact on your own

writing? What books do you keep coming back to? Everyone always says Faulkner.

A. I think I was very influenced by some of the things I first read, which, as I said, tended to be rather outrageous adventure material—*Tom Sawyer Abroad,* the King Arthur stories, *The Arabian Nights, Doctor Doolittle.* But then I got down very rapidly to reading rather solid stuff like Tolstoy and Dostoevski in junior high. They still remain important. I didn't know these were the best things written, but they were. I was very lucky.

Q. What about American writing? You've mentioned Twain.

A. I read Hemingway fairly early, as most people did. I was absolutely bowled over in about the ninth grade by *A Farewell to Arms,* largely bowled over at that time by what seemed to be its extreme sexual daring. And still, now, I look at Hemingway with a lot of tremendous respect and affection, although my work couldn't be more different from his.

Q. When do you have time to read?

A. Actually, I don't do a tremendous amount of fiction reading. I don't have time to, because I'm either teaching—one semester a year—and then I try to write. When I'm teaching, I tend to read what I'm teaching, which is Milton and a class in writing. Then when I'm writing, reading becomes a difficult problem because most writers, whatever else they are, tend to be born mimics, and I always feel that if I read any extraordinary work while I'm writing I begin to feel invaded by that writer's sensibilities—especially somebody as individual as Hemingway, Conrad or Henry James.

Q. What about Faulkner? Even though he's not a major influence, does he have any importance to you?

A. I don't think I even knew of the existence of Faulkner until the day he won the Nobel Prize in 1949 when I was 16. That says something about Faulkner's reputation at the time. Because in a very good high school like Broughton at Raleigh, no one had ever heard of Faulkner until he got the Nobel Prize and then the reaction was horror that this man who wrote *Sanctuary* and other sex books had won the Nobel Prize.

But, someone I had read earlier than Faulkner, and admired enormously, was Eudora Welty. I read her story, "A Worn Path," at Broughton. Then I looked up other stories of hers, and they were very important for me in that the world Eudora Welty wrote about bore far more relationship to the world I knew than Faulkner's—a sort of much more tense, hectic, violent world.

Q. Could you comment generally on the so-called mystique of the Southern writer, as long as we're talking about Faulkner and Welty? Is it overdone?

A. I think it's tremendously overdone, although it is now fashionable in some circles to say that the whole southern thing, insofar as it was rural, agrarian, is really over, that there aren't any more people living in the country.

Well, nonsense. I can get in my car here and in an hour be in the little village I was born in. There are many changes, but they are still living essentially as they were living in 1933. They're telling the same stories, speaking the same language.

What I think is difficult and is true is that Southern writers now, people of my age and younger, are faced with a very great dilemma of living in a region which is already crowded with very distinguished predecessors. We've got Faulkner, Welty, Robert Penn Warren, Flannery O'Connor. We're faced with the fact that an enormous amount of this material has been done over and over. So I think, in my own work, part of the move away in *Love and Work* and *Permanent Errors* was from a conscious sense that perhaps this is a vein that is thinning out.

Q. How is it when you are writing? What is a typical day like?

A. When I'm writing, which I try to make two-thirds of the year, I tend to start about 10 in the morning and try to be available to it all day. I write in longhand and type up at the end of a couple of days. If you stopwatched me, I wouldn't put pen to paper more than a couple of hours in the course of a day. I tend to stay here at the house. Over the period of the whole day, which runs from 10 in the morning until about midnight, I will make innumerable trips to the desk, but I don't ever sit at the desk more than 15 minutes at a time. Then I get up and do some of my little fidgets, listen to the news, make some coffee. Sometimes I think the morning is the most productive time, and then sometimes at midnight, I'll suddenly burst loose.

Someone once asked Mr. Faulkner if he wrote by inspiration or habit and he said he wrote by inspiration, but luckily inspiration arrived at 9 every morning. I know what that means. And there is a kind of magic about keeping the stride once you've got it going.

Q. What are you working on right now?

A. Nothing at the moment. I don't try to do anything while I'm teaching. I really just finished *Permanent Errors* in March. I've got two long things in mind. I've got a year's leave from teaching coming up in February and I want to get straight to work then.

An Interview with Reynolds Price
Ariel/1972

From *Ariel* (Washington and Lee University student literary magazine), 10:2 (Winter 1972), 3-17. Reprinted by permission of Reynolds Price.

Last Spring, under the auspices of the Glasgow Endowment Fund, Reynolds Price visited the Washington and Lee campus for two weeks, Mr. Price gave a reading and a lecture during his stay here. His work was studied in an English seminar which he attended. During the second week of his stay Robert Lockhart, Steve Haughney, and David Olson went to his suite at the Lexington Motel and for two hours conducted the interview that follows.

Mr. Price's books include two collections of stories, *The Names and Faces of Heroes* and, his most recent book, *Permanent Errors,* as well as three novels, *Love and Work, A Generous Man* and *A Long and Happy Life* which received The William Faulkner Foundation Award in 1962 for a notable first novel. So much attention has been centered around this first book that it seemed appropriate to begin the questioning with an inquiry into the creation of Reynolds Price's most famous work.

Ariel: You mentioned that you waited until you returned home from Oxford before you started *A Long and Happy Life.* Do you think that it is an advantage for a writer to stay on his home ground, or do you think that it's just your particular case?

Price: I think it depends entirely on what a writer's relation to his home ground is. Joyce felt that it was necessary for him to leave Dublin before he could begin to write about Dublin successfully. So he went to Paris and Switzerland to spend the rest of his life, the next 40 years, writing about Dublin but what obviously was very much Dublin-in-the-mind, finding Dublin in dream, in nightmare. I've often felt that this finally leads to a terrible failure in Joyce's work—cutting himself off from the roots of his inspiration, and this obsession with the past which really becomes a form of schizophrenia. But to say that Joyce should have stayed in Dublin is entirely meaningless. Joyce might well have gone totally berserk if he'd stayed in Dublin, or have become an alcoholic. He did what he had to do. If it had

unfortunate sterilizing effects on his late work, then that was simply
the choice that his life made for him. I think the novel on the whole,
up till now, has been a form very profoundly rooted in given places.
It's very hard to imagine them being moved out of their locales.
Eudora Welty talks about this at great length in "Place in Fiction";
and she says, could you imagine *The Sound and the Fury* set in
Germany; no, can't imagine it set in New York either. Could *The
Remembrance of Things Past* be set in London; no, has to be in
Paris. People don't behave that way in London. So the novel has till
now been a very local form. And out of the local comes the univer-
sal. But what's going to happen now that people, especially in
America, are becoming much more mobile? You meet a child eight,
or a young man eighteen, and he says, "I've lived several places."
(I've actually been a number of places myself, although most have
been in a circumscribed culture, which was Piedmont and Eastern
North Carolina. Then four years in Europe.) But what's going to
happen when people don't have very profound relations to given
places or when their only relations are with places that are horrific?
Having only metropolitan nightmares.

Ariel: Do you think that this mobility might have some influence
on the seeming proliferation of New Journalists like Tom Wolfe
and Norman Mailer, who are basically urban writers and who simply
describe without really the novelist's concern for plot and story?

Price: I haven't really thought of it that way. I'd be inclined to
think that the two examples you give are people who are not essentially novelists *by talent.* Interestingly enough, Tom Wolfe is from
Richmond and went to Washington and Lee, so he has small-town
Southern upbringing. Why doesn't he write about that? Well, he
doesn't. He's chosen to write about something else.

He was in Chapel Hill recently. I didn't hear his address, but I read
some reports of it. He seems to have stated in a rather firm way that
he thought journalism was it. People no longer want to read fiction,
because fiction can't tell us what life is like any more. Well, I think
that is purest nonsense. I certainly don't think Tom Wolfe's journalism, interesting as some of it is, tells us what *life* is like either; it
tells us what it is like to be Tom Wolfe. And in so far as anybody is
interested in hearing that, then it's interesting, but that's really all it
gives. The minimum thing that any work of fiction, or any work of art

for that matter, has always promised is to tell us what it's like to be the person who made it, or a part of what it's like to be the person who made it. And always our response to any work of art is partially a response to the maker, to the perception that the man who made this thing is either a bastard or a saint or something in between, a nice guy. And part of the trouble with some people who are great geniuses, like Mann and Wagner, is the feeling that comes through their work—however, great the work is—that you wouldn't have wanted to spend any time in a room with the men who made the work.

Ariel: Some people have intimated that the novel is dead. Do you think that increased social upheaval has resulted in a shifting conception of prose fiction that would provoke a statement like that?

Price: Well, I don't think it's dead, by any means. And I've just written an essay trying to explain some of the reasons why I don't think it's dead, why there is no reason on earth why it *has* to die, at least for another 50 or 60 years, assuming that the human race doesn't die. But upheaval is going to endanger it; it already has severly endangered the novel as we've known it, the local place-centered, character-centered novel, because one of the major forming forces of human character has always been *place*. Suppose you had been an Army brat and had ricocheted around America, Europe and Guam. (As most of those kids have.) What would your life be like? You probably know people like that, as I do. I have some good friends who've lived like that. But there always comes this moment when you realize—well, if I'm a human being, they aren't quite, or perhaps I'm a dog and they're a cat, or they're a cat and I'm a panther. There is a lot of relation, but there are also some very strange things that they don't share with me. There are some people who live out of doppkits instead of out of houses; and if they write novels, they are of necessity going to write novels quite different from mine, or anyone else's who has been deeply rooted in *place*. Like Tolstoy, Emily Brontë, Dostoevski, or any other great novelist you can name.

Ariel: Do you think that it is possible for the novel as we know it to grow out of these sorts of relationships and this sort of fluidity?

Price: The greatest of all novels came out of the 19th century, which—had you lived in the 19th century—would have looked like a time of most enormous floods of change. Everything on the move, class warfare getting very firmly underway, fantastic economic problems, pressures, the whole tremendous influence of literacy and mass printing, the easy availability of books and so forth. I'm not sure that society looks anymore fidgety now than it would have in 1860 or 1850. It may be more seriously out of control now than it was then (I'm inclined to think that it is)—for the simple reason that there is a quite serious possibility now that we can destroy the human race. It may even be possible that we already have destroyed it by poisoning all the plankton. I mean we may have already doomed the life-chain of the plankton, in which case we will all suffocate in the next X years. But I don't think most people perceive that possibility. You know, they read about Earth Day in the newspaper; but I don't think they have any deep spiritual knowledge that man is worse-off than he was in 1860. On the other hand, most literate people, the people who like novels, have that sense, I think. A certain sense of doom. And in so far as they are concerned with writing about the present, in so far as they feel any compulsion to tell it as it is now, it seems to me they are already inventing very new kinds of novels—kinds of novels that I'm not really at all interested in, and also this parajournalism that is so popular now. But it seems to me that this is putting the work of the novelist where the work has never been before—all in telling us how it feels to be alive this minute. The novel has always been a very retrospective form—Tolstoy telling you all he had ever known by having been Tolstoy to the age of 40, not what it feels like this instant in St. Petersburg on the Nevsky Prospect. So a tremendous commitment to *Now* seems to me a very dangerous thing, but a lot of young writers and the "with-it" middle-aged writers are terribly committed to right-now. To their great ruin, it seems to me.

Ariel: Aren't these writers attempting to communicate with a fluid audience through a commitment to Now rather than a commitment to place (a common experience that's just not as common anymore), and might not that propel the novel in a new direction?

Price: Well, I think it has already sent a number of people who might have been good third-rate novelists into other directions. They've realized that they are not selling hundreds of thousands of copies of their books; and so they want to do something that seems to them much more relevant, you know, with-it, and they get into

writing up communes and writing up drugs, and writing up Women's
Lib and so forth. Well, you know, some of that is perfectly honorable;
and no doubt it's better for some people to be first-rate journalists
than third-rate novelists. But there has always been a certain amount
of room for third-rate novelists in the world. Still, I think it is probably
fatal for a writer (a journalist) to begin to calculate audiences. He can
only tell you what he knows and needs to say; and if there are any
number of people in the world who want to hear it, fine. If there
aren't, then he can always just deposit his knowledge in time cap-
sules. And hope that when the Martians finally land they will be
heavy readers.

Ariel: Don't you think that has to be a concern for a writer? If he
feels that what he's saying is valuable, doesn't he want people to
hear it?

Price: I think that he wants *some* people to hear it, but then this
raises a question of how large an audience, and I don't know any
serious writers who really sit down and think "Should I do this to this
book in order that it will sell another 10,000 copies?" Now there
have been great writers who did that, people like Dickens who very
carefully calculated what the sales-value of a given turn of plot might
be—the death of Little Nell or keeping alive of Little Nell. But I think
very few serious writers really are concerned about that now. There is
a small audience in the United States—far too small—for any serious
work of art in fiction. There are larger audiences for certain other
kinds of serious art—serious movies and certain serious theatrical
performances—but I couldn't agree with you. I think that the novelist
assumes a *necessity,* and quite rightly so; and I think that he is a
human being. There's a certain kind of race called Human Beings,
and he is a member of that race. And insofar as he is not either a
monster or a psychopath, there will always be a certain number of
other human beings who are enough like himself to be interested in
what his reports are. It's just an assumption he has to make in order
to get his work done. I think it's death to start thinking, you know,
how can I reach more *Americans?* And I think you have to think of
an audience, yes, in the sense that you don't want to speak in private
language. Joyce, for instance, in *Finnegans Wake* is creating a private
language, is nearing the language of a psychopath, schizophrenic.
And he is very aware of that. He said, you know, "I demand nothing

less of the reader than that he spend his whole life understanding my work." That does seem to me the statement of someone who is far gone into some kind of megalomania, and I'm just not at all interested in spending even *hours* of my life in trying to comprehend *Finnegans Wake,* much less the rest of my life. And I think amongst the things in the world that matter, *Finnegans Wake* is towards the bottom of the list. So are my own books, so are the books of Tolstoy and Shakespeare.

Ariel: But a writer has to keep up some illusion that what he is doing is going to be worth something; otherwise, I don't think he could continue to work.

Price: Of course he keeps that illusion. But I think the writer works out of compulsion much more than out of illusion. I think he writes because that's what his faculties know how to do. You breathe because that's what your lungs and your pulmonary muscles know how to do, that's what your diaphragm knows how to do. It is not possible for you to stop breathing by willing to do so. You can stop for a certain amount of time until you black out, and then your lungs quietly start breathing again. A writer writes, I think very largely out of compulsions which he is powerless to restrain.

Ariel: Is that your experience, that the writing of your books has come out of an organic need?

Price: Very much so. I wouldn't do anything that hurts so much if it weren't organic! Organic, metabolic need of some sort. I hate to write.

Ariel: You *hate* to write?

Price: Of course. Don't you hate to do anything you do well? I'd far rather do something like draw or paint, which I do sort of third-ratedly. I can draw all day without ever getting up from the chair, but I can't write more than two sentences without getting up.

Ariel: You wrote poetry while you were an undergraduate, and you said somewhere that you stopped because you realized the verses were bad. Now you've started up again. Why?

Price: Because I think they are getting good again! Well, obviously some of the most recent prose that I've written, some of the pieces that I read the other night, like the short pieces from *Permanent Errors* about my parents, have been approaching the condition of poetry much more nearly than the condition of prose; and several things have come to me over the last couple of years, in the form of poems, verse. As opposed to coming to me in story, or as ideas for novels. And so I've written them as verses. I'm not sure how good they are, but I think they are as good as the most recent prose I've written—in different ways, of course. Also for some years now—for really 10 years or so—I've spent a good deal of time doing translations from foreign languages. Usually languages that I don't know well at all, so that I can just sort of look at a poem and maybe look at another English translation of it and then get out a dictionary and start looking up the words and trying to make, in the English language, a poem that I like which seems to be inspired by something in the original. Often, as I say, I'm not qualified to make a literal translation of the original poem; but what I've tried to do is make an English poem myself. I think doing those started for me as an exercise in sharpening up my own language, my perception of the individual word; but I think that it may also be one of the things which has led me into writing poems recently. The poems that I have written tend to be long narrative poems, to have some relation to fiction in that sense; but I think long narrative poems might be something poetry could use a few of now. No one has written any since Frost died.

Ariel: Do you think that contemporary poetry is suffering?

Price: I don't read a great deal of it—I'll have to confess—for the reason that I don't like it very much. It doesn't seem to me very rewarding. I don't have the patience that it seems to require—that I devote my life to understanding, comprehending it, responding to it. If I'm going to read verse, I'd much rather read the verse of the past from Homer through, let's say, Wallace Stevens. But there are some living poets whom I read with great admiration, like Lowell, Auden and Spender. No doubt I'm omitting a number of people whom I like.

Ariel: Do you have plans for a volume of poems in the near future?

Price: I don't have plans for it, but I certainly hope that eventually a volume will accumulate. I don't have the necessary volume of pages yet. I've got about, I think, 40 pages divided between roughly half poems of my own and half versions of other people's poems, foreign-language poems; but yes, I hope eventually, another several years perhaps, to have a volume of poems and translations.

Ariel: Who are your favorite novelists?

Price: There are a number and I wouldn't say I have, you know, a single favorite novelist. I certainly think Eudora Welty is the living writer that I admire most. Her work I have the most natural sympathy for. Her work I certainly most enjoy reading. But I very much respect a number of living people—Bernard Malamud, Saul Bellow, some of the early work of John Updike, some of the work of William Styron, the detective novels of Ross Macdonald. But I could go on with quite a list that I like. I think they're the sort of people that most everybody else likes who reads much fiction. They're obviously good and, in all the cases I've named, they're rather traditional—traditional in a very broad sense, people who are writing more or less easily comprehensible English and American prose. Traditional as opposed to "experimental."

Ariel: Your own career started out with a very successful first novel, *A Long and Happy Life.* Through recent literary history people who have come out with successful first novels have sort of gone downhill from there. I'm not trying to say that you have, hardly; but Fitzgerald certainly never recovered from the success of *This Side of Paradise.* How has it affected you?

Price: Well, maybe he never recovered personally; but he certainly recovered artistically. I think his work got better and better the longer he lived. His last work—*Tender Is the Night* and the fragments left of *The Last Tycoon*—is the best he ever did. It seems to me that as my work proceeds from *A Long and Happy Life* it becomes more rewarding. It may not become more easily accessible or deeply "popular," but that wasn't the intent.

I think *A Long and Happy Life* was popular for a while for a lot of the wrong reasons—because people thought it was a nice love story; they failed to see that it was a bitterer pill than that. But most people failed to perceive that *A Generous Man* was a most bitter book about a ruined young man, not at all a joyous book about an adolescent on the way into manhood. Which simply means that most people can't read, even the most trained readers. They can't see what's on a page—it's there on every page of *A Generous Man*: already heading over the hill.

Ariel: Has anyone asked you why you changed? As if they wanted you to keep writing *A Long and Happy Life* for the next 40 years of your life?

Price: I don't think I've ever had anyone actually say that to me, in so many words. I've had people imply to me—"Oh, dear. Why have you left the tobacco roads of childhood for the fleshpots of the world?" Well, my life's left; that's why. And in any fiction, with almost any writer, there's always a gap between the having of an experience, the confronting of experience in one's own life, and the time in which that experience demands to be dealt with in the work. It's very dangerous, I think, when people start having experiences on Saturday night which they write up on Monday morning. This has been my worry about a lot of Updike's most recent work, for instance—the sense that Updike goes to a party on Saturday night and writes the story about it Monday morning. In a sense, he's living off his muscle rather than his fat. In my own case, I've found that, with a few exceptions, the experience almost invariably takes ten to fifteen years to shoulder up out of my life into my work. I think that's been true with most novelists, and that's another great danger of people who are trying to write novels about *now*. Nobody knows what *now* is like. Of course, their reply would be, "We haven't got time to wait. We've got to go ahead and say what it feels like now." And it's always valuable to have reports on what it feels like now— which is why something like Mailer's book about the march on the Pentagon is valuable: because it tells not what it felt like to be anyone else then, but what it was like to be this extraordinary exotic creature, Norman Mailer. I think he's gone on, trying to repeat the form; and now it's not very interesting to be told what it feels like to be Norman Mailer on the moon. But it was valuable, once. I think journalism is always valuable in telling us—you know, there are those Victorian journalists, like Mayhew, who wrote about the London poor in the 1850s. It's wonderful to read them, just as fascinating—to me anyway—as to read Dickens, but utterly different.

Ariel: Do you keep a journal?

Price: No, I never have really except for the year and a half that I kept a notebook about *A Long and Happy Life.* It wasn't a diary. I wrote in it every day, many times a day; but it was not concerned with what it felt like to be Reynolds Price. It was concerned with

Reynolds Price's curiosity about this thing he was to begin writing. I never wanted to have that kind of self-conscious relation to my experience—living for my journal. Now there have been great people—great journalists, God knows, and great novelists—who have kept elaborate journals (I think Gide's is much more interesting than his novels); but a journal is primarily an autobiography and I'm not ready for that. I do have a sort of notebook. I have a place, a composition book, in which I enter all sorts of things from my head—a name that interests me or a little anecdote that I hear, a little clipping out of the paper that strikes me in some mysterious way, potentially mineable in my work—but other than that, no.

Ariel: Aside from writing up *A Long and Happy Life* into a screenplay, have you considered writing for the cinema?

Price: Yes, I have. I was just recently asked to write a screenplay for a novel written by a native of Lexington—a man by the name of William Marshall, I believe. He wrote a book called *Sounder,* a children's novel. It won the Newberry medal about two years ago, a very good novel about a young black boy growing up in the mountains of Virginia. It's going to be filmed by Robert Radnitz, and he sent me the novel to read. I realized as soon as I read it that I saw how a good film could be made from it. It's a very unscenic book—mostly "He did this, and three weeks later he did that, and three weeks later he did that, and then six years later he did that"; but I realized that I knew enough about the material to invent the necessary scenic matter. That foundered though because there wasn't enough money involved to make it worth my while spending ten to fifteen weeks of my life in Los Angeles writing up someone else's book when I had something of my own that needed doing.

Ariel: But screenplays seem familiar to you?

Price: Oh, yes. I've had no sense of bafflement about writing screenplays—my premise is that the screenplay of *A Long and Happy Life* is a good screenplay! I think it is. When I was invited to write the screenplay the first two times, I refused; and someone else actually wrote a draft. This was much too literal a conversion of novel into screenplay; and at that point, I stepped in and wrote a draft myself, in 1965 or '66. I felt rather frightened and read a lot of other people's screenplays to see what the form was; and then I suddenly realized—"Well, nonsense, I mean, you know as much about movies as anyone else, because between the ages of five and thirty you must have seen a couple of thousand movies. They're built into your own sensibility just as profoundly as the novel."

Ariel: Do you think the cinema, with its current popularity, is perhaps becoming the modern romance; that is, replacing the novel as the vehicle for romance in the late 20th century?

Price: I think at the moment it's taking over some of the novel's natural audience, which would be young intellectuals, people of your age and slightly older. I also think the movies seem to be doomed in a way that the novel isn't doomed necessarily—that is economically. It's just staggeringly difficult to make a full-length movie now because they cost at least a million dollars to make; and even if they cost less, even if you make something tremendously cheap like Barbara Loden's recent film, *Wanda*—everyone's oohing and ahhing because that cost $180,000: well, my God, where are you going to get $180,000? You can produce a good musical on Broadway for $75,000. Where are you going to get more than twice that amount of money to make your own movie with? So I think what's happening to the movies is maybe also what's happening to the novel and the short story; and that is, their audiences are shrinking down to a kind of hard-core minimum, which may not be bad. The novel started as a popular form, a popular middle-class form; and it's become essentially a form of the upper intellectual classes in the 19th and 20th centuries. I think the movies may finally turn out to be the entertainment of the educated classes, rather than the popular form they were at the beginning. I think the history of the movie may exactly parallel the history of the novel, except that the movie has done it much more rapidly. Movies are only 60 years old now, and the novel is almost 400 years old.

Ariel: Do you have another novel in the works?

Price: In the works to the extent that I'm thinking about making some notes for it. I haven't begun writing the chapters. As a matter of fact, just now I'm working on revising the essays, the literary essays and personal essays that I've written over the last ten years, thinking about making a volume of them.

Ariel: The criticism has been made of Welty's *Delta Wedding* that it is a naive book, politically; and in a sense, one could make the criticism about *Losing Battles* and probably about a lot of Southern fiction, excluding Faulkner's. A story of yours and a story of Flannery O'Connor's were removed from a short story anthology recently and substituted in their place were six stories by black writers. What's your feeling generally about the relationship between white Southern writers and the black man in the south, and why urban critics, mostly New York critics, feel the need to make such a criticism?

Price: Well, what bothers urban critics, or what bothers the people who objected to *Delta Wedding* or to anything of mine on racial grounds, is the reality that lies behind the stories, the social realities. To that extent, *Delta Wedding, Losing Battles, A Long and Happy Life* are tremendously politically conscious stories, in that they report a given social condition at a certain time; it may not be the immediate present. *Delta Wedding* is set, what?, in the late 20s and was published in the early 40s. *A Long and Happy Life* is set in, I think, 1957 and *wasn't* published until 1962; so it's a report on a racial situation in Warren County, North Carolina, really as it existed in my childhood and up until the mid-60s when the situation there began to start moving. The primary error they've made, of course, is living in cities, which it seems human beings really weren't ever intended to do—not if they were ever going to remain human. It seems to me on the contrary that *Delta Wedding* is probably the single most illuminating book we have about racial relations in the Deep South, about the fantastic complexity of how that evil operates, how people of enormous culture, kindness, generosity, goodness like the Fairchilds, with great human richness—human in *nature*—were perfectly capable of living on a base of virtual slaves. On the other hand, so were Sophocles, Euripides, Homer, Plato, Socrates, everyone who wrote in Rome, everyone who lived in the world up until about the 1820s when the notion of emancipation really got going. No one likes the idea of slavery—well, a few slaveowners do—but the fact is that it has existed for most of the history of the human race and has been, like it or not, an important factor in the sorts of cultures that have produced works of art, leisure cultures. We're now entering a kind of leisure culture where you don't have to have slaves to do your work, or you have so much free time yourself that you do your own housework and also write your own novels—although that might ring a little falsely to the housewife who wanted to be a novelist and had three children and lived in a little apartment of her own in Dayton,

Ohio. But this situation has changed very fast—if you want to read an exercise in total silliness, go back for instance to Diana Trilling's review of *Delta Wedding* in *The New Republic,* or whatever it was, in 1941. The dopiest sort of view. No, it seems to me that *Delta Wedding* and *Losing Battles* together give us a far truer notion of what it was like to be alive in the Deep South before the second war than any other novels ever written.

Ariel: Is it your view that the place of criticism is in description and judgment rather than in analysis?

Price: I think you're right. But I think a certain amount of analysis obviously occurs in the process of describing and judging.

Ariel: But that's not the only end of criticism?

Price: No, and I think the most valuable single discovery of modern criticism has been *explication de texte.* Just sitting down and trying to find out what a poem says. I mean, it's a great heresy to say so; but I think that it's possible to give a prose statement of any good poem. The prose statement is not going to *be* the poem, but part of what disturbs me greatly about, let's say, the poetry of Wallace Stevens, which I think I admire enough, though I'm not sure how much, is that I almost can never figure out what the poem *means.* I've been trying to read "The Comedian as the Letter C" all week; and I mean, I'm just no further along than when I started. And all the commentaries that I've read don't seem to know any more than I do, really. They're just talking, fairly rapidly, in hopes no one will stop them and ask a question.

Ariel: In your teaching of Milton, what do you expect your students to respond to? How do you want them to respond?

Price: Well, aside from all the hard work that they have to do, reading the poem, finding out what all the allusions are to, finding out what a given line says, how a given line is constructed, what its mechanics are—now those are important. God knows, very important preliminary steps; but they are only preliminary steps toward the final problem, the destination: discovering the design, what Milton's design upon your life and upon the life of the world is. What *Samson Agonistes* says to you about your life. Then, if you find out what it says to you, you've got to go home and decide what you're going to *do* about what it says; and what you're probably going to do about it is ignore it; but at least never again in your life will you be able to

say that you don't know what commands *Samson Agonistes* makes
to you. I don't think it makes a *single* command; I think it makes
extremely complicated commands. They're not commands that can
be stated in aphoristic form; they can be stated only within the
large structure of the poem itself, which is why it's a poem and not an
essay about human behavior.

Ariel: Do you think it's a mistake to try and make moral euphe-
misms about every work of literature? Could it be that we shouldn't
try to verbalize the organic effect of a piece of literature upon
ourselves?

Price: Well, I think it is possible to say a lot about what they say.
It's quite possible to say a lot of the things that *King Lear* is about. It's
about the relationship between parents and children; it's about the
relationship between man and the mysterious gods, for another thing
(and the two things seem to be intimately related in Shakespeare's
mind, and it's no doubt they are in the mind of God); but it's very
dangerous to try that. I think one of the things that modern criticism
has been is a revolution against the 18th or 19th century view that
literature is largely a set of tracts, sermons; that really the lesson of
King Lear is "Be good to your old Daddy." Well, that's one of
the lessons of *King Lear* perhaps; it's by no means the central one.
The lesson of *King Lear* is the whole play, and that's a very difficult
thing to keep in your mind all at once. But Shakespeare never
promised it was going to be any easier than that; so if you're going to
deal with him, you've got to *deal* with, I mean, really come to grips
with *King Lear*. It's an experience at least as difficult as inventing the
H-bomb.

Ariel: If you had one piece of advice to give to a young writer that
you have some confidence in, what would it be?

Price: What advice would I give? This is assuming that he's gifted
to start with and that he's read a great deal of literature of the past of
the sort he wishes to write—if he wants to write novels, he's read
most of the good novels ever written. Well, I think the only piece of
useful advice would be to say, "Go to your room and write." Pascal
says in the *Pensées,* "Most of the troubles of the human race come
from man's inability to do one thing—sit in his room and work."

PW Interviews: Reynolds Price
John F. Baker/1975

From *Publishers Weekly,* 4 August 1975, 12–13. *Publishers Weekly* is published by R. R. Bowker Company, a Xerox company. Copyright © 1975 by Xerox Corporation. Reprinted by permission of Xerox Corporation and Reynolds Price.

Sometimes the author in person can be easily imagined from the nature of his or her work. You know instinctively that X will be breezy and rather cynical, Y earnest and humorless, Z cheerful and a bit sloppy. Reading *The Surface of Earth,* however, gives no accurate idea at all of what novelist Reynolds Price is like.

The Atheneum author, whose book came out last month to a critical reception that was mixed and even controversial in New York, but was generally enthusiastic elsewhere, has few of the qualities in person that his latest work suggests. Where the book is leisurely, ruminative and predominantly dark in color, Price is high-spirited, often witty, and a long way from the driven Southern writer of the popular imagination.

His career, too, has been a shapely and ordered progress to wide recognition as what Theodore Solotaroff describes as "the legitimate heir of the great Southern writers of past generations." Born and raised in North Carolina, he went to Duke, where he first began to write (and where he came to Eudora Welty's attention). Then he won a Rhodes scholarship to Oxford, and spent three years at Merton College as a postgraduate student. He continued to write, met and won encouragement from such eminent English *littérateurs* as Lord David Cecil and W. H. Auden and ended up, like Robert Frost and Eliot, winning first recognition and publication outside his native land.

"It was at Oxford that I did my first good stories, and where I first began to be taken seriously as a writer," Price says. His first published story was printed by Stephen Spender in *Encounter.* "I guess I was first published by the CIA, in fact. I'm a creature of the CIA—no wonder I've always had such a warm feeling for them!" (Price builds a quick, absurd edifice on this circumstance, and roars with laughter.)

A British publisher gave him a contract for a book, and meanwhile his agent, Diarmuid Russell, was circulating some of his stories here. It was not until the *Encounter* story, however, that American publishers began to show any interest. One of the first who did so was Hiram Haydn, at that time establishing Atheneum with Pat Knopf and Simon Michael Bessie. A contract was signed, and though he had a book of stories, *The Names and Faces of Heroes,* ready, it was actually his novel *A Long and Happy Life* that came out first, on one of Atheneum's earliest lists. "Hiram and Pat kept postponing it until the astrological omens were right," Price grins. "It was fortunate they did, because eventually John Fischer heard about it and published it in *Harper's.*"

Price actually intended the story that eventually became *The Surface of Earth* to be his next novel. "It started as just a fairly simple idea—a father and his son traveling in North Carolina in 1944. Eventually that was the end of the book, and I worked back to its beginnings." As the project grew in his mind, however, there were other things he wanted to write, and he put it aside.

In the following decade he published two more novels, *A Generous Man* (1966) and *Love and Work* (1968), another volume of stories, *Permanent Errors* (1970) and a collection of literary essays, *Things Themselves* (1972). Then he finally returned to work on his biggest book three years ago, and wrote fiercely at it every day for three years (with Sundays off) until it was completed last Christmas.

"I can't remember another book that just came as this one did," he says. "There was hardly any breaking down or stopping. For the first time I got an idea of what it must have been like to be one of the great 19th century novelists who created a world. I'd go into my workroom and close the door, and I'd be surrounded by my characters, and the times in which they lived." Price tries to write about 500 words at a sitting, honing constantly, and once it is done, it is finished: "I don't work in drafts."

It is a huge book, and, alarmed by its bulk, Price went over it when he was finished with a fine-tooth comb, trying to see what he could cut; "but without being at all narcissistic, I couldn't see there was anything that didn't advance the story."

Many of the events in *The Surface of Earth* take place offstage and are then reported, either verbally by a character, or in one of the

many letters that stud the book. "I didn't calculate this, it seems to
me that's just the way things often happen in life. You don't see
something happen yourself, but somebody tells you about it, or
writes a letter describing it." This is one of the ways in which Price
sees himself and his work as clearly products of the South. "You get
used to this way of approaching things—it's a highly oral narrative
culture." The constant use of letters, in itself an old-fashioned sort of
approach to a novel these days, he also sees as true to the time of the
book. "People never used phones in those days—even when I was a
boy, though we had a phone, it was only for odds and ends. For
real communication, people wrote long letters. You can write things
in a letter you can never *say*. Oh, the splendid things I've written in
letters in my time! And usually torn them up the next morning, of
course!"

There is also "a voyeuristic element" about reading someone
else's letters, even in a book. "I remember Nevill Coghill telling me a
story about Auden at Oxford as a young man. He came into his
room one day and found Auden reading his mail. 'Mr. Auden, what
are you doing?' 'Well, how am I going to become a writer if I don't
know what people say?' Auden replied."

Price dislikes being thought of as specifically a Southern writer—
"though of course I've traveled enough to be aware of its difference
from the rest of the country, the gamey flavor that is all its own." Any
similarities among Southern writers, he says, are because they were
exposed to the same kind of life—the storytelling, the climate, the
growing up with blacks—rather than because they consciously imitate
each other. And he is intensely irritated by those who complain that
the South is a narrow frame for a writer to work in. "It's a large
part of the world, in fact, a good bit larger than France, and it has
millions of people. Complaining about its narrowness is like complaining that all the great Victorian novels were about England."

He doesn't care to be compared (as he frequently has been) with
Faulkner. One recent review compared his view of family life with
that of Eugene O'Neill, and this pleased him much better. "In England they also mention Hardy, and that's fine, too." In fact his
fictional idols are Tolstoy (whom he has read and reread ever since
he was 14 years old), Hardy and Chekhov.

Contemporary writers? "I'm afraid I tend to go back and read my old favorites over and over again, and I suspect that most people who don't *have* to read contemporary books probably do that." He recalls the narcotic effect of the reading of childhood—"when books are something that can get you through the time"—and figures that all committed readers and writers can remember something of that sensation. He would like to do an essay on the profound and probably subconscious effect childhood reading has on anyone. He would also like to examine the current nature of criticism: "I think the idea of a regular reviewer is untenable. It requires extreme tenacity, and a very fine rein on one's testiness; it's fatally easy to show off at the expense of someone else's labor." He himself would decline to review a book with which he was not in sympathy, and laughingly proposes a licensing system for reviewers: "One of the criteria would be that they must have been reviewed themselves within the last three years—preferably unfavorably!" Beyond that, he declines to be drawn into a discussion of the brouhaha that erupted in the pages of the *New York Times Book Review* recently between Eudora Welty, an admirer of his work, and critic Richard Gilman, who gave *The Surface of Earth* an unenthusiastic notice.

"I don't like to see reviewers and writers getting so seriously involved," he says: "My books are an important part of my life, but they're certainly not the beginning and end of the world."

Now his big book is safely published, Price has decided to give himself a year off. He has nothing he wants to do at the present, except "read, look out the window, see friends." Writing a book, he says, is a major effort for the unconscious mind, "and now it's time to give it a rest. Maybe not enough writers give their minds a rest like me. There I go again," he laughs. "Patting myself on the back, as is my wont!"

Conversations: Reynolds Price and William Ray

William Ray/1976

From the *Bulletin of the Mississippi Valley Collection* (Memphis State University), 9 (Fall 1976). Reprinted by permission of Reynolds Price.

These conversations began with two friendships. In 1972 Professor Charles Crawford, Director of the Oral History Research Office at Memphis State University, suggested that a series of interviews with Southern writers be undertaken, perhaps to add a literary touch to the odd but appealing diversity of ongoing projects under his direction. Oral History at Memphis State reflects an array of academic and not-so-academic interests, from a living history of the Tennessee Valley Authority to the spoken record of Memphis jazz and blues, each project dedicated to the preservation of the *story* in human history as it is uniquely recorded in the minds of its actors. The invitation to record on tape the Southern writer's story, through the dramatic interplay of seriatim conversation, was *easy* to accept, especially for an enthusiastic amateur. Professor Crawford's own enthusiasm, his and his secretary Brenda Meier's never-failing help, and the flexibility offered by such a do-it-yourself venture have sustained that early pleasure.

Another, older friendship offered further motivation and ideal material for history by recorded speech. Reynolds Price had been a friend, on the page and in person, since at least 1968. His early novels, *A Long and Happy Life* (1962) and *A Generous Man* (1966), and the early stories collected as *The Names and Faces of Heroes* (1963), nurtured in common soil and in the common tongue of rural North Carolina, were established resources of the New Literary South when the friendship began. Since then, other books have enriched that common ground and enhanced that reputation. By 1974, conversations with Reynolds Price seemed not only worth continuing, but worth printing as well. Thus this volume, produced with the generous help of Dewey Pruett, former Curator of the Mississippi Valley Collection of the John Brister Library at Memphis State University, and Jim Simmons of the Memphis State University Press. Special thanks are due Sharon Hesse and Brenda Meier, who transcribed the conversations.

The five conversations cover an active two year period, from June 1973 to June 1975, when Reynolds Price was at work on what is now his longest and most demanding novel. All took place in the writer's home on forty acres of tamed forest and pastureland near Durham, North Carolina. Duke University, where he teaches, and the University of North Carolina at nearby Chapel Hill, where the friendship began, are silent but strong points of personal reference. Points of topical reference in the talks are many. Like Mr. Price's living room, they reflect a life and an art of subtle complexity, organized by sustaining loves and allegiances, looking out on the world with a wide and luminous vision. Special prominence is of course given to other novels and stories and essays by the writer's hand: *Love and Work* (1968), *Permanent Errors* (1970), *Things Themselves* (1972) and, for the reason already mentioned, *The Surface of Earth* (1975).

The talking relationship with Reynolds Price has, for Oral History at Memphis State, been a happy coincidence. He is a master teacher as well as writer. He is a writer-about-fiction as well as a fictionist who speaks forcefully about his chosen craft and his given culture. He talks of the South because he grew up there, and has lived elsewhere. He talks of contemporary writers when he talks of the classical novel and its tradition, because he knows both. He talks candidly of self, of society, and of the arts, even (perhaps especially) when one runs against the other's grain. Like his views, the voice that expresses them is deep, strong, and carefully gauged. He has been a wise and willing conspirator in an act of breaking silence—a silence which, for more than one modern writer, has separated the life from the work and from the world.

These edited conversations should have some value both for general and for scholarly interests, in the several contexts which they touch: Southern culture and letters; American history and writing in the twentieth century; world literature, especially the novel, in its richest traditions. Their themes are many, but not random. Though unrehearsed, they have Mr. Price's impulse for order and illumination. And whether their reader is listening for clues to his life and work, or looking for some light on the larger contexts, they record one writer's voice in moments of truth and humor. For that they were well worth doing and are here preserved.

Conversation 1, 18 June 1973
Ray: Mr. Price, it is often suggested that the Southern writer's life is perhaps more important to him as material or basis for his fiction than anything else. Can you think of anything in your background, growing up in the South in your time and your way, that had to be expressed in fiction or was expressed uniquely in fiction?

Price: I never quite thought of Southern writing or Southern writers in that particular way. I suppose part of what you're saying is that people who live in an essentially rural society or a society of small towns and villages are dependent, are enormously dependent, upon the resources of self and family, of very small groups, of groups consisting perhaps of no more than five or six people, if that; that the pressures of the government, politics, larger movements of peoples, and of societies in general, have not perhaps impinged as directly upon the South, certainly at least since the Civil War, as they have upon citizens of Manhattan. I'm not sure all that's true, but hearing you ask the question makes me *think* that.

Ray: Was your own family a small one and as closely knit as one thinks of a Southern family?

Price: It was rather large. Both my parents were from small towns. My father was from Warrenton, North Carolina, a small town in the northeastern part of the state, which had been a very important town in North Carolina politics in the late eighteenth and early nineteenth centuries. It was the home of Nathaniel Macon, who was Speaker of the House under Thomas Jefferson, and had been quite a center. Warrenton is now, presently, a town of perhaps fewer than 2,000 people.

Macon, which is five miles away, was my mother's home town, the town in which I was born. Macon is presently a town of fewer than 200 people and has always been roughly that size.

I don't know that I could say any particular thing that, as generalization, would set my childhood, my experience with family, very much apart from what I take to have been the experience of other

Southern writers. Obviously, there are an enormous number of
details, both of fact and personal feeling, in my case, which have
emerged in my work, either directly in the form of autobiographical
fact or in some sort of more metaphorical or allegorical form—forms
about many of which I am obviously unconscious.

I do think that as far as I know about the backgrounds of other
Southern writers and really of other American writers in general, my
family background is rather typical—relatively small-town, intensely
based upon the relationships existing between tightly knit family-
groups, paternal and maternal families who had known one another
for decades, operating within the framework of small towns (even
of villages in the case of my mother's family), resolutely middle-class
in income and in outlook, Protestant (in the case of my mother's
family, Methodist; in the case of my father's family, Episcopalian and
Baptist).

My mother's father worked for the Seaboard Railroad as station
keeper—station manager—in Macon for most of his life, and most of
her brothers then proceeded to Norfolk, Virginia and worked in
various capacities for the Seaboard there. My father's father, Edward
Price, was a clerk in the Registry of Deeds in Warren County for a
number of years.

It sounds to me very much like the lives of other Southern writers
that I've known—in my case, at least, a grandfather who himself
remembered and suffered the effects of the Civil War, Grandfather
Price. My own father and my mother, of course, suffered very much
the effects of the Great Depression in the thirties. In many ways a
very typical writer's family, it would seem to me—perhaps most
importantly, a family in which the children were tolerated in close
proximity to the adults. And though there were nurses and maids and
cooks of one sort or another almost universally present in the various
households of my family—black women, occasional black men as
gardeners—though there were those figures always there to tend the
children to some degree, we were never reared by nurses or gover-
nesses of any sort; we were reared by our parents and aunts and
uncles. I remember very much as a child resisting the company of
other children whenever I had the choice of children or adults. The
adults were always having to shoo me out of the house on a Sunday
afternoon because I'd much prefer to sit at their feet and listen to

them retell the family stories and jokes—much preferred that to going outside racing round in the dust with other children. I don't know that there's anything unusual about that.

Ray: It doesn't sound very unusual; and that leads to another question that I would like to ask, without considering the larger implications of the relationship of history to story. The question is: is it more important for a writer like yourself to have a family like that and to be the conduit or expression of a culture than to have a personal history—a personal crucifixion, if need be—to make you write, to provide the impetus for whatever expression narrative fiction necessarily entails? Is the surrounding, the environment, the upbringing, the ambience of your early life more important than the particular emotional or psychological impulse that has made you write?

Price: Well, it's an interesting question; but I would think it's fairly certain to be unanswerable in any sane fashion because it raises the whole basic conflict of psychology—of training, nurture—versus character, innate endowment.

My own conviction, at this point in my life, would be that people are what they are because of *who* they are in a rather narrow sense, because of who their genetic precursors happened to be. The longer I live—and I'm forty now—the more I begin to see, or at least begin to believe that I see, that the basic facts about me are conditioned largely by the fact that I am a *Price* and a *Rodwell* (my mother's family). My parents are dead but I can go back to Warren County now and meet my father's sisters, my mother's surviving sister there, various cousins, and feel immediately at home with them in a way which has nothing to do with present compatibility but with the simple fact that to some very large extent we are simply the same sort of animal. We're the same sort of animal because we have the same kind of chemical predispositioning.

I really do believe that; and my feeling, as a rank amateur to science and as someone who simply reads the latest developments on genetics in *Newsweek* magazine, is that we're coming round much more now to a revival of faith in genetic preconditioning of a sort which was quite popular when I was a child. People were always being told in the thirties that you had inherited so-and-so from your father or your grandmother; so-and-so had cancer because her mother had cancer. Then we went through the forties and fifties in

which absolutely everyone was supposed to have sprung fully grown
from the brow of Time. Now I think we're coming much more
solidly to a view that people have a severe set of conditions punched
into their systems when they're born, through the DNA molecule if
nothing else.

This is certainly not to say that there aren't enormous amounts of
pressure applied to those physical realities, those chemical realities,
which can pull it, shape it, mold it, perhaps even to some extent
basically alter it. But it has been very much my feeling—and I've
been rather surprised by the feeling in the last few years—that I find
myself lapsing into *Pricedom* to some extent: a fairly comfortable
feeling to think that the things I don't like about myself are largely the
result of my carrying in my body certain molecules from Wales and
England, about which I can essentially do nothing.

Ray: You're talking about fatalism, a kind of chemical determina-
tion. I wonder if it's present in such a writer as Faulkner. Are Faulkner's Southerners *fated* within a fated circle, finally, even those who
seem to escape? Quentin Compson, for example, never can escape.
Is this one great Faulknerian theme? And is it a theme shared by you
or by other Southern writers whom you admire and know?

Price: As you know, I'm not nearly the Faulkner scholar I should
be—there are probably half the novels of Faulkner which I haven't
read. My guess would be that there is a burdensome sense of family
as destiny. I don't know really the degree to which Faulkner would
have defined that as a kind of chemical destiny, as opposed to
destiny of environment and conditioning.

I do think (and it's a cliché about Southern writing but like many
clichés a true one) that Southern writers in general have an extraordinary sense of the power of family over individual. But I think that's
simply the merest accurate observation of the conditions of Southern
life, of small-town rural life. The people who were present were your
blood relations. There were no street-car conductors around; you
were not bombarded by street-people coming at you as you would
have been had you grown up in Philadelphia, even had you grown
up in a Philadelphia middle-class family. You were surrounded by,
protected by, and threatened by those people who shared certain
basic structures that were also present in your own body; and therefore your obsessions were formed in the presence of those people

who were most like you. It obviously gave a kind of inner intensity of both narcissism and understanding to Southerners—especially to those Southerners who later, for complicated reasons, became artists of one sort or another. It gave them, I think, a kind of intensity and need for understanding and expression which perhaps is not so strong in certain other parts of the country—a kind of intensity that I, for instance, don't feel in the students whom I teach now at Duke.

It seems to me that with the weakening of the family in American middle-class society an extraordinary diffuseness results. A kind of vacuum is present in the center of a great many young people, space which was once filled by family concerns. I'm not necessarily defending those concerns, because (as is world-famous) the family has also been the hothouse of neurosis and psychosis.

Ray: And this is clearly present in Southern fiction?

Price: Of course. But something rather frightening to consider is that the human being—so far as we understand anything about the evolution of *homo sapiens*—has always existed within the framework of a fairly closely-knit, fairly permanent family. And really only within your lifetime and mine have we seen the break-up of the family in this very dramatic way—both the physical break-up in which people leave the nest early, never to return, and yearn not to have their parents live near them. You know—your parents live in North Carolina; so you rapidly get a job in Oregon if possible, placing 3,000 miles between yourself and them; and finally, when Mother gets to be eighty, you send a check to a rest home in North Carolina and have her salted away there. Whereas, of course, in my childhood and in rural areas to this day, the old person is simply absorbed into the back room of the house; and the family gets on with the rather awful business of presiding over the decay and death of one more human being and witnessing every minute of it—the children witnessing it with every breath that they draw.

I know a great many intelligent, thoroughly admirable young men and women at Duke now who really don't know one thing about human beings older than their own parents, who really couldn't tell you anything about what it's like to be older than thirty-eight for the simple reason that they've never lived around old people. That seems to me frightening.

Ray: And presumably the phenomena of sickness and death are largely unknown to them?

Price: Quite meaningless to them. And therefore, it seems to me, they put far too much emphasis upon the present. They have far too little sense of the mortality of human destiny; there are few *memento mori* strewn about their paths. Of course, there *are* such things; their own contemporaries have died in ways that your contemporaries and mine didn't die—through overdoses of drugs, Vietnam. In short, these particular young people have the problem of living in a ghetto of youth—than which I could think of few things more limiting.

Ray: This unidimensionalism that you note in students in American universities these days—is it characteristic of only their generation, or is it characteristic of a culture cutting across generations? And if the latter is the case, what is its origin?

Price: It's not anything that I've thought much about; therefore anything I say will be subject to extreme shallowness and the sorts of television-generalizations that are not really worth indulging in. But it would seem to me apparent that it runs right through American middle-class civilization—that is to say, all American civilization except the very poor—and it would also seem to me that in the present form it's probably an entirely new phenomenon in American history.

We have those wonderful and bleak and terrifying accounts in seventeenth- and eighteenth-century lore of the young man who set out through the Cumberland Gap or wherever for the frontier, bidding his mother and father farewell and saying he would contact them when he could and simply vanishing never to be heard from or of again (perhaps he got all the way to Kansas and lived out a long life and decided never to write back or perhaps he died before he got to the Cumberland Gap); there was that sort of lean and frightening frontier departure from family, *contingency*. But that was never the rule of the time. The rule was that people stayed on the farm or in the small town and often lived in the house with their parents and their old aunts and uncles for the rest of their lives, surrounded by their own growing progeny.

These particular children that you and I teach now seem to me subject to an especial curse that's been visited upon them; and I don't really know why—why the family's broken down the way that it has. One of the reasons that anything breaks down is because people no longer want to *have* it. And the family *has* caused—at least since the Oedipuses—so much havoc in the lives of individuals that it's entirely understandable that people would wish to destroy it or at least try radically to alter its nature. When I see the desire of a number of young people to move back into the extended family situations in which there are large groups of people living together— everything from communes to much more old-fashioned things in which there were a mother, a father, two sons, their wives, their children, and several spinster aunts and uncles all living in a large house—those situations, I must say, rather appall *me*; I would very much hate to live in situations like that. There are many things about the small family that attract me and seem to me an improvement upon the very neurotic conditions that were prevalent in times when there were too many people living in one house, all of them desper- ately in one another's hair, psychic and actual.

But the fact remains, as I said earlier, that to destroy the family or to alter it radically is to alter the only thing that we really know as a constant in human history. It's almost the only specific invention of man as an animal. The continuing family, bound by love and/or duty, is virtually the only thing man possesses that almost no other animal possesses, as far as I can tell.

Ray: The new tribalism that you have described, negatively: do you see it as a substitute for either the small family that you and I grew up in, on the one hand, or the loner, the existential hero, the isolated man on the other? A reversion, if you will, to an older tribalism, a looser confederation of small human groups in a larger group? And is discipline in that kind of life perhaps an answer to the neurotic laxity of the alternatives that our times have presented? Typically in such writers as Eugene O'Neill for the small family, or Jack Kerouac for the man of the road?

Price: I would suspect that what you call a "new tribalism" *is* a response to the small families who followed the Depression, maybe an economic concomitant of the Depression. I certainly knew by the age of eight that my parents were in such economic straits that they simply couldn't afford to have more than two children between 1933 and 1941.

You know there must be some sense on the part of young people, some hunger for this larger, more teeming atmosphere; and when one sees the smaller family of three, three or four, one understands perhaps why children want numbers.

I myself didn't grow up in a family like that. As I've said, though my brother and I were the only children in our immediate family, we were surrounded constantly by this larger family of cousins, aunts, uncles, who were present almost every day of our lives and present in real and important form. I think I very much enjoyed it as a child. I never questioned it as a condition of my life. I never yearned to flee from it.

But once my parents had died, once I had moved geographically away from the bases of my parents' families, I found that it was a great relief to be out of family. And when I go back to visit now, I find that I enjoy it for a while; but I very quickly begin to feel tremendously *impinged upon* by these numbers of people from whom I've been away too long.

Ray: How far are you now living from Warrenton, your family home, here outside Durham?

Price: It's an hour and twenty minutes, about sixty-five miles, something like that.

Ray: How often do you think you might visit Warrenton, say in a year?

Price: Oh, three or four times maybe.

Ray: For holidays?

Price: Holidays and funerals with fairly depressing frequency now, because my parents—if my father were alive, he'd be seventy-three; and my mother would be sixty-eight; their brothers and sisters, all of them were older than they and are beginning to vanish now.

I was just there last—oh, two weeks ago—for the funeral of my mother's oldest sister, who lived to be eighty-eight. My family, as a rule, have not been very long-lived; and she lived to a greater age than anyone I can recall on either side of the family. I was there for her funeral; and there was a very pleasant—since obviously the funeral of an eighty-eight year-old woman is not an occasion of great mourning—there was an extremely pleasant gathering of the family with the typical kind of Southern-reunion lunch for everyone: lots of ham and pecan pies and a chance to sit around and tell the old stories and jokes.

As always I was astounded afresh by the verbal ingenuity of my
mother's and father's family—the love of words, the precise and very
careful guardianship of language that still exists in the family. They're
not especially well-read people, they're not highly educated people;
but they are people who (like human beings in general until really the
second half of the twentieth century) have treasured the *word* as the
central means of continuance in human life.

Ray: A trait of Southern behavior that is exploited and expressed
in fiction by Eudora Welty in such books as *Losing Battles*?

Price: Well, she's really the great custodian of the oral history of
the South, the old traditions of the talking South.

But I feel it tremendously when I go back and hear one aunt begin
telling a story, which we've all already heard—you know, at a conservative estimate, 395 times in the last forty years—told by this
same woman. And she will tell the story—because I have a good
auditory memory and am able to recite it in my own head silently
two words ahead of her, to know exactly which noun she's about to
use, exactly which conjunction, preposition, even where the articles
come—and suddenly she will reach a sentence, and she'll have a sort
of verbal collapse; she'll forget the appropriate noun.

Ray: So you cue her?

Price: And I will know what her mistake is, but somehow because
I'm still "little Reynolds" in relation to her, I don't make the correction. Someone more nearly her age will make the correction—and
make it rather gently, not simply saying, "No, no, you've made a
mistake" but repeating the sentence and getting it right. That happened six times two weeks ago when I was there for the funeral. It's
just the old, old principle—the transmission of data from mouth to
mouth. And it still seems in many ways the safest means of transmit-
ting the data, if the data is meant to be *memorable*.

Ray: You spoke of the loss of this ability in the second half of the
twentieth century. Would you care to amplify on that observation?
Does it lead anywhere?

Price: I'm not sure that it does, except to more of these potentially
silly generalizations that I'm making. It would almost certainly be a
product, wouldn't it, of the decline of the family, of groups sitting
around retelling the past to one another?

Ray: Thus the observation that students are less and less able to communicate verbally in whatever form we present them? It's not just a foolish function of the premature dotage of English teachers, that our students are less and less forced by circumstance to communicate in at all sophisticated forms?

Price: I think you and I both are describing a phenomenon which we know to exist. Just what the many causes of the phenomenon are, I don't think we can say. I'm constantly now made aware of the fact that all my life I've assumed that almost everyone else in the world had the kind of family I had—extremely talkative people who use the English language very, very well in a rough-and-ready but precise way, as a precise instrument of human expression and delicacy and communication.

Now I know my assumption was wrong! But in my particular case, I was wonderfully blessed with the two large families I had—the Prices and the Rodwells, lovers and guardians of the word. I think that, insofar as I'm a writer at all, it must be a very important fact that I grew up in the presence of language used in its best and most careful ways—for the communication of past love, present and future obligation; above all, for consolation and delight.

I think young people today in America are the victims of already long lifetimes of hearing the English language *very badly used*. Like everyone else in America, I've been watching the Watergate hearings on television for the last couple of weeks, utterly engrossed by them. And of all the causes for horror—aghastment—in the whole situation, the one that most appalls me is the poverty of language amongst those people who have so far testified before the Senate committee, such people as Jeb McGruder and Herbert Porter, even Maurice Stans, an older man: to hear that particular non-language they're using. Jeb McGruder was unable to talk about the *break-in* to the Democratic headquarters, of the *burglary*. He invariably had to call it the "entry," the "entry into Democratic headquarters." *Entry* is a word which has absolutely no moral content whatever.

Ray: Even when allied with the word "surreptitious."

Price: Especially when allied with the word "surreptitious." I heard General Haig yesterday on a CBS interview—the man who's taken over Haldeman's duties as Chief of Staff in the White House—talk about the attempt to put the White House staff onto a kind of "conveyor-belt system" for more "rapid processing of input and output." Well, I'd hoped that Haig was going to introduce something fresh and salubrious into that particular murk; but a man who can say that is not going to effect change.

And I'm reminded vividly and frighteningly in the last couple of weeks of that essay by George Orwell, which I read as a freshman at Duke, called "Politics and the English Language," in which he says the moment language begins to crumble in the hands of men of power, watch out—the worst is yet to come. And it is!

Ray: And Ron Ziegler's word *inoperative* can mean nothing, yet stand for a public declaration.

Price: Exactly. Exactly.

Ray: Is the writer in our time like Yeats's Cuchulain fighting the waves, as he is a user of words? I'm not sure, perhaps you're not sure, that all writers are artistic or judicious conservers of language as we've been discussing it; but is that one function of the writer, for yourself as you see it?

Price: I think I'm aware of that as one of my purposes now in my life—having been a writer or having consciously thought of myself as a writer since the age of fifteen or sixteen, almost twenty-five years. I don't think I thought of myself in that way when I was beginning to publish books in my late twenties and early thirties. I thought of myself much more as a kind of possessed recipient of inspiration, a sort of lightning rod for the gods perhaps! That may have been true—it would be nice to think so. But I think now that, while I'm still aware that whatever gift I possess and whatever work I do is to a large extent beyond my own control, I do feel that *one* of my purposes is to employ the English language, to propagate the English language, in ways in which it is very seldom employed and propagated in America today, even by writers who should know better.

Ray: One of the most obvious characteristics of your own writing is its lucidity, and I couldn't help noticing in your home today a copy of Strunk and White's *Elements of Style*. So I ask you the question: for the fictionist *or* the non-fictionist, *are* there rules of style? And to what extent is the writer aware of such schoolmarmish things?

Price: "Rules of style?" Be more specific.

Ray: As a working proposition for the student of prose, that sentences should be short, balanced, or rhythmic?

Price: I don't know that those particular injunctions are defensi-

ble—few of my sentences are short; very few of the sentences of
most writers are short!—but as a beginning rule for beginning writers,
it's probably a helpful injunction.

No, I think that I would subscribe, as *writer* and *teacher,* to the
classical rules of English rhetoric. I would think that they should be
taught, that they should be obeyed (though not as sacred dogma—
they can always be bent by a man who needs to bend them and
knows how), that they should be seen as the bones of language, the
skeleton of the language: a skeleton strong enough and flexible
enough to have borne the weight of great geniuses, of literature and
politics and science throughout centuries, and capable of bearing that
weight today.

Ray: Among your other activities is Milton scholarship, the teaching of Milton, whom you studied with Helen Gardner at Oxford. I
would ask you: other than Milton, what writers do you find yourself
returning to most often? And what writers—or what works, more
specifically—have impressed you, with time, more than any others?

Price: I've written a good deal about that particular facet of my
own past, I think. The writers whom I admire and return to are
writers most literate people admire and return to—Tolstoy, Milton,
the Bible.

Just in the last two or three years I've been returning to the Bible in
a way which I think has really been important in the fiction that I'm
writing now. I've been doing a series of translations into very literal,
very plain twentieth-century English prose of short narrative passages
from the Old and New Testaments—really attempting to learn, or
relearn, something about the bare bones of narrative; the absolute
principles of what story is and can be, of what expectations: the
simple fact being, obviously, that the narratives of the Old and New
Testaments are the most successful narratives in human history, in
that they have enforced belief and attention upon thousands of years
of auditors; therefore they must contain a great deal which any
narrative artist can learn from. I've been very fascinated and I hope
my novel has been enriched by the work that I've done on those
narratives.

I've also in the last few years done a great deal of reading in
American detective fiction. I know that writers are all supposed to be
famous addicts of detective fiction; but until the last two or three

years, I myself hadn't been that. I perhaps just wasn't ready to appreciate and enjoy it. But I've been making up for lost time in the last few years, reading a great deal of Raymond Chandler and Dashiell Hammett, Ross Macdonald amongst living writers, and really seeing them as what I think they are—and what many writers older than I have known for years: that they are, in the twentieth-century novel, the great exponents of pure narrative, which is certainly why they're amongst the most popular of novels. They're amongst the most popular of novels because they're amongst the best. That is, they're amongst the purest purveyors of *story*. And I'm really convinced now—that what the novel is, is *a long story about a number of people as they move through the acid of Time.* But if it's not a *story*, it can be none of those other things; and it cannot really interest more readers than the author's family and perhaps a few beleaguered graduate students. Such experiments as we've all been subjected to in the last few years in America fiction—you know the kind of novel I'm talking about, which is essentially written by graduate students for other graduate students—those are simply the sorts of flukes which have always been present on the fringes of literature but can have no permanent demand on the attention of audiences, of readers.

Ray: Do you think the readers' perceptions and expectations therefore change little, or less, than some sociologists of literature maintain? Is there no change, with time, in the pattern of expectations for what a novel or a story is? Is it possible that here is a vanguard in the breakdown of narrative form or of narrative expectation in fiction, which we simply may not be aware of as proficient but conservative readers in an older tradition?

Price: Well, of course there are changes. I mean, we've just finished saying that young people today are very different from, say, young people even fifteen or twenty years ago—the young people that I was in college with twenty years ago. And yet I find, say, that when I read them, some brief twenty lines of prose from *The Book of Kings* about the murder of Jezebel, they're utterly enthralled. They didn't know the story existed; they've never heard of the wicked Queen Jezebel or the man who had her thrown out the window. But they're enthralled by something which can only be called *story*.

Someone moved from A to B; and as a result of his physical move
from A to B, C occurred.

These young people are, in some genuine sense of the word, a
different kind of organism from me; yet they and I can sit in a room
in the Duke University Library and listen to something written 3,000
years ago perhaps and be held intensely by it—held to the point at
which they want to go out and learn much more, read much more of
this sort of story.

I don't quite know what to say to you. I don't want to be fuddy-
duddy about experiments in fiction or the possibilities of vanguard.
Of course, these experiments must constantly be made; and even the
most sterile and dry-as-dust experiment may flower in some entirely
unexpected way, generations later, in a *genius.* I'm only lamenting, I
think, the fact that an enormous number of literary journalists beat
the drum in a mindless way for what appears to them new—what
any serious student of literature would know not to be new at all,
certainly no newer than the *Satyricon* or *Tristram Shandy,* which in
themselves encompass almost all the experiments that are now being
foisted upon the American novel.

No, I'm not trying on some sort of turkey-cock conservatism; but I
am trying to be sane about what I think is the tremendous need of
American fiction and of fiction everywhere that I know of its existence—and that is a return to its own roots. It's no accident that
fewer and fewer people are reading fiction, that television is absorb-
ing enormous amounts of the attention and time and curiosity that
used to be directed at the novel and at the short story.

Why is this? I think it's probably because there is in human beings,
the human animal, some sort of appetite for narrative, for story. In
the eighteenth and nineteenth centuries this appetite was largely filled
in Western civilization by something called *fiction,* the novel and
story. Now it tends to be filled by other things—by serials on television, stories in newspapers. And I think if a novel is interested in—
and I as a novelist *am* interested in—recovering some of the territory
that it has ceded to these other forms, it can only do so by returning
to a much stricter devotion to the telling of story: the accessible,
approachable, consoling *story.*

The only caveat would be that I suspect that very few of the people
who are now writing the sorts of novels which I deplore, know any

stories to tell. I think if they knew the stories they would be telling them.

Ray: The novelist is first and necessarily a story-teller.

Price: I have to believe that.

Ray: Well, then we come back around to the question I asked and you evaded for very good reasons earlier. Why must you tell the story you tell?

Price: Because I know it.

Ray: But you know other stories. How do you choose your story? How does your story fashion itself?

Price: I think it really does choose you. That's certainly been my own experience.

Ray: Must there be fascination?

Price: What does "fascination" mean in that context?

Ray: What would happen to the story as you fabricate it, as you express it, as it comes into being: a fascination with or love for the characters.

Price: Of course, it's as simple as that. It is fascination; it's mesmerization (if there's such a noun) with the organic growth of something as complicated and as simple as a plot.

For the last eighteen months I've been working on a novel which is approximately, I think, half-finished now—it's going to be a very long novel. It concerns the fortunes of two families in the years from 1903 to 1944. When I began writing it, I had only a very skeletal sense of the movements of these people, the movements of this story, and of its ultimate outcome; so the great pleasure for me—the great joy of the last eighteen months of work and my great appetite for what I hope will be the next eighteen months—has really been founded in my delight at having this elaborate story invent itself day by day as I go in to my desk, not essentially knowing more than a day or two in advance precisely what's going to happen next.

Ray: What kind of control do you exercise over your material thereby? How can you say that the novel is half finished, for example, if it's a daily combat with the narrative? That's not a fair question, is it?

Price: It's a fair question, but I think it's really like asking a highjumper how he gets over the bar—it's what his muscles know how to do. I could go into a fairly elaborate explanation of the structure and the architecture of the novel, which would be premature, which I wouldn't want to do now; but I think essentially it's a matter of feel. I simply know that the story is almost half told.

Ray: Have you chosen a title?

Price: I don't have a title which I'm absolutely convinced about yet. That's beginning to disturb me a little. A title always represents, the discovery of a successful title for a book always represents for me, a kind of seizure—a final seizure upon the meaning of the book. I have one or two candidates for the title now, but I'm not utterly convinced that any of them is right.

Ray: So the title for you is an expression of theme. Is this necessarily or always the case? Can the author pull our leg, for example? Can he play with titles? And have you ever done that yourself, in a story if not a novel?

Price: Anything I would say would apply only to my own practice; I don't know about the practices of other writers. I'm sometimes a little appalled at what I take to be the flippancy of writers about the titles of their works, but I can't even give you examples of that at the moment. I just remember the emotion sometimes in the past, even occasionally in the works of my friends. But I must say I treat the matter of title with great solemnity and try to be as responsible about it as possible, as helpful to the reader.

Ray: We wouldn't expect therefore from you, as we have had from Philip Roth recently, something called *The Great American Novel*?

Price: I don't know. I'm a great admirer of Philip Roth's, and I haven't yet read that novel; so I don't really know whether that's a good title or not—the book is apparently comic—but it surely has cheek and gas.

Ray: Would it be too inane to ask you if there has been *a* great, *the* great American novel? No doubt there have been many great American novels; but is there such a thing as *the* American novel, or *the* English novel for that matter? A characteristic work? A work which can stand for the genre by some kind of metonymy?

Price: I hadn't thought of that, but I suppose the obvious thing to say would be *Huck Finn*. I'm not sure that's at all true; I'd want to think about it much more. I suppose it's the offical American novel in the way that Norman Rockwell is the offical American painter.

Ray: Twain would probably find that an odious comparison!

Price: I'm sure he would but I'm afraid it may be true. I don't know what the official English novel would be, unless it were something like *Pickwick Papers* or *Great Expectations*.

Ray: Necessarily a Dickens novel?

Price: What else would you suggest?

Ray: I would think of *Tom Jones*, for academic reasons I suppose.

Price: Yes, maybe—though that has social-class limitations which Dickens avoids. No, I wouldn't want to get in the business of picking, you know, the greatest English or American novel. I could certainly say what were my *favorites*, but that would be a matter of autobiography and not of comment. There's far too much of this business of *ranking*.

I'm pretty sure that there hasn't been an American novel yet that can really stand up in the same room with *Anna Karenina* or with Proust; that can really say, "I as an elaborate intellectual and emotional and aesthetic construct can stand beside the greatest monuments of human intellect, human architectural power." I don't really think we have that in American literature yet. I'm sorry that we don't—American literature is very young; and in any case, there simply may be conditions in the world which preclude the writing of such books any more. I don't know. I strongly suspect that there may be such conditions—that for a very long time to come novelists, like the great bald eagle, may find it difficult to lay eggs whose shells are not too soft.

Conversation 2, 18 June 1973

Ray: Mr. Price, you've mentioned older Southern writers in particular and novelists in general whose work has been important for you. Are there contemporary writers, friends of yours perhaps, who are instrumental or influential in your own writing?

Price: There are certainly writers whom I admire greatly and to whom I feel grateful for the existence of their work and for specific kindnesses that their work has done to me and to mine. I've spoken and written about my gratitude to Eudora Welty and my tremendous admiration for her work. There are writers of my own age like John Updike and Philip Roth for whom I have strong admiration and with whom I feel a kind of contemporary brotherhood perhaps. We were the class of the early thirties, as it were—I think Updike was born in 1932, and Philip Roth and I were born in 1933. I've always felt a sort of late Depression kinship with their work. I think we are largely formed by the same sorts of social conditions, and our work has a lot of interesting internal relations.

Ray: Despite the geographical disparity?

Price: Despite the geographical disparities, I think.

Ray: Well, I would make the association with Updike, not only on the basis of relationship to background, to a place—his New England, yours border Southern—but also of a similarity in approach. I think especially of the scene of Updike's in which the hero of the story—rather clearly autobiographical—leaves the hospital where his father is dying. The kind of thoughts he thinks and what he expects his father to do sound more like Rosacoke Mustian, one of your own characters (my favorite and I'm sure many of your readers' favorite character), and the way she would think somehow about her father if she found herself in that situation. I don't, however, see a connection with Roth on the basis either of relationship to background—in his case far different from yours—or of approach to material or theme. Could you see a connection yourself, or a point of contrast?

Price: I never thought it out, but I don't think there has to be a *connection*. It's perfectly possible for polar types to attract and admire one another. If pressed, I might say though that the great similarity between Philip Roth's work and my own would seem to be a shared sense of the comic nature of existence, to be pompous about it—a wild sense of the ludicrousness of most human effort.

Ray: Is Eudora Welty's fiction also expressive of this?

Price: It certainly is. Perhaps our great living comic novelist.

There are many other living writers whose work I admire and whom I wish extremely well, but it would only be accurate to say that I don't read regularly or systematically or voraciously in the work of my contemporaries in fiction or poetry.

I think that's perhaps true of most writers. They are so absorbed in their own work that they probably do very little reading, of a heavy sort anyway. My own reading when I'm working on a novel or a story, as I am now, tends to be something that's really either extremely light—magazine or newspaper reading—or something that really has nothing to do with fiction—a biography, travel, something utterly different—because the last thing one wants to do after having spent a hard day at the desk writing a novel is to go up to bed and start reading another novel.

It's perhaps one more explanation of why so many writers are addicts of detective fiction. That's the sort of thing one can lull one's brain to sleep with, without getting very deeply or intellectually engaged, without in any way feeling impinged upon, threatened by, the particular nature of the intellect or the stylistic resources involved.

The last thing I would want to read while I was writing a novel of my own would be some very highly flavored writer like Conrad or Henry James, because I think by nature, by necessity, all novelists are born mimics. And if one starts reading work that's that highly seasoned, that gamey, there's almost invariably going to be a certain amount of mimicking that simply turns up the next day in one's own work—certainly in my case.

Ray: Has this been the case, do you think, for Southern writers following Faulkner? Almost inevitably, does one have to come to terms with Faulkner in some way? Or is that no longer a burden?

Price: I've talked and complained about that a lot; so I wouldn't want to expand much on it here, except to say that I think that's an interesting case of Southern writers, almost to a man, *not* being involved in an imitation or mimicry of Faulkner but of Mr. Faulkner and other Southern writers being involved in an imitation of a given original, of a common original—which is the way men and women have talked in the South in the last fifty or sixty years. As you know, no doubt, from living in Memphis and having grown up in piedmont North Carolina, people in the South, with certain limits and certain regional variations, tend amazingly to speak in very much the same way. It's the last great regional language in America, and it's a language which occupies an enormous geographical area. As I've said in several essays, the South is a country larger than France; and I can travel from Durham, North Carolina to Jackson, Mississippi, which is a distance of 800 miles, and find that people are still speaking almost *exactly* the same dialect that I have grown up with and known all my life, whereas I can go from Durham, North Carolina to Philadelphia, a distance of 400 miles, and find them speaking an utterly different dialect. I can go from here to Baltimore, Maryland, which is 300 miles; and a quite different language is being spoken. So it's not so much a matter of geographical distance as it is of a prevailing tradition over a large part of the country.

And Faulkner was one of the great early recorders in the twentieth century of that particular language. The reason that Robert Penn Warren or Eudora Welty or anyone else may happen to sound to readers a good deal like Faulkner is simply because Faulkner sounds like Southerners talking—and thinking.

Ray: And therefore provides at least a model?

Price: I don't think he provides a model; he just provides a *reminder* perhaps to certain young writers that the kind of language that they have grown up with and known all their lives in their kitchens and front porches is a language which is potentially the vehicle for works of serious fiction. And for me that particular under-standing came not from Faulkner but from Eudora, whom I read and admired long before I ever got to Faulkner. I read Eudora Welty's early stories as a high-school student and knew immediately that I had grown up hearing stories exactly of this sort, knowing people who expressed themselves in exactly these same comic idioms, metaphors, similes. And my natural conclusion was—my own experi-ence constitutes the potential building blocks for works of fiction, works of art! That would have been the chief thing that Eudora Welty's work did for me as a writer. As a human being, it's given me enormous pleasure and insight and understanding; but as a writer that was the great gift of encouragement her work gave me, I think, when I was fourteen, fifteen years old.

Ray: You've suggested a number of traits characteristic of Southern linguistic behavior. I wonder if we could elaborate on them. You've suggested a capacity for storytelling, quite literal, quite com-pelling, quite dramatic; a capacity for anecdote, especially comic anecdote; for verbal witticism, for outlandish (or what would nor-mally or elsewise seem outlandish) metaphor, simile-making. Are there larger rhythms in Southern speech? Are there patterns of diction, of usage? Should we speak abstractly, or can we speak more concretely of what makes Southern verbal behavior, for the writer especially, different from that of other Americans?

Price: Again, I haven't thought about this in any consecutive and abstract way. I have in the last year or so, in visits to my relatives, been struck by *one* fact that I think sets them apart as unusually gifted Southern practitioners of language, that sets them apart from talkers in other parts of the United States. And that would be that their language, and I think really the language of the South in general—the old South, the traditional South—is a language of *vision*, that is to say a language based upon an intensely *visual* experience of life. It is a very precise, pictorial form of language based almost entirely upon the information delivered to the brain by the eyes.

My father's family, the Prices and the McCraws (my father's mother was a Miss McCraw), have a great genius for simile and metaphor of a generally comic sort. And the metaphors are invariably, of necessity, based upon visual perceptions. I remember my Aunt Martha Reynolds, who was along with my father the verbal genius of the Price family—my Aunt Martha Reynolds, having gone to the sheriff of Warren County's daughter's wedding, remarked at the end that the sheriff (who was a very short, very round-headed man) came down the aisle leading his daughter in her white dress; and she said the sheriff's face looked exactly like a *cheese*. It was a brilliant perception, a visual perception expressed verbally about this particular man's appearance—a large hoop cheese walking down the aisle on a man's shoulders. No, I would think that the genius of Southern language has always been that it's remained in extremely close touch with the eyes.

Ray: Will this characteristic live as long as there is a Southern rural culture beyond the outskirts of Atlanta or Memphis or Houston? Or can it change with time, within the culture itself, has it already changed with the urban contact?

Price: Oh, it's already changed enormously. I mean, one teaches students who come from Memphis and Chattanooga and Houston and Atlanta; and they don't talk in this way. They don't have these sorts of perceptions. I don't quite know why; but the obvious thing would be because most of what their eyes deliver to their brains is material of such *awfulness*, visual *awfulness* (those strings of fried-chicken franchises, shrimp-boat franchises, car washes, pennanted gas stations) that their brains simply refuse to handle them, that their brains are simply clogged and junked up with visual debris from which they are not able to select and have no desire (quite rightly, I would think) to select verbal signs, symbols. I think that it's perfectly

possible to create a civilization so awful that no one wants to look
at it, and I think we're in the very *rapid* process of almost completing
such a civilization.

Ray: . . . Any more than we'd want to listen to it, as you suggested
earlier.

Price: Exactly.

Ray: Well, you yourself live in one of the most beautiful sections of
one of the most beautiful states I know, in a corner of Orange
County in piedmont North Carolina, on rolling hills and meadows—
near one of the uglier little North Carolina cities. This leads to the
question: why have you come back after living elsewhere? Is it
important for the Southern writer generally—for you individually—to
return to this proximity, to this place? And how do you feel about
staying here? Have there been alternatives to this particular geographical bond?

Price: With the exception of four years spent in England (and with
the odd trip to the Continent) at Oxford University, as a student after
Duke University, I've really spent the rest of my life within fifty miles,
sixty-five miles of where you and I are sitting right now; and have
no intention of spending the rest of it anywhere else, certainly no
hope of spending the rest of it anywhere else.

Some of the reasons, I suppose, would pertain to a kind of natural
laziness, a desire not to have to alter my direction, not to have to get
up and learn an entirely new way of life, an entirely new set of signs
and signals and language. But I would really think it required no
defense. I would think it's a basic reason most human beings, until
the 1940s, in the United States, have lived out their lives within a few
miles of their birthplaces (most of the human race still does so—
because after all most of the human race does not live in the United
States of America or even in western Europe)—and that would be
because, as a creature surrounded by other creatures, one learns the
life of a given place from the moment he's born. He learns the
language, the local dialect, which is the case of people living in a
small village in eastern North Carolina or people living at the edge of
a small rice paddy in Cambodia; that language may vary if you walk
500 yards to the next little hamlet. You learn a language; you learn
what the angle of someone's head and eyebrows means as he speaks
to you. You learn all the signs of social approval and disapproval that

can be conveyed by the shrug of a shoulder or the turn of a hand. You not only learn those things and take warnings from them, but you take great delight in them. You take great delight in being a skilled practitioner of a given culture.

And so when I go away from North Carolina or even when I go away from Orange County, North Carolina (why, I'm a perfectly exportable commodity! I have no great neurotic fears about going away or entering a different culture or different social situation), I find that I always sigh with relief on getting *back* to a place in which I can go in the post office or go into a grocery store or dry-cleaning establishment and know *exactly,* the instant I enter it, the instant my eyes record what the girl in the drive-in looks like, I know exactly how to talk, how to behave, what to say, what questions to ask, what tone, what speed, what rhythm. Obviously I don't think of them consciously; those are simply internal changes of gear that take place as a result of forty years of living in this particular place.

It seems to me that the only thing in the world I am truly an expert upon is the experience that *I* have had. And since that experience began and, for some twenty years before I really began writing seriously, occurred in this place, why should I leave it now and be doomed to being an exile and a stranger in some other place, where I would have to spend the next forty years beginning to acquire a kind of second language? It would never be more than that.

Ray: Even within the continental United States? Only outside the South?

Price: I think that's very true. Yes.

Ray: Is the Southern writer necessarily an exile if he has left the South? I think of Truman Capote, for example, one Southern writer who it seems to me has not exploited, in his stories and novels, the linguistic patterns of Southerners. Is he still identifiable as a Southern writer, or is he exiled as such? Or Thomas Wolfe, who thought of himself in quite these terms?

Price: I don't want to get in the business of issuing judgments upon the geographical movements of other writers, but it would seem to me that very few Southern writers who have left the South cannot be said to have paid a very large set of travel tolls for having gone. Some of those people are close friends of mine, and I have great admiration for them. But it's a matter of grave seriousness to leave the country which one knows and to live in another country. I think it would be just as serious a decision for me to move to Wilmington, Delaware or Princeton, New Jersey as it would for me to move from here to Marseilles, France. I don't think that involves any hyperbole at all.

Ray: Probably less pleasant, too!

Price: Probably considerably less pleasant!

Ray: I wonder in fact if in Marseilles you wouldn't find closer, more immediate elective affinities with its culture than you would in a Northeastern urban setting, for example.

Price: Very likely. Mind you, I'm perfectly aware that the small-town and rural South—the small-city South, for that matter—contained forms of frustration, repression, suffocation which made it all but imperative that some people get out. I'm not denying for an instant that there were serious writers—and, no doubt, will continue to be serious writers—who simply had to move to New Hampshire (not that New Hampshire doesn't have its own particular forms of emotional thumbscrewing!). But it does seem to me that perhaps they might have entertained the idea of moving to a small, to the next-size, Southern city as opposed to having to go to, let's say, New York or Los Angeles.

Ray: You've spoken several times about the perspective of age—of your generation, your age—and mentioned that you recently turned forty. Does it seem to you a different perspective from, say, that of five years ago or ten years ago, when you were writing your earlier novels? Will your writing be very different by virtue of age or by virtue of time, beyond such development as we would normally expect in style, vision, and so forth? What can you attribute specifically to age, from the special vantage-point of forty years?

Price: I don't think I'm the person to decide that or even to speculate about it. If anyone's interested, they can look at the work that I wrote, the first novel I wrote, which I began to write when I was twenty-five, and the work I'm writing now—if they're interested in that sort of chronological stratification.

The things that I could say would be sort of incidental and emotional, such as that I enjoy my life a great deal more now than I think I have at any previous point. There's a sense of familiarity with my life, with my own nature, and with the purposes of which I'm conscious in my life—a kind of ease of movement within my inner and outer life—which gives me considerable pleasure. I'm very aware that that sort of ease is always of extreme fragility, that it could be altered tomorrow by an illness, by some sort of external accident. So I hope I ride quite loosely in that sense of pleasure, that I don't hold onto it with any hysterical fervor. But I think that's certainly one of the gifts that can be given one by time, by early middle age. I don't really think I could tell you anything about forty that I don't like—I mean, about being forty. I would adamantly refuse to be any age before twenty-five again, I can tell you that! And there's no age between twenty-five and now which I'd rather be than now.

Ray: Well, in your latest novel (we'll discuss it only briefly in terms of getting ready to write), do you find that the approach to a novel now is different from *A Generous Man* or *A Long and Happy Life*?

Price: Yes, it's much easier. I don't think it's easier because I'm more of a hot-shot craftsman than I used to be or because I've learned any enormous secrets of skill or technique that I didn't formerly possess. I mean, one obviously does gain certain kinds of expertise—certain little, not secrets but short-cuts of craft, that one didn't know fifteen years ago.

No, I think the main thing I feel I possess now that I didn't have in my early books would be—it wouldn't be accurate to call it self-confidence; I think it would be confidence in the mysteriousness of one's abilities. That is to say, in another metaphor, confidence in the unconscious mind, in the fact that the work, such as it is, is to a large extent compounded and finished and delivered to one from levels of the brain—the heart, if you like—which are quite beyond conscious control, beneath conscious control, and that I've now—I think; I hope—learned to trust in that essentially irrational green-house, hothouse, laboratory, and to wait for its deliveries. Luckily I have found, at least in the past eighteen months of work, that those deliveries occur on schedule daily, six days a week because I work six days a week without really permitting myself any exceptions except for illness.

Ray: Could you describe a routine working day?

Price: I sleep eight hours every night. I sleep eight hours from the time I go to bed (and I don't have a regular bedtime; but I tend to be in bed by midnight, and then I sleep eight hours). And I get up and I have breakfast—my mother said you can always tell when someone's middle-aged when they tell you that breakfast is the most enjoyable meal of the day; I now think that breakfast is the most enjoyable meal of the day. I have breakfast and then perhaps I sort of putter around the house for half an hour or so reading a magazine or doing something essentially in the nature of warming up, and then I go into the study and just begin to write; with brief pauses for cups of coffee and listening to the news on the radio or something, I will work from perhaps nine or ten o'clock until noon. And then I will shave and dress, then drive into campus, where I have my mailbox, and get the mail and eat lunch in what's called the Dope Shop on Duke campus (perhaps called the Dope Shop now more appropriately than in some years past!). Then I can go and do chores that I do, like getting the laundry or getting a tire changed on the car. I come back home in the early afternoon. Then I take a nap; then I get up and eat supper, normally with friends, and spend the evening doing something pleasant, going to a movie or watching television or talking to friends.

I do like to have about three or four nights a week, at a minimum, which I spend at home alone just doing something utterly idle, reading casually something rather light or watching television or writing letters; something like that, just to have periods of quiet, unpressured quiet, in my life. Then I always take Sundays completely off; I don't allow myself to write a line or to type it up on Sunday. And then on Monday morning I start again. Boring as it is, that's the way I do it. I think it's the way all writers do it, give or take the odd quirk.

Ray: Well, the tape recorder can't record an image of the very beautiful farmland on which you live. Presumably you spend some time just walking around in this very beautiful place.

Price: Not much. I mean, I'm the original indoors person!

Ray: Even with the little Wordsworthian lake just outside?

Price: My childhood was just a *nonstop* broadcast of my mother's saying, "Why don't you go out and get some fresh air!"—because I was always huddled over a book in the corner or huddled over my sketchbook, since I spent an enormous portion of my childhood drawing and painting. No, I love the idea of Nature with a capital N— trees, grass, flowers, and so forth—and I did this spring plant a

number of azaleas and rhododendrons in my yard, largely because I
wanted to abandon ever having to mow the lawn again. So I covered
the whole lawn with pine straw to kill the grass and planted lots of
plants. And I *enjoyed* planting them. But once I've planted them, I'm
perfectly prepared to abandon them to their fate—I don't go out
every day to feel the leaves and look at the buds or anything.

Ray: After all, the book is waiting to be written inside!

Price: I think I'm very eighteenth-century in that way. I like the
idea of Nature through glass—"Nature under glass." Oh, of course, I
go to walk every now and then; but really not nearly as much as I
ought to or as much as friends think I do, considering the fact that I
live where I live.

Ray: You mentioned that you type up what you have written. Is
your first procedure to write in longhand, always?

Price: Yes.

Ray: And then do you type up at the end of the day?

Price: Oh, I normally type up once a week, something like that.

Ray: Is there much revision at that stage?

Price: Very little at that stage—almost none at all. Maybe two or
three words on a page might get changed in the typing-up process.

Ray: Have you managed to save all your manuscripts?

Price: Yes. I love writing longhand. I can't imagine how anyone
can write on a typewriter. I mean, some marvelous writers do—
Shakespeare *didn't,* for instance. But I love the sort of physical
process of making it with my hands, and I've said somewhere in an
essay that I think writing is to a large extent a manual art. It is
something one makes with one's hand, and there's something very
important for me about the speed with which I can literally make the
characters in ink. It's very important for me that I write with a real,
old fountain pen which uses liquid ink and not with one of those
horrible mucilage-holding ball-points.

Ray: Another aspect of the *visual* quality of language?

Price: Again! And also for me an important matter of speed. I can
type much too rapidly. I can type much more rapidly than I can *think
interestingly.* I think a very serious study could be done of the
deleterious effect of the typewriter upon the American novel. It's
assumed now—I mean the sort of cliché *Saturday-Evening Post*-
Hollywood image of a writer is of a young man hunched over a

rather old office typewriter surrounded by lots of cigarettes and whiskey and unknotted neckties. Who would have been the first serious novelist ever to have used a typewriter? Really the novelists of the twenties, wouldn't they?

Ray: Well, I read recently that Mark Twain's *Life on the Mississippi* was the first piece of American fiction to be written on a typewriter.

Price: That's interesting. I wouldn't have known what it was. Of course, as is famous, Henry James's last novels were dictated directly to a typist who sat there and typed them in the room in which he was dictating, which is a horrifying spectacle, both auditory and visual! And I think obviously it says a great deal about the nature of those last novels—their monstrous syntactical nature is largely the nature of a voice speaking as opposed to a pen writing.

Ray: Would you care to make a comparison with Milton dictating his last, great poems to his daughters?

Price: I never thought of that. That's very interesting.

Ray: In the sick room?

Price: That's very interesting. Why had I never thought of that? Of course they transcribed for him.

Ray: Do you ever find yourself reciting dialogue as you write it?

Price: No.

Ray: Actually speaking? Is that ever necessary?

Price: After I've written a line I might say it aloud, just every now and then to myself, to see if the rhythm is right or if I like the assonances and dissonances involved. But no, I don't declaim to the walls. I talk to myself in other ways around the house—which our old cook used to call "talking to the dog." We would walk in and catch her talking to herself in the kitchen; and she'd say, "I was just talking to the dog." And I do a great deal of that, just stand in the kitchen and say, "Oh, damn!" or "What did I do that for?" or "Will I never learn!"—all those things people say aloud to themselves, especially if they live alone.

Ray: To ask a question the answer to which, I suppose, one already knows: do you like living alone?

Price: It's not so much whether I like it or not. It's the fact that I seem to *need* to live alone. People do what they have to do, don't they?—give or take the odd session on the rack? I think I've been for whatever reasons—most of them obviously utterly unrecoverable—

a solitary all my life. I was an only child; I was eight years old when my brother was born. We lived either in the country or very much on the edges of small towns so that I had very few playmates and had, from my earliest times, to invent my own forms of entertainment, which took the forms of reading and painting and the invention of imaginary games, which I played with myself. For whatever reasons, I like to live alone. Well, I *need*—I wouldn't say *like,* although I certainly wouldn't claim that I was unhappy living alone. If I were unhappy living alone, I'd do something about it; wouldn't I?

Ray: You make it sound very logical.

Price: No, it's not logical. It's very mysterious. But it's probably unalterable.

Ray: There's yet another aspect of fatalism. Are your characters fated? To what extent can you impute free will to them? And I wonder, especially in the next novel—a chronicle novel, a saga, as you said, of two families over a forty-year period: is free will, a volition, a desire—whether it's mental or emotional in origin—a real and discernible factor in the behavior of your characters? That is to say, do you think it is a discernible factor in human behavior?

Price: Yes, I'm sure it is. I believe that both from observation and really by dogma, because I believe in it as a believing Christian—that man has free will, that he both suffers from and is blessed by free will. I also believe that he has, both from observation again and from dogma, something called "Original Sin," that he has certain burdens that are upon his shoulders simply as a result of having been born, of being a human being. And perhaps one of the meanings of the metaphor of Original Sin is that we bear upon us the accumulated genetic propensities-to-folly of man. We are all men, but specific brands of men—i.e., I am a Price and a Rodwell and a McCraw and a White and so forth and so on all the way back—you know, two grandparents, four great grandparents, eight great-great grandparents, etc., back until finally, of course, everyone's related to everyone else in some sort of immense genetic pool. But I would assert the existence of free will.

I know, in the case of my own family, in my own life (without at all proposing myself as a hero of the human spirit!), I know of times when I simply stood up against the specific gravity of my own conditioning and of my own genetic past and said, "No! I'm not

going to do that! I'm not going to go *that* way. *That* way would be
the easier way. I don't *need* to go that way." Many, many other
times, of course, I've gone the way my body demanded to go. And
that hasn't necessarily been the wrong way. Quite often it's the right
way to go—the wisdom of the body.

Ray: Well, the exercise of that kind of free will sounds to me rather
intellectual and certainly demands a maturity of age if nothing else.
Do you think that maturity is possible in a young person? The kind of
young people, like Rosacoke Mustian, you have to write about in the
kind of books you write?

Price: I know it's possible in them because I think we're seeing
young people now living in times which are a good deal more
difficult than the times that I had in the 1940s.

Ray: Difficult in what way?

Price: I think I had as miserable an adolescence as any human
being can ever have had—at least outside the novels of Dickens—but
in fact it was an adolescence lived in a time which really was a rather
simple time, the years from 1944 to 1947. There was, you know,
an enormous war going on, but 3,000 miles away. My problems were
simply the problems of being an unpopular kid in a small town who
was always being beaten up—partly through my own fault but to a
large extent through just the malice of my contemporaries.

But I know of a small number of students at Duke now who have
really made mammoth efforts of the will to throw off their own backs
curses laid upon them by their parents, their high-school education,
their experiences with LSD, their bad involvements in wasteful and
destructive sexual relationships; and I have seen people (admittedly
few and rare, strongwilled people) simply say *no* to certain dead-end
roads upon which they've discovered themselves. Other people
proceed blithely—not blithely, but glumly—to the ends of those
roads and die in the impact against the wall at the other end.

Ray: Do you write about both kinds, both Wesley Beavers and
Rosacoke? Do you find one more interesting, more tractable than the
other?

Price: No, I don't. I don't find one more interesting than the
other. I think I *do* write about both kinds, because the world consists
of both kinds. And of course to say two kinds simply means that
those are the poles; and most human beings, as with all considera-

tions, fall in some gray area between those two poles. Nobody is the total victim of his genetic or environmental fare. All people make certain decisions at every moment—Doctor Johnson's famous demonstration of Free Will consisting of kicking the stone.

Ray: "Thus I refute the Bishop!"?

Price: "Thus I refute the Bishop!"

Ray: Well, I keep coming back, skirting back, to a question we brought up earlier, and that I still haven't phrased successfully. But it relates to the life and the work of the writer. I would quote Yeats here and ask to what extent it's true that the writer must choose perfection of the life or of the work? And to what extent your work is the expression of life needs as well as life experiences? To what extent you are able to live, to maintain the equilibrium, the serenity, to make it possible to enjoy life? I don't mean to say that writing has to be therapy, or to ask you about the last neurosis that a psychiatrist may have hauled out in front of you (if you've ever been to a psychiatrist). But to what extent, if any, can you see writing as the fulfillment of real need for you?

Price: Oh, entirely.

Ray: It is not volitional? It *must* be done?

Price: Yes, I think it *must* be done. I think it's a need of my *entire body,* just in the way that the hair on my head is some sort of need of my body. It's a need of my body to produce this stuff on top of my head, to produce these nails at the ends of my fingers. My body also, amongst its many other secretions and products, produces these things which are parcelled up into volumes of fiction and essays. But I would want to be *very* careful about trying to define the nature of that need or of being too specific about that need.

I think the dichotomy of perfection of the life and perfection of the work sounds splendid and memorable in Yeats's poem, and I think one knows to a certain extent what he means, but as with a number of those dichotomies in Yeats, I think upon examination they're a little more flashy than they ought to be. I was just reminded the other night by a student who was proudly quoting Yeats's poem "The Scholars" ("Lord, what would they say / Did their Catullus walk that way?")—and remembering that when I was at Oxford, Auden, in his inaugural lecture as Professor of Poetry, said that we only know of Catullus because of the grim pedantic labor of little scholars sitting in monasteries and universities over the last 2,000 years. So it was really very shallow of Yeats to make that condemnation of scholars. However, anyone who has taught in a university knows what Yeats is talking about—although he has certainly over-expressed himself, as he so frequently did, and as any poet, any passionate man does.

What would a perfect life be? I suppose a perfect life would be the life of a man or a woman who discovered very early in his years the nature of his work, discovered the skills with which to do that work, discovered very shortly thereafter another human being whom he could love and cherish and whom he could imagine tolerating for the rest of his life—tolerating in close proximity; living with that person, that is—that those two people would then produce progeny who were physically and mentally normal, who would grow up to become sturdy and self-starting mechanisms, and that that life would proceed through seven or eight decades toward a lucid and painless death. Well, whoever had that?

Ray: So we choose what portion comes to us?

Price: Well, of course we do!

Ray: And smile for it?

Price: Yes!

Conversation 3, 21 August 1974

Ray: The last time we talked you indicated that you were at work on what promised to be your longest novel. You now indicate that you are within sight of the light at the end of the tunnel. I'd like to ask you how long you've been working on the book, and if you would describe how you began. How do you begin a novel?

Price: I've actually been writing the book for about two and a half years, since January 1972. It's a book that I have consciously thought about and planned for since 1961. Shortly after I finished *A Long and Happy Life,* my first novel, I thought that this particular novel would be my second. In fact, I actually tried to make a beginning on it at that time but made very little progress. So I put it aside and kept an elaborate notebook about it through the years; and began it, as I said, in '72—twelve years later.

I began it as late as 1972, thinking that it concerned itself exclusively with events of the summer of 1944 in Eastern North Carolina; and I wrote nearly fifty pages set in that summer—which is the

summer that I was eleven years old myself, in my own life. I wrote
fifty-some pages and realized that I had begun the novel much too
late in terms of its own necessary chronology; that, in fact, I had
to go back to the beginning of the story and write from there. So I
stopped in the winter of 1972 and thought my way back—figured my
way back—to what actually was the beginning of the story. Which
essentially meant inventing the beginning of the story—because I
hadn't done that. It meant inventing the grandparents, the lives of the
grandparents of one of my characters in great detail—beginning with
them, setting in motion a genetic relationship, through marriage,
that survives and flowers two generations later in the boy whom I
initially thought I was exclusively writing about. So after having
written fifty pages, as I say, I stopped and went back and began in
1903, with the elopement of a young girl and her high-school Latin
teacher, the birth of their son. For the past two years, I've been
involved in bringing those characters down from 1903 to 1944. And
now I have them within fifty or sixty pages of a conclusion, I hope.
That's what I've been doing.

Ray: Who is the boy, and has he appeared in a previous novel or
story?

Price: No, he hasn't. His name is Hutchins Mayfield—Raven
Hutchins Mayfield—and he's not the central character in the book; I
don't mean to imply that. He was the character in the book that I first
thought of—one of the two characters that I first thought of, he and
his father. But he does stand at the end of the line. He's the third,
really the fourth, generation of Mayfields with whom the novel is
concerned. He's the last visible male heir in the book. He's fourteen
years old in 1944; and he precipitates, to some extent, a partial
solution—not by any means an entire solution—to some of the
problems that have plagued his two families, his mother's and father's families, for three or four generations.

Ray: It occurs to a reader of all your work that family relations,
family history, family problems, fundamentally circumscribe your
characters' visions of their lives. This is true even, one would think, of
the last novel *Love and Work,* which takes us out of Warrenton,
North Carolina—rural North Carolina—and into a more developed
and urbane mental world. Is this the case, as would appear, with the
new book? And how has your vision, your treatment of the family,

changed, if at all, from say the Mustian or the Gupton families of rural North Carolina in your first two novels?

Price: Well, I would agree that all my books are certainly family obsessed. I can't think of a novel which isn't really, by anyone. I certainly can't think of a novel that I would call a great novel, a novel that I love or have great admiration for, which doesn't seem to me very profoundly concerned with the family. I'm sure you could think of exceptions; and I could, if we had long enough (perhaps family isn't very important in Henry James, especially in late James; but then perhaps one could argue that it's very important, certainly in *The Golden Bowl,* family relationships). But no, mine are very drenched in family; and that's because *I'm* drenched in family. In our earlier conversations I've said some things about the sorts of families that I came from and the sorts of influence that I can calculate or begin to guess those backgrounds had on me, as a child and as a developing witness of the world. How far that particular personal experience has shaped the new novel, I can't really say; or how far the new novel differs in its views of the family and statements about the family from statements that might be abstracted from early novels by me—I really don't know. I think it would take me a good while before I could look back at the book and have that kind of distance on it.

I think we talked earlier, again, about my growing sense, as I have aged in my own life, of both the potential tyranny and the potential blessing of one's genetic heritage, as opposed in fact to one's emotional conditioning or at least as working very strongly along with one's emotional conditioning. And I think the new novel, as you will probably see, is fairly explicitly concerned with a person's almost chemical identity—what it means to be the actual blood chromosomal heir of a particular person; how frequently in one's life facts like that have an importance which we try to deny, which we try to ignore, which we're often unaware of—and almost always at our own peril. But I think this, if indeed a truth or a part of the truth, is a truth that can only occur to one or be visible to a human being when that human being has lived enough of his life to begin to feel himself settling into his own solidified character and begin to realize that, like it or not, he bears indissoluble and undeniable relations to other members of his family which probably aren't entirely matters of conditioning or environment. And now that I'm in my forties, I think I begin (as I think I said last time) to realize that *family,* in that sense, has taken on a new meaning for me. I don't mean to imply any sort of Hardyesque nineteenth-century determinism about it—people constantly conquer or evade or destroy the messages contained within their chromosomes—but it's certainly a constant fact.

Ray: One also remarks in reading your fiction from the first a change in the quality of the vision, the quality of consciousness of your main characters. I would remark in the last novel, *Love and Work* again, that humor is by and large missing from the oppressive responsibility and guilt of the adult protagonist by contrast with the immensely responsible and prematurely mature younger protagonists, Rosacoke and Milo Mustian, in the first two novels. Can you yourself see from this vantage point, from the novel in the making, that you've returned in any way to a Mustian mentality? Or is that change in the quality of consciousness a part of your life vision and therefore necessarily to be found in any character you come up with at this time, no matter what *his* place or age?

Price: Again these are questions on which I can only offer opinions, certainly not truths. I would not agree that there's no humor in *Love and Work.* The humor is not found in the same place; it's not found in the mouths of the rather small cast of characters, the rather intense, oppressed husband and wife who stand at the center of that book. The comedy in that book is contained in the essential absurdity of Thomas Eborn's stance in relation to his own life and the lives of his parents. For me, at least, a large part of the pleasure is at the end of the book, in which there is the ghostly vision of his happy parents; that for me is both an awesome ecstatic moment of unanalyzable reality *and* a very comic moment when this man has his own fairly simplistic, neat, tortured, fashionable twentieth-century ideas about love and marriage challenged by the ghostly parents, people whose lives have been simpler but in fact perhaps more complicated—certainly better.

In the new novel, I would think that the humor and the comedy are in both places; are in the actual structure of the book, in the intermeshings of the characters and their fates and their actions, and also in their mouths. I think there's a good deal more verbal wit in the new novel than in *Love and Work.* But the situation in *Love and*

Work, as always in any serious book, is a response to the particular characters and story of that book. There's very little in *Love and Work* to be funny about; at least there's very little for those two people, Thomas and Jane Eborn, to be funny about. There's an awful lot for the Mustians to be funny about in their lives. They happen to be people who perceive their lives with a great deal of wit and humor. Part of Eborn and Jane's trouble is that they are such whey-faced, serious observers of their own minds that they have little time for the kind of verbal pageantry that comes as second nature to the Mustians—and, I think, to the Mayfields and the Kendals, who are the two leading families in the present novel. Which is not to say that the present novel isn't in many ways the darkest of the books. I think it's full of darkness; and it's full of many things better than darkness, happier than darkness. But it's by no means a romp through forty-one years in the lives of two families.

Ray: What I'm asking about, I think, is continuity in your writing. The most often remarked feature of your work from the very beginning to the present, to the last group of essays *Things Themselves,* is stylistic grace, utter clarity: what's been described as "pellucid grace." This is clear. Your mark is indelible here, quite as much as for example Faulkner's. Some writers are not as characteristically stylistic. What I'm asking for now is a similar and answering continuity of theme, approach, tone, vision—whatever vague synonym we choose—which I at least feel has been submerged in the last novel, and indeed in the stories of *Permanent Errors.* I'm not as a reader asking you to go back. That wouldn't be possible and it wouldn't be desirable anymore than in life—to return. I am asking you, though, whether there is a vitality which you would grant as missing from the strained neurotic modern consciousness of the Eborn couple, but which we can find again here. And whether this is salubrious, both for your writing and life. Is this a better way of being? Is the Mustian mentality, insofar as it is possible anymore, preferable for you to the Eborn?

Price: You must remember that I think that *Love and Work* is the best book I've written before this present one. I wouldn't agree that in any sense, in *my* mind, it's a less good or less rich novel than the first two. On the contrary, I prefer it; and I prefer the stories of *Permanent Errors* to almost anything I've written until now. (Obviously, I think the novel that I'm working on now is the best thing I've done; but then most writers think the thing they are presently working on is the best.) *Love and Work* is very different in many ways from the earlier novels; it's much less superficially attractive. But it seems to me a more complicated and interesting book, despite its brevity. I think that part of what you feel, and what I think a great many of my friends felt about *Love and Work* and *Permanent Errors*, is a kind of tension, a kind of tightened-forehead atmosphere of which I was very aware when I was writing them. They are both books which—without going into elaborate autobiographical statement—feed out of and off of emotions fairly recent in my own life at the times I was writing them. Therefore they have that slightly febrile quality that highly personal, confessional material sometimes has. This is not to confess that either the characters of *Permanent Errors* or *Love and Work* are literal representations of moments of my own life, because they really aren't; aside from the few pieces in *Permanent Errors* which are about my parents and one or two pieces about friends of mine, they are very much about invented characters.

Ray: But you're not that kind of writer.

Price: I haven't yet been that kind of writer, I think. But certainly emotionally—psychically—those books feed out of my fairly immediate experience much more directly than the first two novels did. It may be one of the reasons that I especially like those two books, that they bear that very near relation to my own heart.

The new novel does again seem both a more distant and a very close reality to me. It basically concerns itself with characters who are not *me* in any of their aspects, a quite large cast of characters who spread themselves over, as I said, forty-one years—in fact longer, because there's a good deal of recollection of the lives of people who lie outside the actual time-scheme of the book, so that the book really concerns itself with virtually a hundred years of time. It's been a pleasure to write; it's been a joy to write, I think, in the way that *Love and Work* and *Permanent Errors* weren't, because a large part of the joy of doing it over these nearly three years has been the joy of inventing from day to day the lives of characters who were quite different from myself. That sort of diverse Dickensian joy in making up a world—whereas in *Permanent Errors* and *Love and Work*, there was a very small, narrow, almost classical French stage with bare

properties, bare settings, and continually one or two characters
speaking in very intense voices.

If asked and pressed, as you've just done, I would certainly see a
very strong continuity in all the books. We've already suggested one
of the continuities, which is the obsession with the primacy of family
in all human lives and the various views of family which are taken,
the various angles which the four novels take on the spectacle of
family life, the different kinds of spectacles of family life. Certainly I
can think of other persistent obsessions which the books have.

Ray: For example?

Price: Certainly a very continuing fascination with the relations of
whites and Negroes—in *Permanent Errors* the relations of whites with
American Indians. Exotic, interracial relations of that sort have very
much concerned me in the work: as they would have to concern any
Southerner of my generation, which was the last middle-class generation of whites to be reared by Negro women.

Ray: Which came to adulthood in the 1950s, roughly?

Price: Yes.

Ray: And that has changed because of Civil Rights?

Price: And various economic conditions. There are still white
children who are nursed by black women, but it's nothing like as
common. Anyway, as I have said before, my family was very far from
being well-to-do—on the contrary, suffered badly from the Depression—but there was almost invariably a Negro woman in the house
who cooked and took care of the children, simply because you could
get a maid for about eight dollars a week. She would come at seven
in the morning and stay until nine at night, and be glad to get the job.

There would certainly be the obvious concern with the supernatural, the relations of the visible world to the invisible world.

And those concerns all continue, I'm quite aware, in the new novel
(most of the concern with family in the book is with the filial relation,
the child-parent relation). There's also a very continuing concern in
all the novels, as there is in this new one, with relations of men and
women, the erotic, irrational magnetism of the sexes for one another—and of people of the same sex for one another, of fathers and
sons, mothers and daughters, friends and friends. I think the books
are very erotic; the books are highly concerned with Eros as a force
in human life. They are not very explicitly sexual except for a scene

or two in them, but they seem to me deeply concerned with Eros as one of the two great forces in life.

Ray: Love and Work being the two great forces?

Price: No, just Freud's two: Eros and Thanatos, Love and Death.

Ray: But your deaths are always so natural and unselfconscious, except the obsessive death of someone like Eborn's mother, for Eborn. I think again of the earlier book of stories, of the death of Papa Mustian in *The Names and Faces of Heroes,* which is a very natural and uncomplicated affair.

Price: Most people's deaths are very natural, I think, except for wars.

Ray: The complication in the experience for Rosacoke comes across the hall, as I recall, and this I remember from the story is the most lasting effect one has—that strange, mysterious last rite that she wanders into, led by erotic fantasy for the son of the dying man. Well, I'm concerned with the point you brought up a moment ago; and that is the presence—the apparently rational, in your case unselfconscious, credence given to the supernatural. One almost misses the ghost of Tommy Ryden in *A Generous Man* because he wanders on and off stage so naturally, so noiselessly that really one almost fails to stop to ask the question, "Who the hell is this? What's going on here?" You are certainly a realist, of the kind implied by a title like *Things Themselves,* your last collection of non-fiction pieces. How do you account for what most of your readers are bound to find of questionable reality—in the ghostly, the ghastly?

Price: Well, that seems to me the problem with twentieth-century readers, the problem with the twentieth century, our old friend the Loss of Faith; I just happen to *have* it. I think to go into *why* I believe the things that I believe would involve me again in saying things that wouldn't convince anyone who didn't already believe them himself, so it would seem a fool's errand. I believe perhaps like Tertullian, because it's absurd: *Credo quia absurdum est.* I've believed all my life; and I think I have had elaborate proofs in my life that what I believe is to a large extent, in some perfectly describable way, *true.* I would hardly need to add that before about 1914, let's say, or 1920, virtually every distinguished writer in the history of the world also believed. Western art is, like it or not, essentially Christian art—until we get into the twentieth century (with a few minor exceptions like

Voltaire and some of the rather selfconscious nineteenth-century atheists), religion is the great motive force of all art, from cave paintings on, so far as we can tell.

More than that I don't know how to say, except that the books, without at all being insistent about it, try to state certain realities that I believe to be true. The ghost of Tommy Ryden in *A Generous Man* is introduced, both realistically and I hope amusingly. As someone said, he's the only ghost in fiction who assists in the change of a flat tire. It is easy to miss that he's a ghost. A lot of people, including a lot of essayists and reviewers, missed the fact. The book says quite clearly that he's a ghost—if you actually read the particular sentence in which that's stated. (It's the last thing that most reviewers can do, read a sentence.) I've met a few people who've seen ghosts. My mother saw the ghost of my father the night before she died. Told a neighbor about it the next morning and died late that afternoon, not knowing she was going to die—died suddenly. Everyone who has ever described to me credible ghost stories—a first-hand experience of a reality that, for better or worse, has to be described as supernatural, at least not understandable by our normal rules of evidence and logic—everyone who has ever described such an experience to me has stated that the experience had about it, while it was occurring, the absolutely unexceptionable air of reality. Ghosts, in the experience of people I know, seem only to be perfectly real human beings sitting in a room or standing in a room. They don't seem to be diaphanous floating objects, clanking chains, through whom you can see the pictures hanging on the wall. If you see the ghost of your mother, you just suddenly walk into a room; and *there* sits your mother, in the chair. It occurs to you about two seconds later or four minutes later—your mother has been dead for fifteen years. You probably know this if you've read any of the proceedings of the Society for Psychical Research in England (they have careful case reports on sightings of supernatural beings of one sort of another)— they so frequently have a perfectly normal human reality about them. So in the ghosts that have appeared in my work—Ryden in *A Generous Man* and the parents at the end of *Love and Work*— considerable pains were taken to establish that they have corporeal reality for the people who see them.

Ray: We remember, for example, that Milo Mustian hears and

feels the breath—shallow, but the real breath—of Tommy Ryden.
And certainly gets a real knock on the head. Could I ask you if the
work, at Duke, of Dr. Rhine in parapsychological research, has had
any particular interest for or effect on your thinking over the last
several years?

Price: I had an office in the same building with Dr. Rhine for
years, though he didn't know I was there; and I never met him. I
respect him as a pioneering figure (and I discovered as a graduate
student in Europe, in the mid1950s, that if one mentioned Duke
University, one got a kind of Rorschach response from every educated European—"Dr. Rhine!" They knew of his work and respected
it a great deal more than Rhine's contemporaries in America. I can
remember as an undergraduate at Duke being told by various of my
professors in the English Department that he was a fraud and a
charlatan and that the University should ride him off the campus on a
rail), but I've never read a book by him. It seems to me that the least
exceptionable thing that can be said is that he's done some valuable
pioneering investigation. Obviously his tools in many cases have
been crude and unreliable, and his raw materials have often had to
be highly fishy. (I can attest, as a young English instructor having an
office in the same building, that one was constantly being asked by
very unstrung, unusual individuals *indeed* how one found one's way
to the third floor to Dr. Rhine's office, people who presumably
wanted to come and prove their psychic powers to Dr. Rhine.) It is, in
fact, one of the deductions that one makes from his work and from
the work of most pioneers in psychical research, or really in the
arts—that people with special powers of various sorts don't have to
conform to our own particular ideas of human respectability, or
intellectual or moral or ethical likability. But as to Dr. Rhine's having
any specific effect on my work, I wouldn't say that he has. I'm
perfectly prepared to believe that the world is not only more complicated than we know but than it is ever *possible* for us to know, simply
because we are limited as human beings by the capacities of our
sense organs. There could be incredible visual phenomena actually
occurring in this room right now which you and I simply can't see—
no doubt they *are* occurring—because our retinas are only capable of
responding to a very short portion of the spectrum of light. The room

could be filled with angels, you know, dancing nude—and we
wouldn't know it.

Ray: This sense of a super-charged atmosphere, whether seen or
merely felt, occurs again, I think, most dramatically in *A Generous
Man*. That is a book filled with psychic energy because Milo Mustian,
those three days of his life, age fifteen, is full of a mysterious energy
that a blessed few perceive, drink, and are changed by for life. Does
this accord again with your own experience of human nature? Are
there persons in life from whom we drink psychic energy at the level
of excitement and drama that occurs in that very dramatic, exciting,
and (I think I would maintain) *symbolic* narrative, *A Generous Man*?

Price: That's a marvelous question, and I think it's the most
exciting thing about human life. The answer of course is yes, there
are such people. They are enormously rare; and it's both tragic that
they are and—for them, at least—marvelous, because they are
always sacrificial people. They are always lambs in whose blood we
bathe, whose blood we drink, as you say. They are always—I very
much hate to use the word—but they are always "Christ-figures" of
some sort or another, to use the tiredest cliché of 1950s criticism. I
certainly don't have any conscious perceptions of Milo Mustian as a
Christ-figure—Christ only in the sense of the god whom men kill and
eat.

Ray: Let's say an Adonis then.

Price: An "Adonis-figure," to create a new cliché. Yes, I've known
such people in my own life; and certainly one of the statements that
the book makes about Milo is that though he, as you say, has this
enormous, inherent immanent energy for those three days in his life,
one perceives as he enters the house at the end of the book (one is
certainly meant to perceive, and certainly if one sees the person he
turns into years later in *A Long and Happy Life,* one sees) that
that energy was taken from him; that it perhaps is given by a god and
is taken away by other human beings. In an essay that I wrote about
the book, I actually quoted those lines of Donne—you remember the
ones in which Donne says of love that "his first minute after noon is
night." And so Milo's "first minute after noon is night." Many people
who discussed the book in reviews and essays spoke of it as, you
know, a young boy's coming to manhood. Well, it is that. It's his
coming to manhood and also, in a sense, his entering senility, enter-

ing old age, as he enters that house at age fifteen or sixteen—
whatever he is—at the end. His life is essentially over; the *good* part
of his life is essentially over when that book ends.

Ray: If Rato had not come back, if Rato's bloody shirt had been a
true omen of his death, would Milo have gone on, and would Lois
have followed him? Can you visualize that for Milo, or was it all the
bravura of his age and the romance of that moment?

Price: I've talked about this before, maybe not to you; but I don't
think it's bravura—I think he really means it. I think he really has a
vision of the horror that awaits all of his kind. Certainly when he is in
the woodshed with Lois, when he describes growing tobacco for the
rest of his life, he says that line that I still love; he says, "Hell, I don't
even smoke!"

Ray: Spoken like a true North Carolinian!

Price: But it isn't bravura; his vision is not bravura; it's a genuine
vision. But then what on earth would Milo have done had he left
home? All right, suppose Rato is actually dead; suppose Lois really
agrees to follow him; what the hell is he going to do? At *best* he can
go to Raleigh or Richmond or Norfolk or some nearby city—Henderson, North Carolina—get a job, you know, working in a carwash or
feed-and-seed store. The boy is quite unequipped to pursue the sort
of knight-errantry that he seems to have in mind, that he seems to
feel is required by the situation of the world.

Ray: Becoming, thereby, Wesley Beavers.

Price: Becoming thereby Wesley. He's doomed. He goes on to
become this rather raucous, burnt-out jokester that we see, who
disgusts even his sister. Though when I wrote the screenplay for *A
Long and Happy Life* a few years after the novel (I think I published
some of those scenes in *Things Themselves,* scenes that relate to
Milo), I really tried to give Milo a slightly better shake—the grown
Milo—and I think there are some moments of tenderness, of the old
Milo that glowed up there, in some of the scenes, especially the
scenes around the birth and death of his first child. And maybe there
is some hint of that in the novel. I haven't read the novel for ten
years at least, but I suspect that there are scenes in the novel when
he and Rosacoke are still a little oblivious to her pregnancy and her
own descending crisis. It's very limited, however, because whatever
that adolescent grace was, it was taken from him.

Ray: I could not be sustained, by definition—impossible of suste-
nance? Or could it have been nurtured?

Price: I think there have been people who have sustained it; they
are people that we call saints. I think that's what we mean by saints;
President Nixon said, leaving office just the other day, in a statement
which was both appalling and perhaps true, that his mother was a
saint. He said, "Most people would say that their mother was a
saint." *I* adored *my* mother; I don't know that I would say she was a
saint. I would say that I've known a saint or two in my life, one of
whom was in my family. I think my mother's sister, the one who
reared her, the second oldest of her sisters, was a saintly person in
the sense that, all through her enormous personal difficulties, she
dispensed a kind of extraordinary psychic generosity and grace to all
the people around her and lived a long life—on into her late seventies.

Ray: A Long and Happy Life?

Price: I would think that one or two of the great writers I've
known in my life have had saintly qualities about them.

Ray: What writers?

Price: I don't think I'd like to say; it would embarrass them very
much if I said it. But living writers. This is not to mean that they
are sanctimonious or goody-goodies. In fact, they are rather thorny,
problematic, difficult human beings like everyone else; but I think
they dispense (and not only in their work, their genius) an extraordinary form of human generosity. I mean, that's the greatest triumph in
human life, to be able to maintain that kind of magnanimity; but
once again, all the people that I've known who were saintly were
sacrificial. They are that at a tremendous cost to themselves. My aunt
had an immensely unhappy life; she brought enormous happiness
to various people around her. And the two particular writers that I'm
thinking of, that I'm being cagey about, are people who have had
very solitary lonely lives and yet who have given the most enormous
love and generosity to their friends—people who came in contact
with them.

Ray: The two words that occur most frequently in Milo's mouth in
A Generous Man are *need* and *give*. He's very conscious of these
essential qualities of his mission and he feels the responsibility of that
mission both in bed and at the family table; a man who is a discom-

fort to his mother and his sister, a good deal, because they're losing their family grip on him. I'm surprised (and this is not really a question but a comment, if you'll pardon me), I'm surprised that the utter simplicity of the fact that we *need* from others and they sometimes blessedly and mysteriously *give* to us had managed to escape me until I confronted that feature of *A Generous Man. Need, want,* and *give.* Is this what makes the drama of the early books comprehensible thematically? And how would you see *Love and Work* first, then the on-going novel, under this theme?

Price: Well, I must say that you may have found out the theme of all the books! I've never thought of it. I never realized that needing and giving are that important in *A Generous Man* as words and as themes, but I would certainly think they are absolutely central to the new novel. Needing and giving, as you say, begin in bed. They begin with the actual conception of a child; and they continue from the moment of his birth, in his relations to his parents and then to the people whom he loves, the people whom he needs and desires to have in his life, in his bed and at his side. I would agree, I think (without having previously thought about it) that the drama or one of the forms of the drama of all the novels, including the new novel, might be said to be strung between the poles of needing and giving, needing and refusal—because obviously need implies both things. Someone can need you and perfectly obviously you can refuse to answer the need.

Ray: Eborn, for example, to his wife?

Price: A large portion of human need is refused, which is presumably one of the major causes of unhappiness in the world—refused needs. Auden says in a poem, the title of which I've forgotten, "When shall we see what should be clear as day? / We are not free to choose what we shall love." That seems to me an unquestionable statement about human need and affection. Our needs are delivered to us at birth—no doubt at conception—and once again, this comes back partly to our chemical heritage, our genetic constitution, as it's formed in contact with our parents, our siblings, the people who rear us and who inhabit our childhoods, who become the world for us and therefore predispose us to certain psychic and physical needs. And our lives can certainly, from one perspective at least, be charted as cycles of need and acceptance, need and refusal.

The most baffling thing about most of our lives is why we need the things we need. The most baffling thing I'm sure that you must have felt about many of your young friends or your contemporaries throughout your life is why on earth is X doing Y? Why on earth is X pursuing B? The answer is X is usually helpless not to pursue Y or B. "When shall we see what should be clear as day? / We are not free to choose what we shall love" . . . and/or need.

Nor are we really free to choose what we will give to other people. Obviously our reason frequently tells us that we should give certain things to certain people who want them from us; but we are really psychically prevented from giving those things, at least giving them truthfully. Sometimes we give them lyingly, give them insincerely. That's not always a bad thing to do, I think; but it is a very tricky and potentially disastrous thing to give forms of love and affection to people for whom one cannot actually profoundly *feel* love and affection.

Ray: For example, Thomas Eborn again, in *Love and Work*, simulating orgasm for his wife because she needs to know that he has been satisfied; that it's still all right, when it isn't—it's no longer possible.

Price: That's an example, yes, a very common example, I would take it, from the lives of most human beings, at least in twentieth-century America . . . now that we know impotency is on the rise, shall we say, in America, according to all statistics.

Ray: James Dickey, describing your work, made account of your non-fiction prose: your essay on Hemingway I think he described as—"*stunningly* good." I'd like to ask you as a critic now, as a teacher, as a thinker about the writing of others and of yourself, dispassionately: if you were to describe your fiction in continuity, in development, from the early stories to the present novel, would you find yourself spending more time talking about surface, characterization, description, narrative structure; more time talking about style, the ironic tone that I think is very much present even as early as *A Long and Happy Life*? Would your own be a rhetorical viewpoint, or would you find yourself coming out for symbolic pattern—something very complicated, even mythic? (As I'm convinced exists consciously in the narrative structure of *A Generous Man*; the names give that away from time to time early in the book.) If one were limited, say, to one viewpoint from which to most fully explore your work, how would it fall in the spectrum of critical approaches, critical possibilities?

Price: I wouldn't ask any reader to share my own concerns about the books. A number of the possible readings which you suggest strike me as being potentially absurd and evasive ways of dealing with the books. My only interest in the books, insofar as I am very interested in past work—and to be perfectly honest, I'm not terribly interested in it. I respect it; I'm glad I did it; I'm always delighted when people tell me that they've read it (especially when they say that they've read it and liked it); but I don't go around thinking about my old work with any kind of continuity or depth, simply because I'm always so concerned with the work I'm doing now. Very few people, of what I could call mental health, spend very much time brooding on their distant past.

Ray: Whether personal or creative?

Price: Whether personal *or* creative. But *if* I talk or think about my own work, I find myself thinking about it in the way that most critics think is awfully old-fashioned and corny and nineteenth-century— simply as books about people, as books about other human beings. If I want to talk about my people, I essentially want to talk about (in the way we were just talking about Milo) what Milo's life is or is not like as it seems to me; about what I think there is, in a very old-fashioned way, to learn about human life, human behavior, from the contemplation of a life presented truly and a little more neatly and visibly than would actually be possible—presented in a novel that way. I don't mean to say that I'd do that other corny thing, which is to sit around and wonder, what is Rosacoke really doing now? I don't have the faintest idea what Rosacoke is doing now; to that extent I really don't care. I mean, her life for me essentially ended as the book ends; so did Milo's. I don't know whether Milo is at a crop-dusting meeting tonight or whether he's drunk in a bar in Norfolk. I'm not *nuts* about the characters. I don't think that they really have lives which continue after the book ends.

Ray: But those two characters went through two novels.

Price: . . . Plus that earlier short story. They really occupied my emotional energies for the years from 1955 to 1966, for eleven years. The first story, "A Chain of Love," was written in 1955; and *A*

Generous Man was published in 1966; so for eleven years of my life I was fairly continuously thinking about members of that family. I no longer am. But someday I might again. I'm not trying to make light of them or dismiss them in any way. I'm just saying that when I find myself thinking about Rosacoke or Milo, I'm thinking about them entirely within the framework of the book in which they existed for me. I'm not thinking, "Well, is Milo today an army sergeant somewhere? Has he joined the army because he can't make a go of farming?" No, I don't know that. One morning I might wake up and know and start writing another book about him, though I don't anticipate doing so. I did briefly, as a matter of fact, about two years ago think of writing a short novel about Rosacoke and Wesley some ten years after *A Long and Happy Life*; but then I began to feel that in a way it would be a gimmick, that it would be cranking up a machine which probably had done honorable work and should be allowed to rest as I had previously abandoned it; that my life had carried me on to points in which I was perhaps no longer in direct touch with them and their lives.

Ray: You're not even haunted by the Guptons?

Price: Not really. I'm amused and delighted by the reality that there are such people, but I haven't known any for years. That's part of the reason that one ceases to think about his characters, because certain characters cease to feed into one's books out of real life; you simply get beyond those points in your life. The characters in *A Long and Happy Life* (once again, need I caution you by saying that the characters are by no means literal transcriptions of anyone I have known) are the sorts of people with whom, as I've told you before, I was in grade school in eastern North Carolina in the late thirties, early forties—people who ten years later began to demand treatment and appearance in my work. I haven't had intimate contact with people of that sort—country people from eastern North Carolina—since 1947, twenty-seven years ago; so it's hardly likely that they're going to have any great urgency in my psychic life again.

The sorts of people that I knew when I was a graduate student at Oxford in the mid-fifties only surfaced in my work in the mid-sixties when I was writing the stories in *Permanent Errors*—the rather intense intellectual people who populate *Love and Work* and *Permanent Errors*.

Now in the new novel, again, there are people who will perhaps be more nearly like the characters of the first two novels. But they are eastern North Carolina, southern Virginia people of quite different social backgrounds, social classes; much more nearly an upper middle-class milieu than the upper working-class milieu of *A Generous Man*. More the milieu of my own parents' families—that's what I'm saying.

Ray: Latin teachers.

Price: Latin teachers, small-town businessmen, cheerful drunks.

Ray: We've talked before about the names of your characters. Some seem consciously significant, some merely funny or euphonious or cacophonous. *Gupton* couldn't be better for those people for example.

Price: A real family from our town; a real name.

Ray: How do you come to a name like Mayfield, for example, as the family name of the new novel? Just *sounds* right?

Price: It just sounds right. I wrote the name down in my notebook probably twelve years ago for the family.

Ray: Has the idea of the boy and his . . . not his history, which you said you had to create, but the idea of the eleven-year old . . . has that been on your mind all that time?

Price: Yes. When I first conceived the book, I conceived it as an intense study of the relations of a father and his one son after the mother had died. And in fact I would think the actual title story of *The Names and Faces of Heroes* comes nearer containing the kind of psychic energy that I thought this novel was going to contain when I first tried to begin the novel in 1961. As I said, the novel wouldn't begin in 1961; but I did write that short story in 1962; and I think I managed to get into that short story the particular kind of energy that was obsessing me, which was very much energy about my own father and my own complicated relations with this man whom I loved very deeply and very complicatedly and who had just died in 1954. And that story was a penultimate transaction with his ghost, as it were—*Love and Work* being perhaps the ultimate transaction with it. The new novel, as it finally developed, does indeed end with a complicated relation between a father and son but of a rather different sort and a relation which is only the last step, or the latest visible

step in a very long chain of causes and effects and accidents in a
family over a period of nearly a hundred years.

Ray: If we could glance back at "The Names and Faces of Heroes," the story, and another story (a sketch really, "Uncle Grant")
in that book, it seems to me that the two are the most transparently
autobiographical, personal, and for that reason in one of the two
cases the most difficult interpretively. "Uncle Grant" to me is marvelous. It fills out the father, the man, and sees him from an objective,
an historical point of view; sees him doing things relating to the black
man, for example, to his family, to his economic situation—in a very
uncomplicated, totally convincing way. I felt, in rereading that story,
that this is utter simplicity; this is *history*. Now "The Names and Faces
of Heroes" remains an enigma to me, and I know it does to other
readers as well. Something is going on, palpably impalpable, in this
boy's mind as he lies in his father's lap and as he comes to terms with
the enormous burden of his relationship to his father, finding a hero
in this unprepossessing man. Do you think the story succeeds?
That may not be a fair question, but I'll ask you to comment on that
story any way you would because I think it's the most problematic of
the early stories, the most ambitious certainly.

Price: I think it's that. All I can say is I've met a number of
strangers, people who didn't know me and didn't know my life and
could therefore have no sense of what the relation of that story to my
life was—I've met numbers of people who told me that they liked
the story, that they admired the story, people who seemed in fact to
understand the story in the way that I intended it to be understood.
That, for me in my life, has always been a kind of touchstone of
whether anything works or not; if you can meet at least three people
whom you don't know, who are not friends of yours, who've actually
sat in their own rooms and read the book and then come to you and
given you a description of the book which matches your own vision,
then the book has succeeded (at least three people who are not
yourself, your mother or brother).

I'm certainly aware that it's a very complicated and in many ways a
difficult story, perhaps a little more difficult than it ought to be. It's
certainly a love story. It's certainly a story containing an enormous
amount of Eros. And I may say that I think it's one of those very rare
stories in English which deals with the reality that English and Ameri-

can writers have found almost impossible to face or talk about, which is the degree of Eros, the overwhelming amount of Eros, that exists between many fathers and sons. There's a great deal of that felt in James Agee, for instance, a writer for whom I've felt a lot of kinship (and who just recently, through genealogical discoveries of my father's sister, I find that I probably was rather closely related to—I have a direct ancestor from the eighteenth century, a French Huguenot who entered Virginia, whose name was James Agee; there can't have been two French Huguenot families in America founded by an immigrant who was called James Agee). But the story certainly contains strong energy of that sort. Perhaps what's mysterious in the story is the end in which the boy has a supernatural vision of what his father's death is going to be like, which is what my father's death was like—a death from lung cancer, over which I as a man of twenty-one presided. But again, those are things that it's almost impossible for me to know about because *I* wrote the story; and *I* know what I think the story is about. It's awfully hard for me to sit in the brain of an intelligent reader and know how much of the story is registering.

Ray: Well, one reads the dream-sequence, the vision of the death, as a calculated and enormously eerie—unnervingly eerie—nightmare, explicitly Freudian, if I can use that word and bend it too far perhaps. We see Thanatos and Eros coming together; the boy is literally pulling away the sexual life, the life of his father, without guilt—he's too young for that, I assume. And yet I wonder if that dream requires some kind of exegesis, like the Bible, to make sense of it. Does it require a Freudian analysis, a Freudian explanation? And if it does, can it succeed as the capstone, the coda, of the story?

Price: I certainly wouldn't have thought it did. There are a great many dreams in my new novel, for instance, as there are a number of dreams in *Love and Work*. But I think they are dreams which are not meant to have any heavy drugstore-Freudian reading pressed upon them. On the contrary, I don't think that even Freud was able to read many people's dreams. I think that dreams, insofar as I understand anything about dreams at all, are primarily interesting or revealing as events in our lives—perhaps no more revealing, no more real than you and I just having had dinner in Hillsborough and eaten barbecue and string beans. The dream that I might have tonight might very likely be no more illuminating to a bystander than the spectacle of me eating barbecue and string beans in Hillsborough, North Carolina. So I would say that I think, insofar as I can really remember the intentions and the effect of "The Names and Faces of Heroes," the intention of the dream was simply to state a truth that I feel about many children, especially about a child who loves his father as much as that child does; and that is that children so frequently have this sense of being fathers to their fathers, of being in a position of protector to these rather helpless adults.

I think children who love their parents almost invariably feel that their parents are hopelessly incompetent, and indeed most parents *are*, as indeed we all are when we are adults. We don't realize when we are children that we are going to be even more incompetent as adults than we were as children. And I think—I know—that I as a child who sometimes used to travel with my father (he was a traveling salesman), that my affection and love for my father were always darkened and deepened and made frightening—made more in-tense—by my perception of my father's mortality, by my perception of the fate that I felt almost certainly waited for this man fairly quickly. My mother's father had died when my mother was very young, when she was eleven I believe; and she had told me in great detail about his death many times, so I was very impressed as a child by the fact that your parents can indeed die when you're young. I guess I used to have fantasies which were no doubt partly hostile to my father and were partly just loving and fearful that he would die; and so when I came to invent that sort of dream, that sort of precognition for Preacher, the young boy in "The Names and Faces of Heroes," I simply gave him a dream which is a fairly literal account of my own father's death. No, I wouldn't ask a reader to place a heavy reading on the dream; I would only ask him to see the dream as just another event in the narrative of that story, an event which in fact *I* know happens to be what really happens to Preacher's father years later. The reader can't be expected to know—although the story states it, I believe—that the dream is a piece of knowledge, a precognition. No, the story once again is a transaction with the supernatural, with the unreal, and therefore risks being unconvincing and unsatisfactory for many readers. But that seems to be a risk that I am constantly taking in my work and I trust will go on taking.

Ray: Well, perhaps I simply have the adult and cynical perspective of Thomas Eborn in *Love and Work,* when he commends the spare narrative by his mother, in the diary account that he discovers the day of her death, of his father's death. What he cavils at is the false sentiment, the clichés; what he admires is the lean and really balanced sense of the sequence. He even, as I recall, mentions her shift in tense as the inspiration of a born writer. My point is simply that the dream is complicated, complicating an already complicated situation, and that "The Names and Faces of Heroes" remains more interpretively difficult even than *Love and Work.*

Price: I love what Eborn's mother says about her husband's death too—I admire her greatly, as I said—but I would answer to that that I think Preacher's perception of reality is a great deal more complicated than Eborn's mother's conception of what's going on in her husband's death. She's making a fairly plain, deeply moving response to the rushing abandonment of a mate, of a life-long love; and this young boy of great sensitivity and precocious intelligence in "The Names and Faces of Heroes" is responding to a considerably broader range of facts and possibilities.

Ray: Did you as a child have a nickname?

Price: I had several, one of which was Preacher. My father often called me Preacher Jones. I never knew why.

Ray: Because you were precocious perhaps?

Price: A rather solemn little boy.

Ray: Well, that's changed at least. If we can shift gears just a moment and return to a point that I raised earlier—what I would call the chiseled finality of style in your writing. There's almost never a sentence that doesn't seem perfected (and I say that not in flattery; as a statement of fact, a judgment, it's as objective as it can be). I wonder often when I read writing like this, of this fitness, how long you have to struggle for the sentence; or if there's ever a struggle past the early development of style, since we've seen this as a constant in your writing. Yeats, for example, struggled, he said perhaps exaggeratedly, with a line a morning and spent all afternoon revising that line. Do you find yourself struggling with the word, *for* the word, with the sentence, with the rhythm of the line, cancelling, going back? Or has writing become—and when did it become?—a secure craft, so that now the puzzlement is in structure, point of view, and things beyond mere wording?

Price: I risk giving away far too much any time I answer any of those questions—far too much to one's critics. You are kind to say that it has a chiseled finality. I would like to believe that that's true myself, obviously; but as you are also aware, there are a number of readers and critics who don't feel that—who feel that it is floundering and maundering and meandering and precious and baroque. The other thing that's dangerous to give away is the fact that the longer I've written, the less effort I have felt in the work. I proceed fairly slowly through a book, as I think I've said several places before, at the rate of one to two pages a day, for about six days a week, fifty-two weeks a year. But if I look at a page of manuscript after I've passed on to the next day's writing, I find that there's very little crossing out; there's very little chicken-scratching on the page. For better or worse, the prose simply arrives at my fingertips in more or less its final form.

It's just the thing that I know how to do. You know, I never knew how to do any of the things that children were supposed to be good at when I was a child. I was absolutely hopeless in sports; I was hopeless in getting along with other children; I was very bad at all the childly skills. I think the one thing in the world that I know how to do is be other people and to write narrative prose well. I do think I know how to do that, and I think I know how *absolutely* by the grace of God. If I looked back at the manuscript material of my first two or three books, I would expect to see a good deal more laboring over the prose—a beginner's labor. But I would say that from about *A Generous Man* on (this is all very rough memory because I certainly haven't looked back at the manuscripts and tried to figure out the percentage of fiddling and revision), I would say from about my third book on I began to get a kind of stride, a kind of access to a natural vein within myself which in the present book at least has flowed with great speed and (for me) great joy. I deeply enjoyed writing this novel in a way that I don't think I could say that I deeply enjoyed writing any of the previous books.

Ray: Well, you said earlier that you see the present manuscript going to 800 pages. That's at least three times as long as the longest novel, *A Generous Man*. How to account for this major change in scope and range? How to account for it in a case like Eudora Welty's *Losing Battles*? Does this presage something in your development, and is it a plateau? Are you fearful that this is a peak that won't be reattained, a pleasure that won't be refound? Or do you accept it in stride, thankful for it?

Price: I'm very thankful for it. No, I'm not afraid; I'm not yet afraid, that is. I have a normal seizure of *post partum* depression after every book is finished, as every writer I've ever known has. It's a perfectly normal human response to having been very busy at something for three years and suddenly having that thing trundled out of the house, having it kidnapped from the crib.

Why is it more than three times as long as *A Generous Man*? I don't know—because I'm forty-one years old and I know a lot more than I knew then.

Ray: Knowledge?

Price: Yes. A novel is, alas—for better or worse—a function of experience and maturity. Why are there almost no good novels written by people in their early twenties or their teens? There are almost none. It's one of the great problems of teaching writing to young people—you find talented young people, eighteen or nineteen years old; you try to teach them some skills; you try to teach them some awareness, some craft and discipline. But you are also aware that you're getting them all dressed up with no place to go for about ten years, because they've got to wait until they've settled into their own characters and into their own lives, until they *know* something in their lives; and then their good fiction, their good narrative, will begin to come out of them in their middle and late twenties—I believe often not until their early thirties. This particular novel that I'm hoping to complete in the next five or six weeks is, I think, a kind of summary book of a large part of what I know as a person who has lived his life and watched many others for four decades.

Conversation 4, 15 June 1975
Ray: Mr. Price, your latest and longest novel has just been published by Atheneum, *The Surface of Earth*. I would ask you, to begin with, to describe continuity from such earlier novels as *A Generous Man, A Long and Happy Life,* and *Love and Work*. The statement is often made that some writers spend their lives writing one book—Yeats for example, or Joyce, or even Faulkner. If this is at least provisionally

true in your case, how does *The Surface of Earth* both carry on and elaborate the vision of those earlier three novels?

Price: It seems to me a very different kind of book, and yet I suppose inevitably it's a book made out of many of the disparate elements which are in those early books. I think in many ways there's a combination in *The Surface of Earth* of the kinds of materials and the kinds of relations to those materials which were visible in the books before, say, *Love and Work*; and there's certainly a strong flavor of the sort of material that came into the books with *Love and Work* and *Permanent Errors*. In fact, though, as you know, I never saw a sharp break in the work, a sharp discontinuity in either the kinds of treatment or the material of the books as they proceeded out of those last ten or twelve years. I didn't see it because I was very conscious of having been *me* the whole time, of having lived a continuous Heraclitean life; and I was partly conscious of the degree to which the books were arising out of that on-going experience of life and out of the long past that lay behind the books before I ever began writing. *The Surface of Earth* would certainly seem to me now not only the longest (I suppose it's as long in terms of words, or longer, than all three previous novels combined) but also the fullest in the sense of using the most, of making the fullest use of the materials of both my life and my observation, my emotions and ideas. As I think I've said to you before, a large part of what has gone into the size and the length of *The Surface of Earth* is the fact that I've now lived more than forty years and, for better or worse, this book contains a large part of what I think I've learned, witnessed in those years.

If that seems to imply—as it always does to literal-minded critics and readers—any sort of direct transcription in the novel of the experience of those forty-two years, autobiographical transcription, again there is no such literal transcription. There is certainly elaborate metamorphosis and transformation; there is certainly the continuing process that one finds in any serious writer's work of ongoing *spiritual* autobiography; but no—no direct literal transcription.

Ray: I'd like to return to the autobiographical relativity; but for now venture a critical estimate, perhaps prematurely: that for at least a first reading *The Surface of Earth* offers by far the most satisfying aesthetic experience of any but a few of the stories that I especially

112 Conversations with Reynolds Price

like and that I think we may have discussed before in what you mentioned as your last collection of stories, *Permanent Errors*. Given the length and the scope of a book that begins its direct narrative in 1903 (although we go back long before, intermittently) and takes us to a June night in 1944—that's a forty-one year span in which you alternate with, I think, great architectonic skill, straight narrative, character-interpretive narrative, and epistolary narrative—I would ask you, was the book written as a sequence of episodes, in order? Is there anything different here from your daily, weekly, yearly writing routine as you've described it before? Is there anything different in the how-many-year preparation of this novel?

Price: Slightly less than three—about a month less than three years. I was actually involved in writing it, beginning in January 1972, and running through, I believe, mid-to-late November of this past year, 1974. The difference, perhaps, in the procedure was to a large extent a difference of length—a function of the length of the project; of realizing, after I was forty or fifty pages into the book, that I was really writing a book that was going to run in manuscript seven or eight hundred pages, which it finally did. That meant that I worked with a kind of gathering momentum, which one never gets, for instance, in writing short stories—simply because they're short; they end very shortly after you begin them; and then the whole machine of that story dies and you have to wait and crank that machine again, overcome inertia, before you can begin another story. Or if you're writing a shorter novel, it takes a shorter period of your own life and perhaps develops less sheer momentum of its own as it goes. That was the pleasure of this book which I've referred to, the sheer ongoing drive of it; the weight of its elaborate and gathering narrative pressing upon me, and the whole process of writing the book through those three years.

I've always written sequentially. I find it extremely difficult even to believe that some writers don't, though apparently there are very fine writers indeed who don't. I write page one and then I write page two and then I write page three. It's very necessary to the way that I've worked in the past, at least, to have the story invent itself to a large extent from day to day as I proceed.

What *was* out of sequence in the writing of the novel, as I think I may have mentioned before, was what I attempted when I began writing the novel in January of '72; I thought the novel began in June of 1944 and that it would occur almost entirely within that summer, with a few excursions into memory and recollection of a deeper past. I wrote fifty or sixty pages set in that summer, as I've said, and then began to realize that there was too much excursus into the past. People were having to stop for far too long and give each other these Wagnerian summaries of past events, which were getting in themselves very burdensome and much too mystifying, I thought, for me and for the reader. So I did stop and go back in my own mind to try to discover where I felt the actual narrative began, the actual story which would bring us to this father and his son in the summer of 1944. When I got to the writing of Book Three of the novel some two years later, I found that most of the initial fifty-page segment that I'd written fitted very neatly into the on-going stream of the novel. That was the only piece which I recollect as having come in any sense out of sequence.

Then when I finished the actual writing of the book this past November or December, in the act of rereading it I perhaps added a total of six, seven, or eight manuscript pages here and there; a paragraph at a time, a sentence or two here and there which came to perhaps a total of fewer than ten pages. I remember adding one or two very short letters to the various sections of letters where I felt a slightly more meticulous link was needed between letters, but those were the only major additions.

Ray: Well, at this point you've reached the age of full maturity at which many, many writers have done their longest lasting, their best work. Let's again provisionally assume that this is, if not your best, at least the first full maturity of your style and vision. I've already implied that the satisfaction for the reader rests in the seamless garment of narrative that is a relatively unflawed depiction of very complicated, subtle relationships and changes. If life is process, then you've caught the process of emotional and physical change in a rather wide array of related and often no-so-related lives over a rather wide and distended space of time, or set of sequences in time. I'd like to ask you if, in addition to growing strength, the vision or conception of this book was stronger or more vivid or better worked out—if you could briefly summarize the conception of *The Surface of Earth* as it's carried out in narrative detail.

Price: Do you mean the architecture of the book, what I think the themes of the book are?

Ray: Not theme, but narrative. What is being said? Whose story is being told and who are the major actors on the stage? And, finally, what shape does their drama take in your mind? What did it take or does it take, before we go then into interpretive meaning?

Price: I initially contemplated the book for nearly twelve years before writing it.

Ray: Beginning in?

Price: 1961.

Ray: You were then working on what?

Price: I had just then finished *A Long and Happy Life* and was assuming that this story, which ultimately issued in *The Surface of Earth,* was going to be my second novel. It became the fourth, a dozen years later. As I was, through those years, contemplating the story and making notes about it, I assumed always that the story was primarily, indeed thoroughly, concerned with the man who is now Rob Mayfield and his son, who is now called Hutch Mayfield. It was only a month or so after beginning the actual writing of the novel that I realized it was about a great deal more than that—although when I stopped in March '72 and realized I was going to have to move back in time to 1903, I don't think I had any conscious conception of what an elaborate view of complicated family interactions was going to proceed out of that action on my part, that narrative leap. But in the instinct, or perhaps the unconscious decision, to go back to the beginning of the story, I landed myself in an elaborate web, the web of family; and the only way to trace my way out of that web back towards what I thought was my initial story (this is getting to be a very complicated metaphor) was simply to tell the whole story, was to circle the web, touch every strand. And that involved making, in the end, a considerably more complicated and elaborate story than I had ever . . . I started to say dreamt of making. Perhaps I *had* dreamt of making it. I hadn't been *conscious* that my mind was planning such an elaborate story. I think if I had really known consciously that I was planning anything so chronologically and architecturally elaborate, I would have been very frightened and filled with anxieties at beginning the book. I wasn't at all. I cheerfully dived in and more or less cheerfully swam out.

It's about, I suppose, the irreducible fact of human life, which is family. The only means ever devised by *historic* man, at least, to get on with his life and with the continuance of the generations. The family—presumably the oldest of all human institutions, that survive at least, and obviously the institution which most affects or *has* most affected the whole spectacle of human history. I think the book is, among many, many other things, about the ways in which two families blend, or refuse or fail to blend, in a marriage, in the creation of children; and then affect one another, for generations, even centuries, to come.

Ray: The focus here being Eva Kendal and Forrest Mayfield?

Price: I think the focus really being *the* Mayfields and *the* Kendals.

Ray: But their marriage—consummating and rearranging this complex web.

Price: Their marriage is the vital act in the on-going present of the book. Their act, the act of their elopement and marriage and their commitment to bear a son, is the act which trips the action of the book. But so, for instance is a quite different act, which is the absolute first act in the book; and that is the question which Rena asks on line one of page one—" 'Who told Thad she was dead?' Rena asked,' " In many ways it's the only question anyone asks in the book, and the remainder of the book is an elaborate answer to Rena's initial question. The tragic narrative of the birth of Eva's mother and the death and suicide of Eva's grandparents as a result of that birth might be looked upon as the act which begins the blending of these families, which ultimately drives Eva from her own home into the arms of the man in the world perhaps least able to satisfy or hold her for long. But then what act propelled Thad, years before 1903, to insist upon fathering a child upon a woman on whom he had been told not to father a child? And what act then propelled his suicide on her death? There's no true beginning, I suppose to any story. All beginnings revert, yield, to the *creation,* the literal beginning of humankind, of human life, and will go on until the extinction of the race or the metamorphosis of the race into whatever else it might become.

Ray: There's a fascinating circularity, in other words, from the beginning of *The Surface of Earth,* in which the question is, why did Thad, the maternal grandfather of Eva and Rena and Kennerly, feel compelled to father a daughter on a wife who could not bear safely? Why then did he offer himself, a double sacrifice, on her dead body at the birthbed? And at the end of the book, when Robinson May-field, now almost forty-one, has for fourteen years lived in a kind of dead end, a blind alley, since the childbirth and death (their second try) of his wife, and who is in the end in the closest possible physical and emotional contact with the son Hutch—contact gained with great suffering, especially to the father, but I think also to the son—deciding not to die, sacrificially, but rather to make out of that same tragic accident two generations later a kind of at least temporary victory and to find in this son, this remnant, at least half of a promise that he had made at his wife's death—if God would spare the child, he would be a man and accept his responsibilities, see responsibility for what has to be the first time in his life; he's at least half willing to do that now. Were you conscious when the first and last scenes happened that this kind of seamless circularity was at work in your conception of family process and the three underlying and recurrent motifs of this, and I think your earlier novels and stories as well: love and work and death? Did this just happen, or is there a con-sciousness, an art that conceals art in such fabricated tales?

Price: I think it conceals itself so well that it concealed it from me most of the way through the book! It's awfully difficult to talk about this; but I have said before to you, and to other people, that the major thing I think I've learned as I proceeded through what's now roughly twenty years of thinking of myself as a writer by profession; what I've learned is essentially that my work is done by something that I would only be able to call the *unconscious mind*; certainly done, at least 85 or 90 per cent, by that portion of myself.

I was obviously aware, as I proceeded through the book, of extraordinary recurrences. Chords of repetition and recurrence and cycle were beginning to sound (here I'm speaking very roughly because I haven't read the book since I finished proofs a couple of months ago and haven't thought a great deal about the process itself) by the time I was reaching the end of Book One in the actual writing—by the time Forrest was encountering his lost father and hearing from his father the narrative of that particular, frighteningly vital, wasteful, blighting life. It really, though, was only about a month or six weeks before finishing the novel—when I realized that the actual end of the novel was going to complete the history of a physical object, of a gold ring—that I began to realize what you call the circularity of the novel, the ringly nature of the novel. That gave me great pleasure, to realize that one of the things the novel had been about was the history of a ring.

Ray: Like many an ancient saga . . .

Price: Like many sagas, indeed. Rings, I suppose, still remain in the lives of most people in Western civilization the chief emotional symbol, the chief physical symbol. The ring, the cross, one or two other tangible objects that still seem capable of bearing large emotional freight for us, for great numbers of people at all levels of society. So I would say that one of the things a novelist is is an organism which makes elaborate constructs of which it is not entirely conscious; constructs which nonetheless, if that person is a good novelist, have true complexity, elaboration, and strength of structure, which are in no way (in works of art as in life) dependent upon our actual, conscious, waking awareness that such construction is underway.

I think that that basic novelist's gift, that basic procedure of the novelist to work largely out of the unconscious mind, is not only a lovely and also frightening fact of the novelist's existence; but it's a lovely and true metaphor or allegory of the shape of most human lives—if those lives can be looked at from a distance, from the aspect of time, decades. That is what I think is perhaps the chief way in which this novel differs from any of my previous novels—it looks at certain characters long enough to begin to see those lives taking on their natural unconscious shapes, their natural patterns, their natural recurrences, their natural . . .

Ray: Destiny.

Price: Destinies. I begin to understand now truly what various great writers and critics of the nineteenth and early twentieth century have said, which is that the novel is unavoidably and gloriously and indispensably *about time*—and I suppose I've written this somewhere—that the novel is essentially a vision of human beings as they move through time and are dissolved in it.

Ray: The novel then is a kind of map of the fatal geography of time. In *The Surface of Earth* you have mapped more fully, in greater detail (I think in no more loving detail; I wonder what more loving detail is possible than *A Long and Happy Life,* for example?) the interconnected fates, the process of accumulation and derangement in time of physical and emotional resources, by a very large group of people. I'd like to characterize the novel now, briefly, as a Southern phenomenon. We've done this before, and I'll have to insist on it again. *The Surface of Earth,* it seems to me, may be your most characteristically regional work; and I'd like, with your correction and help, to list the reasons why.

First, it is more conscious of the pressing facticity of Southern life, in this case eastern North Carolina again, and Virginia—really from Norfolk to Roanoke—but for the most part in a small hill village, Bracey, and Richmond, with a touch or two in Washington, D.C. More aware of such things as the on-going, never-dying emotional facts of the Civil War and Reconstruction in the lives of those whose grandparents, at least, witnessed the events and lives which (Negroes especially) carry that living memory. At the other end of the novel, in the last two books, the Second World War and the toll that took in the lives of all young Americans and the emotional effect it has on the life of a young Southern boy, our final protagonist, Hutch Mayfield.

Price: The end of the First War was important too for Grainger, as you remember, who served in France.

Ray: Correct. A fact he'll never let anyone forget!

Price: As no one *would* who was ever in France in the First War. My childhood was a chorus of old men, not-so-old men at that point, talking about France and the trenches. Indeed, they should have. I suppose it was the most memorable event in the twentieth century, if that's possible to categorize.

Ray: From beginning to end then, what facts of life in North Carolina and Virginia, from the turn of the twentieth century to almost mid-century, to the end of the Second World War and some would say of American innocence—what facts seem to you to be most important in your vision of life lived in this time and this place? I would ask you to mention anything as concrete as the likelihood of having to patch your tire fourteen times on a road between Goshen, Virginia and Richmond on the mountain highway, driving whatever car you drive in 1925, as Rob Mayfield does. Or facts as mysterious as the relationships of black and white, especially black women and white men as they issue, for example, in Rover Walters in the novel? What makes yours a distinctly regional voice, a regional vision or version of the "novel idea" that would invite comparison (this is by now an old thing) with Faulkner's *Absalom, Absalom!*, to which it is I think probably closest?

Price: Like most of the Southern writers I know, I suppose I'm pretty thoroughly bored at actually talking about the *Southernness* of it. This is one of the things that I was conscious of in the on-going act of writing. It seems to me a very *American* novel; to talk in many ways about, or to show many facets of, what it really means to have been American over the last hundred years. Much more so than *Southern.* I suppose the two things in it that seem to me most powerfully Southern are two things which are not uniquely Southern but are certainly very major realities in Southern life. Those two things would be the enormous force, even tyranny, of family organization in absolutely every aspect of Southern life until down perhaps into the 1950s and 1960s, when it seemed to begin at least in urban areas to relent something of its grip on the South. . . .

Ray: With the "Americanization of Dixie"?

Price: Insofar as there has been any of that outside Atlanta or Charlotte. The other thing would be one to which you've already alluded, which is the enormously complex symbiosis of the races that has existed in other forms, I assume, in other countries in the world where thoroughly disparate racial groups have been brought into intimate contact with one another but in America has only existed in the South in the last 300 years.

I was extremely fascinated in working out the story, over the three years that I wrote it, by the resort that I was able to make to my own very intimate relations with Negroes from the time I was born. (The earliest photograph of me, a day or two old, shows me held in the arms of a black woman.)

Those would be the chief ways in which the book would seem to me Southern. Otherwise I'm not really sure that I'm conscious of anything worth saying. There are obviously the large and small accidents of Southern life that fill the book, that flesh it out, give it its local habitation and its name. Everything from the living memory of the Civil War to the living memory of slavery, to the reality of country roads in Virginia in the 1920s. (The thing that you mentioned about

flat tires was a thing that delighted me when I was a child—my aunts
and uncles talking about the early days of driving in the South and
how tremendously perilous a journey one undertook when one set
out to drive five miles away from home. There were no paved roads,
and tires apparently—I never looked into the actual construction of
automobile tires before 1945—were made out of something like
cigarette paper because there were always these epic numbers of flat
tires. They were called "punctures." You would have fourteen
"punctures" between Raleigh and Henderson if you were trying to
rush somebody to the hospital or on some equally urgent mission.)

The book, I'm delighted to be able to see, is filled with the
accidents of Southern life and the deep features of Southern life; but
it does seem to me a more thoroughly American novel than
Southern.

Ray: I was skeptical about the number of punctures that one
would receive on such a road, so I checked it out with an authority,
my grandmother, who lived near and used to drive country roads
between Elkin and Winston-Salem, North Carolina in the teens and
early twenties, and she related an anecdote that is worthy of you and
sounds more like Reynolds Price than it does a family event: that is of
her older sister, Ruth, having a husband who suddenly became ill in
Elkin and put off going to the doctor in Winston-Salem, the hospital
fifty miles away—a long day's journey by car—until one morning the
discomfort was too great; and they set out, and had just left sight of
the house when he stopped the car, pulled over off the little dirt road
and simply lay down on the steering wheel and died. Apparently the
fifty miles of dirt road between one small town and another to get
to the hospital overcame him! There's humor in that, of course, if it
occurred—and admit that it could, please—just that kind of thing, in
this book—though the humor is perhaps more livable on the page
than it is in the memory.

Price: Sandbars were another great feature of my childhood
exposure to anecdotes of that early driving in the South; people were
always saying, "We struck a sandbar and swapped ends." It meant
that the car hit, literally, a bar of sand in the road, presumably fine
dust or sand; and these were little light-weight cars with bicycle tires
on them—the car just "swapped ends." It described a 180-degree
turn in the middle of the road; and you'd have to get out and lift the

car or jack it up, dig it out, or whatever. There was also a lot of this hitting animals in the country.

Ray: The perils of large pigs in the road, as in the novel?

Price: Right. Rob described striking a pig and having the farmer run right out and butcher the pig. I think those are things which could have happened in New England, in New York state, anywhere in America in the twenties, when there were no roads.

Ray: With the same radiant laughability, though, I wonder?

Price: I don't know about that.

Ray: You've mentioned humor before. Let's turn then to the novel as novel rather than as Southern phenomenon. You said, for example, in an earlier interview that there was an element of humor in *Love and Work,* which I, for one, had missed, as I took it to be a somber or rather bitterly thin slice of life in one troubled, urbanized, Southern American intellectual's life. Here I think the novel is laughing, jubilant, almost Rabelaisian, thoroughly successful as a joke— and this is where the Southern writer again has often been most successful. Do you find that the humor or potential humor, potential jokes, in the affairs of these troubled individuals just happens naturally as a quality of the life you are rendering, or again do you construct consciously the effect that the reader takes away? Do you want the reader to laugh, to behold what is essentially a comedy interrupted by tragedy?

Price: I'm glad you feel the comedy in the book, because several of the readers whose opinions I respect greatly, while they claim to have liked the book, have felt it a *very* dark and perhaps even depressing book. I didn't myself, in the act of writing it, feel it to be that. I certainly felt it to be in some real sense of the word a full comedy, though by no means a funny book or a joking book.

No, I didn't meticulously plan the occurrences of laughter. When laughter enters the texture of the book, it just enters naturally because that's what comes at that moment; that's what I think would happen in the lives of those characters at that instant. I suppose occasionally I'm aware that a scene or an episode is perhaps painfully heavy for the reader and, as in life, would be mitigated or accented or relieved by a moment of humor. A certain amount of Rob's vital humor in his life is a necessary decision both by him and by me

that his plight could become dangerously lugubrious if it weren't
leavened by all sorts of wit, which I think it is.

Ray: And in fact the novel, in its wonderful diversity of temperament and character, offers no example of the sloppy, crying drunk,
the lugubrious yet humorless sentimental. Each of these characters,
even at his most self-pitying; I think of Aunt Hatt, for example . . .
Poor Aunt Hatt, always alone . . .

Price: . . . She has a lot to pity herself about, one might say . . .
Makes a joke of her poor red face and her waning vision and her
slightly addle-pated memory.

Ray: The crux of negative criticism of your earlier fiction, which I
have echoed myself, is that your characters, almost all rural, whether
young, middle-aged or old, are (1) capable of moral intelligence or at
least moral consciousness, (2) articulate, especially self-articulating,
and (3) given to often rhapsodic self-examination. There's the sense
of a giant, wonderful, living symposium in each of your books, and in
the stories in a minor way. Yet life doesn't offer, does it, characters—
men and women, boys and girls—who can speak as well, as fluently,
as lovingly, and as truly of themselves and others as yours do? Is
this fact, if it is so—this difference, this critical crux—answered at least
partially by your own family, your own genetic equipment: word-
loving, word-using, word-rejoicing people?

Price: I think the reality of self-knowledge, self-justification, self-
explanation which is offered in *The Surface of Earth* is offered as
bald realism. It's a reality which I have lived with all my life in my
own families, my mother's and my father's, and which I've observed
in other families. It's a reality which—if you want another absolutely
guaranteed witness to—you can find in that long and fascinating
volume of letters called *The Children of Pride,* published by Yale over
three years ago, in which we see an enormous Georgia family
exchanging literally thousands of letters over a period of thirty or
forty years. The reality is rare, but I know it to have existed in my
own life; and in other countries, and especially in other levels of
culture in this country, one encounters fluency of observation and
verbalization of a sort that I think my book records quite literally. It
doesn't seem to me in this case a heightening or even a *slight*
falsification of reality. Certainly I'm aware that there is a heightening

of literal reality in a book like *A Generous Man,* but there seems to me none in this book.

Ray: In what sense is reality heightened in *A Generous Man,* as an aside?

Price: Well, I've written about it in an essay on the book, as you know, but. . . .

Ray: In *Things Themselves?*

Price: . . . Yes; but there are very few Southern boys, even of Milo's grace and charm, who are capable of telling one quite so freely and eloquently, I suppose, about their choices, their hopes and visions. They are however perfectly capable of *feeling* that elaborately and *feeling* with that pressure and eloquence and intensity. But my own experience of those types when I was a child or an adolescent didn't include many people who had the kind of unbounded, non-stop eloquence of the sort encountered in Milo.

I call that book, as you know, a romance; and I think we expect from romance that kind of heightening of daily life. It doesn't at all seem to me a falsification; it seems to me a sort of allegorization of daily life, a truthful "raising of the ante."

Ray: Hawthorne's sense of romance then—as with *A Generous Man*'s ghost? The stray ghost, the stray vision?

Price: It has a great deal of the equipment that one normally expects to find in romance, yes.

Ray: But *The Surface of Earth* is not a romance—is a "reality play," if you will?

Price: A novel.

Ray: Which is different from a romance?

Price: A romance is not a novel, yes.

Ray: Hawthorne's distinction again . . .

Price: . . . and Robert Louis Stevenson's.

Ray: The instructive comparison here, I think, is between Hutch Mayfield at age fourteen—discovering what his choices are, and in discovering them and pursuing one, acting as a kind of a catalyst or alembic for his father's own rejuvenation which, at the end, gives that wonderful affirmation, that closing off, that joining of the circle and marshaling of energies toward the future and his father's plateau, Rob's plateau—and Milo in the earlier book, though in fact the Milo

in this novel, if he's here, is Robinson Mayfield in the middle sequence of the novel, 1923–29, up to the death of his wife.

Price: I hadn't thought of that, but I suppose Rob does have some
of the same kinds of energy that were so attractive in Milo.

Ray: "The Christmas tree on which God has hanged all the gifts,"
for man, woman and child and animal, to seize, to claim. Robinson
Mayfield, like Milo Mustian, finds that the claims cannot be answered,
and that in his failure to answer one he often destroys another that
he would have perfected. His life with Rachel, for example, is rendered incomplete by failures that have already happened in him—
failures not so much of will as of consciousness. And in that sense
Robinson Mayfield's story is a kind of adult *Bildungsroman.* Yet
instead of tracing the emotional and intellectual growth of a notable,
distinguished, or favored young man, we have a second life, vouch-
safed to Rob at age forty, at least as interesting a reading experience
as Dickens' young heroes, with all the manifest and instructive
differences between the two. Can you answer in one word or another
whether *The Surface of Earth* is essentially Robinson Mayfield's
story?

Price: I think I would resist the idea of any particular character's
being the central figure in the book. Once I had committed myself to
this elaborate cast of characters, I was not conscious that any particular character was central. I think in a real sense the novel comes to
rest on the not very broad, but as we begin to see, quite strong
shoulders of Rob's son Hutch.

I think what you may be saying is that Rob is the most *likable* adult
in the book; and I would probably agree with that, except that I
suppose my personal favorites varied from month to month as I was
writing it. Perhaps the most consistent favorite while I was writing the
book was Rena. I'm not sure that Rena would be my favorite if I read
the book again ten years from now. Polly is another valiant soul,
whom I love.

I would want to think more before I committed myself to choosing
a center for the book. I think the center of the book is invisible. But
it's nonetheless there.

Conversation 5, 15 June 1975
Ray: One of the most obviously beautiful things about *The Surface
of Earth* is the colorful dust jacket which you designed for the book. I
wonder if you would describe and interpret it.

Price: The emblem on the jacket is an illustration of a passage which is for me very important in the book, and which occurs very near its end. Perhaps I'll read a couple of paragraphs from pages 471 and 472 which clarify, for me at least, the significance of the design. Rob's son, Hutch Mayfield, who is fourteen, has gone out on a sketching trip with a woman whom he's only just met—Alice, who is in fact his mother's old best friend. And since art, drawing, is Hutch's chief ambition in life, he finds himself with Alice, who is an art teacher, drawing a mountain landscape in this small Virginia town which was his mother's home. As he draws the mountain before him, he begins to meditate upon his own problems and difficulties as a graphic artist; and through those meditations, particularly concerning his difficulty in drawing trees and leaves, he works himself into a memory of a particular childhood puzzlement, a bafflement which lies behind the emblem you mentioned. On page 471 he looks at his drawing which is in process and thinks, "It was one thing he *had* made this morning, unaided, from what the earth offered of its visible skin—the surface it flaunted in dazzling stillness, in the glaze of rest, to beg us to watch; then grope for its heart."

Then he goes on to meditate about the difficulty of adding leaves to the trees and how he has the chance simply to take out his eraser and pretend that it's November and not June—strip the trees and solve the problem. But he decides that he will leave his rather incompetently drawn leaves on the trees. "So he spared the trees now. He trusted to wait till the secret of leaves, if nothing more, came into his power. First the power to watch one green leaf in stillness; then the dark banked branches in all their intricate shifting conceal-ment—concealed good news (that under the face of the earth lay care, a loving heart, though maybe asleep: a giant in a cave who was dreaming the world, a tale for his long night) or concealed news of hatred embellished with green (that a sight like this or a shape like Rob's was only the jeering mask of a demon who knew men's souls and guided their steps). It seemed, now at least, that any such power would come here if anywhere. This place was an entrance. He'd need to wait here."

So when my editor at Atheneum asked me last December, Janu-ary, if I had any suggestions that might be passed on to an artist as to a jacket design for the book, I remembered this passage and did, myself, a design which, in my own fantasy at least, was Hutch's rendition of that childhood fantasy of his, that childhood curiosity about what lay in the center of the earth as opposed to what was on the surface of earth. It was a fantasy that I had in a slightly different form as a child of five, six, seven. I remember the age precisely because I know the house we lived in when I used to have the meditation. It's very Platonic, a naturally Platonic notion that I've later found many children have—I would frequently imagine that, and be quite convinced that, the visible world was a dream being dreamt by a giant who was asleep in a cave; and concomitantly I realized that if the giant ever woke up, our world would vanish like "the baseless fabric of a vision." Hutch has that, as it turns out, rather common child's meditation in his own form. And that's what is illustrated on the jacket.

Ray: Is that a beneficent giant rather than the cruel body of Rob embellished in green? His is a powerfully smiling face.

Price: I'm not so convinced that He's smiling and I'm not convinced that He's malevolent either. I would think it's. . . .

Ray: Morally ambivalent? Or beyond that?

Price: I would think it's simply an inscrutable reality.

Ray: The "dream of a sleeping giant." It sounds like Henry C. Earwicker's "wake-dreaming" rendered by Joyce.

Price: This one isn't asleep, I think. His eyes were meant to be open, though He has no pupils in his eyes—has no pupils in *Its* eyes, I should say, because It's . . .

Ray: Of course, asexual.

Price: Also supremely neuter.

Ray: The epigraph in the novel is puzzling, from the *Confessions* of St. Augustine. Will you read and comment here as well, since this is at least as indelibly your imprint on the final product as the cover is?

Price: It's my own translation of the Latin lines which are either the literal last lines of the *Confessions* of Augustine or within a few lines of the end—"But You, the Good which needs no good, rest always, being Yourself Your rest. What man can teach another man that? What angel an angel? What angel a man?"

I found as I came near the end of the novel, and as I began to think of what had not come to me in the course of writing the

novel—that was the title—I began to find myself consciously searching my memory of the novel, my experience of the novel, for an
appropriate title, for an appropriate phrase which would be emblematic of the totality of the book and yet not be so specific and so
special that it *over-directed* a reader's interpretation of the many,
many things that I thought the book was about. I found myself aware
of a very powerful strain in the book, which might be called "the
yearning for rest," on the part of almost all of the characters there—
their ultimate realization of the deep hunger really for stillness, for
stasis, for harbor. Each of the characters would describe his or her
notion of rest, need for rest, in different terms. So I was trying to
formulate a title which would embody that concept; and I came up
with various candidates, all of them later rejected, which it's not
important to recall here. But in the process of thinking about the
theme of the drive toward rest, serenity, peace, even death in life, I
remembered that the first thing I wrote down in the notebook which I
began to keep for this book in 1961 was Rex Warner's translation of
those short lines from the end of Augustine's *Confessions*; and I went
back to the book itself and studied them in their context and made
my own translation and found that they deeply defined for me what *I*
think the center of the book is.

We concluded our last talk with speculations about the center of
the book; and it does seem to me, in my own mind (I wouldn't insist
upon it for any other readers) that the center of the book is an
invisible need, an invisible power, an invisible force—God, a giant in
a cave, whatever any individual reader might wish to call it—toward
which all the more visible, more tangible, less perfect creatures in the
story yearn. That "Thing" (for lack of a more adequate word) which
almost all of us perceive to be at the heart of the earth, at the *center
of the world*, and toward which all bodies tend. An enormous
amount of suffering, the cruelty, the remorse which is experienced by
the characters in this book, is experienced, I know, because of their
failure to deal adequately, either mentally or emotionally or spiritually, with that invisible center of their lives—which is at rest, which is
perceived by all of us to be at rest, and which rest we ourselves seek;
but alas, and invariably with tragic results, we seek it in other created
bodies. "What man can tell another man that? What angel, an angel?
What angel, a man?"

The epigraph defines for me also another strain in the book which is very important to me, the relation of men and angels—*angels* not being used at all in the supernatural sense but in the literal Greek sense of "messengers."

Ray: As Rob dreams of a man dressed in normal street clothes, who nonetheless radiates the message, the dream, later in the novel?

Price: That and also, more specifically in the terms that I'm thinking of just now, the relation between blacks and whites in the novel—the blacks who are in many senses of the word *angels* to their white employers, owners (even blood relations), who bring to those toiling white brothers and owners of theirs all sorts of vital and necessary and generally unheeded messages, messages which often seem to me to come from that restful center toward which, or around which at least, all the striving of the book occurs.

Let me warn every reader—I'm not claiming supernatural status for black people in this novel. I am claiming that they serve in this novel, as they have served in my own life and I think very richly in the life of the American South and the whole American nation, very richly as messengers, tale-bearers of quite other orders of existence from the prevailing norm of American and white-Southern life.

Ray: Well, come to think of it, every Negro character, player on the stage of this novel from beginning to end, is of some service either as minister or messenger or both—some dark angelic service—to some Mayfield, some Kendal, some Hutchins.

Price: It's very often a condemnatory message. It's by no means always a benevolent food-bearing, gratuity-bearing service. It's very often a service of accusation and condemnation of a very merciless but just moral sort. Grainger says, doesn't he, late in the novel—or Hutch remembers or recalls to his father that Grainger actually defines black people as "angels" in relation to white people?

Ray: There from the very first black character who encounters Forrest Mayfield on his trek. . . .

Price: Bankey Patterson.

Ray: . . . . Bankey Patterson, who later, it is apparent, is father to Della. What is the relationship?

Price: It seems likely that he's a direct ancestor of Della's, her great-grandfather. The novel doesn't work it out in really verifiable detail.

Ray: His strange, mysterious rite of symbolic murder as surcease of sorrow for Forrest, as he applies the knife silently to Forrest's sleeping wrist, is the troubling, at least bemusing detail early on which is clarified only cumulatively, like much in this book—a very long, very cumulative story.

I do think that there is a distinction to be made though, interpretively, and you've raised it in reading and talking about the epigraph. Isn't Augustine describing here a kind of Platonic, if you will *Hindu* Absolute?—the self-sufficient divinity, the Good which needs no good (capital *G* good, which needs no small *g* good). And isn't that difference somehow beyond Nature? In some sense creative of and manifesting itself in relative time and space, but also self-sufficient beyond it? Isn't that then the Platonic Idea, the Hindu Ground of All Being? Isn't that very different from your sleeping giant at the center of the earth, the child Hutchins' dream-vision or Shelley's Demogorgon for example, in *Prometheus?* The sleeping giant who expresses the necessity of natural change which will bring down a tyrant, will change the world in due course? Isn't the center of your earth, the center of *this* earth's surface, here and in your other books as well, very much a *process*-force, a father *of* and *in* Nature rather than beyond it? And aren't we therefore going far astray when we try to make God or an immanent divinity or an absolute force, self-sufficient unto itself, the center toward which your characters tend? Don't they tend toward a *natural* harmony?

Price: What's a "natural harmony"?

Ray: A harmony that is in tune with its own genetic rhythms and which marks its genetic rhythms by emotional human associations rather than in the frenzies or reveries of prayer, transport. Your characters are not religious in the absolute sense. Often there is a witty, at least a funny, counterpoint between their Bible-quoting and their praying on the one hand, and their failure to darken the church door in twenty years on the other. What I am driving at is that your characters are natural men and women seeking their inmost nature, self-sufficient but also bound in complex webs of relationship and responsibility which they often come only too late to realize, too late to save. Whereas the good, the absolute metaphysical Good, the Ground of All Being, is not a part of that framework. It stands above and beyond it. You say your characters seek stasis. I'll accept that or I understand that if you mean a harbor in time, a falling into the rhythm of one's own natural change and an acceptance of one's own natural—and that again usually means familial—responsibilities or relationships. I find it difficult to see, however, how the epigraph, as I think Augustine intends it from my reading of the translation—how that illuminates your characters. They are not seeking the Good, capital G; they are seeking a good, small g, in their lives—a coming to terms with their natural destiny, their genetic fate, and understanding it.

Price: They're seeking rest; they're seeking surcease from pain; they're seeking the cessation of pain and struggle and unhappiness, as I fear all created beings are. They, like you, make the mistake of assuming that the solution to the search, or the end of the search, can be achieved "naturally"; that is, within the human frame on "the surface of earth." Augustine says it can't be. So does *The Surface of Earth*.

Ray: And which of your characters builds a bridge to the center? Which strips away the skin of the surface?

Price: Rena and Grainger.

Ray: Rena and Grainger?

Price: They, for me, would be the central ones who do. There were other important contributors to that bridge-making.

Ray: Well, all Rena does is tend her garden.

Price: Alice.

Ray: And all Grainger does is bring a ring back home; back to rest on the left hand which it fits naturally—not supernaturally.

Price: To that extent he brings about the partial amends which occur at the end of the book.

Ray: Are there permanent errors, as an earlier title of yours avers?

Price: In natural life, yes.

Ray: In the novel, for example, what relationships are permanently marred? Can we list a few and draw some lines of distinction between the complex and subtle?

Price: Just absolutely off the top of my head, I would say they are *all* permanently marred; with the possible exception of Hutch and Grainger's, Hutch and Alice's, Hutch and Della's. Permanent marring certainly does not mean cancellation or destruction. It just does mean permanent marring, permanent scarring.

Ray: For which there are only partial amends?

Price: For which there are only partial amends.

Ray: In the natural world?

Price: In the natural world.

Ray: Beneath the surface? In the final rest? That, I fail to see in the book; and I fail to see its need in the book. I guess I'm satisfied, naturally, with the natural radiance of joining and the beautiful resolution.

Price: I'm not, as I said, at all insisting that anyone bring to bear any particular set of spectacles on the reading of this book—only clear clean ones.

The book seems to me, first and foremost, as I've said in our last talk, a thoroughly realistic view of the kinds of human life that have been available to me in the last forty years. If I have certain readings or interpretations of the lacunae, the absences, the lacks in the lives of these characters, those are not absences which I would insist be defined in my way.

Beyond that I really wouldn't want to talk because, in the first place, I'm not a trained metaphysician. In the second place, because to talk about it is only to encourage more rigid categorization by some readers of a book which seems to me to wish, at least, to *resist* categorization and easy schematization.

I obviously feel that life has many meanings and some few meanings which are much more important than others. Those meanings, either of greater or lesser importance, seem to me to impose very powerfully their own patterns and shapes, their own architecture, upon related human lives when those lives are seen in time, over long periods of human time. But I would say finally, and I think as truthfully as I would know how to say it, that the book itself—the lives of its characters—is my only way of looking at those realities and those patterns, and certainly my only way of making any useful statements about them.

Ray: Let's make at least one list then. What are the particular human relationships illuminated and explored by *The Surface of Earth*? I would think they might number at least a dozen. Can we begin a partial list, in a way a partial amends to that last question?

Price: All right. Just to start on page one—sister-and-sister; sister-and-brother; daughter-and-father; son-and-father; daughters-and-sons-and-mothers; grandchildren and their grandparents; children and their aunts and uncles; adults and their servants; children and the servants of their parents; the relationships that broadly speaking are called friendship: male-male; female-female; male-female. What else?

Ray: Fathers and sons.

Price: Fathers and sons, very crucially in the last book of the novel and certainly other books as well.

Ray: Can we focus on that last crucial vision in the novel? A vision without antecedent in my knowledge in modern fiction, in which a son, age fourteen, lies with a father recently found, refound; in an attempt to love, relove; to revitalize—a son lying with father, age forty—against whose back the father rediscovers, for what must be his last chance, his last time, the contour of his own fate and his own responsibility. And who whether or not he's able to forgive himself for the mother, Rachel's death, who whether or not he can come to terms with others in his life—other lost causes, permanent errors that have strewn his path for 400 pages—nonetheless has that moment of affirmation, if not quite revelation, at the end of which he lays his head against the shoulder of his son and completes what, I think again, is a unique moment, a unique kind of relationship that startles and satisfies, and that I would ask you to comment on to this extent. What do you intend for the reader to believe of Robinson Mayfield, whether or not we can agree that he's a personal center for the novel? What do you mean for him to discover, learn, reflect, or intend for his and his son's future? Will he stay with Hutch? Or is he ready to relinquish—a final relinquishment but in this case a blessed one at the end of the novel? By virtue of this uniqueness, a scene which I think bears much reflection.

Price: I think the only thing I could truthfully answer to that would be to point to a sentence on page 488. It's Rob's meditation in the third person: "His whelp was here now, a twin to his flesh. With his lips on the bone of the boy's left shoulder, Rob promised again, though he did not speak or forget as he promised how he'd failed other times after fervors of hope. Then he turned away and slept in a minute, a rest like warm blood, no scrap of dream."

As I said in one of our earlier talks, the consequent lives, the future lives, of characters in my books, after the books themselves end, are essentially of no continuing concern to me in the sense that I don't sit around inventing what Rob and Hutch Mayfield did in 1945 and then 1946, and what they might be doing today if they're still alive. All I could say truthfully, and not hedgingly at all, is simply that Rob makes a promise; that I think we know for the first time in his life, at least, that he has powerful reasons, powerful new understandings and new admissions which give that promise a better chance of succeeding than it ever has had in his life before. But we also know that *he* knows how frequently he's failed his promises in the past.

Ray: Everybody else knows that too.

Price: *Everyone* else—the famous fact to the family of his generation; and he's a man in his early forties: it's very hard to teach an old dog new virtues.

Ray: Even if the old dog still has a puppy's body and perhaps a puppy's resiliency.

Price: Hutch has an orderly and lovely plan for them or even a series of plans of how he might improve their lives; simplify their lives, and, like so many children, Hutch is right. Hutch understands certain large, simple primary facts of life which are forgotten by adults and will be forgotten by Hutch, one assumes.

Ray: And which are, for example?

Price: The simplicity of happiness; the minimal nature, the minimal constituency of human happiness; the possibility of intercourse in all its richest and most rewarding senses; the possibility of rest *in* the natural world—temporary rest at least. All children have such knowledge; all the children I've ever known. All children *lose* that knowledge. What evolution that particular knowledge will follow in the case of Hutch, I don't know. It does seem to me that Hutch has either learned or inherited genetically or been given perhaps by the grace of God certain forms of knowledge and control and understanding which were not previously visible in any other member of his family in the past three or four generations.

Ray: Since who?

Price: Well, since the earliest mentioned members of either the Mayfield or the Kendal families, going back as far as Thad on page one, and going back as far as Forrest's Grandfather Mayfield, who I suppose is the earliest mentioned member of that lot.

Ray: The first Forrest?

Price: The first Forrest, who built the house in Richmond.

Ray: We might pause again to ponder the autobiographical here. I've asked you before, in the process of writing this novel, whether you were in love with or in fatal fascination with the lives of any of its particular characters. I wonder if you might choose one character or one relationship or one episode in the novel and at least diplomatically suggests its provenance in your own experience or your own store of anecdote. That might be instructive for the readers who find a critical crux working against other improbabilities, though realistically elaborated. Say, for example, the rather high incidence of black-white symbiosis which of course suggests a cultural condition. Could we focus on one that we could plainly and safely discuss?

Price: Let's talk about dangerous childbirth because several readers of the novel have suggested to me that it's about as dangerous to get born in this novel, both for mother and child, as it is to be a child in a Dickens novel!

Ray: Poor little Nell! Will she ever get born?

Price: I myself had a very difficult birth. My mother had a very dangerous and nearly fatal labor which nearly involved both our deaths. I, born in 1933, was born in the last decade—in the Western world at least—of truly dangerous childbirth. Antibiotics became widely available in America during the Second World War and in Europe immediately thereafter, and hospital facilities and techniques rapidly increased in sophistication to the point at which we now happily can see childbirth as not nearly such a perilous journey for mother or child.

So my own birth was of considerable difficulty, a fact which resonated through my own childhood in the very fluent recollections of my mother and father—and aunts and uncles—about the difficulty of that birth. I was born in my mother's family home in Macon, North Carolina, not in a hospital (the nearest real hospital, I suppose, was Durham, sixty miles away). I was told as a child, *frequently,* of other childbirths which had resulted in the death either of the mother or the child or both at times—births which invariably precipitated tragic consequences amongst their survivors, especially precipitated an enormous weight of guilt in the surviving husband who was left for the rest of his days to bear the burden of having instituted in a woman that action which ultimately caused her death.

I would like to think, and would suggest to readers, that the "high incidence of perilous childbirth" in the novel does not represent an obsessive concern of my own with birth trauma or mother-child hostility of any sort but does represent a strong and, I would argue, historically accurate memory of conditions that were much present and enormously influential in human terms as recently as thirty years ago—and certainly are ever-present in large sections and classes of American society today. Look at the infant mortality rate, the mother mortality rate, among the Navajo Indians, for instance. In Arizona and New Mexico it's still enormously high, appallingly high.

I think that heightening by danger of the act of birth, the act of childbearing and birth, lent to the relations of husband and wife and mother and child, a lifelong intensity which is little understood now, especially by Americans who have been born in the age of antiseptic, relatively safe childbirth. Mothers, as is famous, existed primarily to bear children. Their anatomical destiny, if you will, involved their volunteering to sacrifice their life each time they had a child. It was a reality of womanhood which bore no counterpart in manhood; no anatomical function of the male regularly involves him in volunteering to risk death.

Ray: Since the hunt.

Price: That was not an anatomical function; that was a social function of maleness. An anatomical function is something that your body is made to do, compelled to do.

Ray: One might argue that the social function which the male is anatomically prepared for.

Price: Yes, yes. And I think that certainly many of the attitudes toward women of males in American society—Western society, and as far as I can tell, in the society of the world—have been profoundly formed and affected by the realization on the part of men through all human history, up until about 1947 or 1948, that in the act of being men, in the act of even being human beings—that is, being born—they imperiled the lives of the other half of the human race. And I think very little has been said or thought by feminists, male or female, today about that profound immovable fact in the history of male-female relations over the centuries, over the eons.

Ray: But it is now movable and in process of transformation?

Price: It's physically movable. I'm not sure that we yet know very much about the psychic complications and traumas of childbearing and birth. We certainly don't know what the effects upon those functions of such modern interferences and impediments as birth control, chemical birth control especially, and abortion and all the other modern family arrangements are going to be. And it will be no doubt centuries before we do know.

Ray: *The Surface of Earth* spans two full generations: early twenti-eth-century rural Southern American life. Did you intend a chronicle of modern America in change? You say you prefer to think about the book as an American novel, not a Southern one—a point we've raised and answered before. Do you intend to be a chronicler of a time, not just a people or a group of individuals *in* that time? Of the mysteries of the body; the conditioned mysteries of the soul, condi-tioned by the body, naturally? But in a particular time, as in no other?

Price: Not consciously, no. What there is of chronicle in *The Surface of Earth* (and there obviously is a good deal of it) is concomi-tant upon what I did perceive as my intention, which was the discov-ery of as whole a story as is possible to a human being; as whole a story of the basic human visible reality—which is family life. Because my families were Southern, middle-class, small-town, white in origin, the families in this story are that largely, with certain outriders. The country which is explored most intimately by the novel is the coun-tryside of the piedmont and mountain, middle and upper South.

The passions and hungers which lie at the hearts of the characters seem to me certainly no less than human, no smaller than human in their occurrence, in their locale; but I would think that there were certain powerful colorations and accents placed upon those charac-ters by the fact of their being Americans, floaters on this enormous raft drifting in what has seemed to be a very dark and unmapped sea.

Ray: Isn't it true that most Americans, especially serious novel-reading Americans, no longer perceive their families, or perceive *any* families since the period chronicled by the novel, as enacting these myths, sustaining these relationships, cherishing, treasuring, some-times ravaging these fine networks of fated relationships? What limitations does that place on the novel's readership, on its potential

reputation, and on the possible contours of your future work, as you
see it from here?

Price: I don't think those are questions that I could answer with
any profit to anyone. I certainly am as aware as you are that the
family, at least in white middle-class America, has taken a very severe
buffeting in the last twenty or thirty years. The fact remains, however,
that all children are born through a physical process fairly old in
nature and still apparently indispensable and that they require anywhere from twelve to twenty years of fairly close nurture by those
physical parents before they are launched or prepared to be
launched upon even the world of the 1970s. So my guess is that our
obsessions with, interests in, curiosities about, passions for knowledge, information, insight, and story about the human family remain
of great constancy in our lives. I would have no way of being able to
predict that that is in fact the case.

It would seem comically unnecessary to point out that the ill health
of the family as an institution in middle-class America in the second
half of the twentieth century is perhaps the merest pimple upon
the history of the oldest and most powerful and pervasive human
institution—an institution which still in all the other social classes in
America and apparently in the most populous countries of the world,
the Asian countries, still rides supreme as maker and life-long arbiter
of the lives of all human beings. We tend certainly as white middle-
class Americans to extend our own very limited realities to the rest of
the world and the rest of time, but the rest of the world and the rest
of time apparently couldn't care less.

Ray: Will you write another novel like *The Surface of Earth,* or is
that utterly unpredictable?

Price: Goodness, will I live for the next five minutes? I couldn't
know. I certainly hope that I would live to write numbers of good
novels. What they'll be like I wouldn't dream of attempting to guess.

Ray: And what, briefly, are the standards of novelistic excellence
which you would meet for yourself, and hope your readers to find?

Price: I would think most of them are implicit in all the thousands
of words we've said over the last couple of years. *Breadth, depth,
entertainment*—because, second to truthfulness, my greatest desire
as a novelist is not to be boring; is indeed to entertain and to
entertain in the specific way that the novel can. That is, with story;

with surrogate life. And finally perhaps—*illumination? Help?* Maybe I should stop there.

Ray: Maybe we could continue if I ask you, finally, illuminations *of* what and help *for* what? Can we circumscribe the mystery of the earth, the earth's surface?

Price: Oh, I don't think it's very mysterious. I think it's illumination of the problems of life. It's as simple as that. I think it's tragic that the novel has undergone in the last fifty years a metamorphosis away from its old function, its chief function—and perhaps the chief function of all literature—and that was *instruction,* the conveyance of information and, one finally hoped, of wisdom. The Greeks, at least the classical Greeks, looked upon the *Iliad* primarily as a book of instruction—how to be a good and valiant man.

Ray: Or wife.

Price: Or wife. Some of the great novelists of the earlier twentieth century began to think of the novel as something decidedly other than that, as some of the distinguished poets of the early twentieth century began to see other purposes for poetry. My own guess would be, as a fairly well-informed onlooker, that the *tremendous* loss of readership which serious fiction and serious poetry have suffered, not only in America but in all Western Europe in the last twenty or thirty years—my guess would be that that loss is to a large extent attributable to fiction and poetry's abdication of two things: their old contract to entertain, to amuse, to divert; and their old contract to help, enlighten, advise, illuminate, expand. To *educate,* to lead out of the lonely desperate self into the wider world of other like and unlike human beings.

On Women and His Own Work: An Interview with Reynolds Price

Constance Rooke/1978

From *The Southern Review*, 14 (October 1978), 706–25.
Reprinted by permission of *The Southern Review,* Constance
Rooke, and Reynolds Price.

Rooke: In speaking of Hemingway's *Islands in the Stream*, you
define the author's theme as "parental devotion, filial return," and
you list three other possible human relations—"with God, with
the earth, with a female or male lover or friend." Is one of these
relations of dominant importance in your own fiction? Could you
possibly rank these four in terms of their importance for your work?

Price: I would think that, certainly in the early work, the poles
would be parental love—familial love, familial relation—and the love
that we, for lack of a better word, define as erotic. In the more recent
work—say from *Love and Work* on—added to that has been, on my
part at least, a more conscious sense of a supernatural element in the
lives of the characters, though it's present in *A Generous Man* too.
That element is largely detectable by its absence from their lives,
rather than in any conscious obeisance they make to such a reality.

Rooke: I would be interested in knowing whether you see the
supernatural element in your work as a more general way of communicating a reality you experience as Christian. Are the ghosts in part
an attempt to generalize from private belief?

Price: I think that's an accurate reading of what I myself am
conscious of in the work. There may be other things—no doubt there
are—of which I'm unconscious. I think the work has consciously
striven to avoid dogmatic or doctrinal limitations. I certainly consider
myself a Christian. But while I'm technically a Methodist, I haven't
been an active member of the church for over twenty years. Insofar
as there are Christian values visible in the *books*, they tend to be
what Aldous Huxley called the perennial philosophy, the basic values
present in all the great religions—values of charity and selflessness,

which seem to me actually at the center of any possible durable ethic for human continuance on the globe. Insofar as my personal convictions about Christianity (or about a man called Jesus) are concerned, I'm not sure that any of the books requires from the reader any special information on that subject. Say in the way that some of Graham Greene's novels, or some of his plays especially, demand that they be looked at through a Christian set of spectacles. Or Flannery O'Connor's two novels.

Rooke: Would you say that it is your Christianity which accounts for your belief that existence is comic?

Price: Very much so. I think insofar as I understand anything about comparative religion, that most of the great religions of the world would ultimately assert that reality is comic—if comic be taken to mean that ultimately all things tend toward order, serenity, the dissolution of the self in some larger intention which, in its broadest sense, would imply comic reality: just in the sense that Dante means his poem is a *Commedia*. He obviously doesn't mean it's a joke; he means it's a comedy. All things end, unavoidably, in happiness—divine will—though that will's schedule is generally a good deal slower than human beings like.

Rooke: You asserted after *A Generous Man* that your own work was basically comic. Is that the sense in which you were using the term?

Price: Yes.

Rooke: Do you think that's altered since *Love and Work*?

Price: No. In fact, I think *Love and Work, Permanent Errors,* and *The Surface of Earth* are both more comic and—if I may say so—funnier than my previous books. Readers have tended to look on the two Mustian novels as the more laugh-filled of the books and to have thought of the recent novels as considerably bleaker. In writing them, and reading them, I've felt exactly the opposite. That's one of the few things that has disappointed me in the response to *The Surface of Earth*—how many reviewers, even the most sympathetic, have said that the book contains no comic relief. *I* think it's a very funny book, in addition to having a great deal which is tragic, wasteful, and appalling.

Rooke: And you think *Love and Work* is a very funny book?

Price: I do. I think in many ways it's a very satiric book also, about this very self-important, whey-faced pair of intellectuals who are—you know—struggling through their attempt to have a little modern marriage, "a meaningful relationship."

Rooke: Does Eborn love Jane, incidentally?

Price: Does Jane love him?

Rooke: We don't know enough about her really, do we, to answer that?

Price: We don't know a great deal about her. We do know that she is capable of accurate hostility against him, which she has learned through years of living with him. I don't know if we could say they love one another or not. By the end of the book, Eborn would seriously doubt that he has ever loved anybody. In the apotheosis of his parents' love, which he feels at the end of the story and towards which the whole action of the novel has moved for him, he comes up ultimately with the conclusion that his own life is condemned by the reality of love—which he feels to be rare to the point almost of non-existence but not quite. I would have said myself in recent years—just from observing the marriages of my own contemporaries and from people, say, a decade younger than me—that married love in the American middle and upper middle classes is becoming a near impossibility.

Rooke: I'd like to get back to that later. [*Laughter*]. Would you agree with Wright Morris' assertion that any serious writer will be found on close inspection to have been hammering away at a single theme throughout his career? And is this true of your own work? To go on a bit, you have identified Hemingway's lifelong subject as saintliness. Could you identify your own, or would you perhaps not wish to? Is it something of which one shouldn't be altogether conscious?

Price: Well, I have certain senses about what the obsessions and the themes are; and I don't mind divulging those, provided any reader or listener who happens to be listening doesn't take that as an insistence on my part that that's the case for anyone but me. It seems to me they are books about human freedom—the limits thereof, the possibilities thereof, the impossibilities thereof. I have gradually become conscious that the books are an elaborate dialogue with the whole notion of free will and freedom, free will and compulsion. They're also, incidentally, dialogues with a great many other things, as you can well imagine—especially a book as complicated as *The Surface of Earth*, which occupied virtually—literally—every day of three years of my working life and twelve years of planning before I actually wrote it.

Rooke: I suppose such a central subject would always be a debate of sorts, but do you have anything like an answer to provide about the question of human freedom?

Price: No, I don't think I have any answer that would be reducible to any terms smaller than the books themselves. And that isn't meant to be a cop out. It's meant to be an affirmation of the fact that I'm a novelist and not a metaphysician or a psychiatrist, a head-doctor of any sort.

Rooke: Leslie Fiedler speaks of yea-sayers and nay-sayers, preferring the latter. In which camp would you place yourself, if you think that is in any way a useful distinction?

Price: I thought that was only a distinction that is made by, you know, Luce publications—L-U-C-E.

Rooke: I ask simply because *affirmative* is a word that comes into question a good deal in reviews of your work.

Price: Yes. I think it's been the cause of a lot of misunderstanding about my work. A lot of people who thought of themselves as yea-sayers rather jumped on the bandwagon of my first two or three books—thinking of them as joyous, rambunctious, yea-saying books—and then found themselves abandoned in the middle of the road when they read *Love and Work*—not having seen, of course, that they'd misread the first three books. Well, without being more pompous than is usual for me, I'd like to think that I've tried to be a truth-sayer rather than a yea- or nay-sayer. It would seem to me the truth contains large elements of both. So does any religious vision.

Rooke: The knowledge in the first part of Hemingway's *Islands in the Stream*, you say, is to "avoid dependence, contingency." Would you say that knowledge informs your own work?

Price: I don't think it *is* knowledge in my own work, and I don't think it's an aim in my work. I do still think it's an aim in Hemingway's. I think it's part of what Hemingway's work is about, the attempt to achieve that independence. I would think on the contrary that my work comes much more out of a psyche of a person who by

either nature or nurture has found himself too independent and
desires contingency, who also obviously has extremely complicated
feelings about contingency—about the yieldings of freedom that are
involved in any of the various brands of contingency. I would have
thought all my books really see love in a kind of Greek way; they see
it as Eros and Aphrodite, as both the greatest reward of *human* life
and also one of the greatest terrors and dangers of human life. In
many ways—I hope the parallels don't imply a false, unearned sense
of camaraderie—but writers as diverse as Racine and Tolstoy have
seemed to me much closer in their vision of human love to my own
than any American writer I can think of.

Rooke: Does your work in any way celebrate or defend the claims
of solitude?

Price: I can't think of a solitary character in any of the stories.
Uncle Grant lives alone in his story, as in many ways he did in our
lives; but he had elaborate relations with my father and peripheral
relations with my mother, me, my brother, and various other white
people on whom he depended. I think some of the genuine heroes
of *The Surface of Earth* are basically solitary people, people like
Rena and Eva, Grainger, Sylvie, and Alice; those are the people who
seem to me the heroic figures in *The Surface of Earth*.

Rooke: Some of those people seem to have wrested solitude from
the familial relation.

Price: They've wrested it, but also they're very aware of the
terrible cost to themselves at which they've wrested it. Rena says that
wonderful thing, I think; she says, "A single life is a dry rag to suck."
It is, but she also has one of the best lives in the book. And ultimately
one feels she knows that too; she knows both things. My father's
family were a family of women who wrested solitude out of familiality
in an extraordinary way—in ways which I think were both rewarding
and maiming for them. Some of these things I learned from those
women are contained in the characters of *The Surface of Earth*,
though none of the characters there is closely based on any of my
father's sisters.

Rooke: Is there some special feeling you have about women that
you are defending in that novel, do you think?

Price: Very much so. I don't think it's primarily a novel about
women. I think it's a novel about both sexes and the various shad-

ings between the sexes. But certainly I was tremendously aware in
writing the novel of—for me, at least—a whole new depth of concern
with the reality of being a woman, of being various kinds of women
because I don't think there is one kind, really. I think there are
very few things that we can define as being *woman*, as opposed to a
series of women.

Rooke: What are those very few things?

Price: I think the basic absolutely unavoidable thing that is *woman*
is the fact that women possess ovaries and uteruses which yearn to
bear children, physiologically yearn to bear children.

Rooke: People have commented on the number of deaths in
childbirth in *The Surface of Earth*. Was that a conscious thing after a
while?

Price: Oddly enough, it wasn't. And actually, when I reread the
book—read the paperback proofs of the book—I felt that since
there'd been so much comment on the number of childbed deaths in
the book, I would count them. I could only count three, maybe four,
in a five-hundred-page novel, which—given the absolutely ghastly
childbed death statistics of the nineteenth and early twentieth centuries—is perhaps even less than normal. I was amazed to discover
how quickly women, for instance, have forgot what a perilous matter
childbirth was until 1945 or 1946 when antibiotics became generally
available in the United States and when hospital care became generally available.

Rooke: Perhaps the heightened consciousness on the part of
many readers about the childbed deaths has something to do with
the feeling on the part of various children in the book that they may
be guilty for the pain or injury caused the mother.

Price: I was very aware of that as a reality in the relations between
parents and children, especially sons and mothers, and between
husbands and wives. As you yourself well know, from reading any
biography or set of memoirs of an eighteenth- or nineteenth-century
Englishman or American, the normal rule was that a man who lived
to be fifty or sixty years old had gone through two or three wives—
having lost one or two in childbirth. Nowadays the United States is
filled with all these old women who have outlived their second
husbands. And the simple explanation of that is penicillin and sulfa

drugs and hospital care, plus twentieth-century tension which has produced all these coronaries in the poor husbands.

Rooke: Do you think a good deal of hostility between parents and children, or between husbands and wives, is based on the pain and risks of childbirth?

Price: Yes, I do. I'm amazed that ideological feminism has taken so little cognizance of this fact in what I'd take to be its first chore— which is to understand *why* men have oppressed women, why men have been hostile to them. Feminism has been so bent on attempting counter hostilities against men, which are understandable if not admirable, that it's had little time to understand the sources of that original hostility. After all, men just didn't make up antifeminism out of the blue, out of sheer unattached power drive. The one thing that can be said about every man who ever drew breath on the globe is this, *he was born out of a woman's body.*

Rooke: And that it hurt her?

Price: And that it *hurt* her, by definition—that it killed many of them, maimed many of them. I nearly killed my mother. I did indeed maim her. Many, many men in the history of the human race have been able to say that, have known it, been told it time and time again by their mothers. It was one of the major means of power that women had over their sons—"I nearly died in order that you might live." And don't think they didn't tell their sons that. Of course they did! How did husbands feel, who every time they slept with their wives risked the possibility of their dying nine months later? Milton— whom I teach, you know, once a year at Duke—Milton *killed* two of his three wives by impregnating them. Don't you think that dawned on him?—that the chief physiological function of joy and love in his life was also potentially lethal to the object of his love?

Rooke: Do you feel that men have generally repressed that guilt?

Price: We've repressed it tremendously. We've had to in order to get on with living—witness the fact that so many people have been surprised at and have objected to the number of childbed deaths in my novel. They aren't objecting because it's unreal; they object because they don't like to deal with the idea that that was a reality. And still is a reality. For all the girls that you and I know who now come to us wreathed in smiles, singing hymns to natural childbirth, we still know that having a baby in the age of almost perfect childbirth technique is a perilous adventure. The fact that perhaps one generation of western middle-class women in recent years has managed to get through childbirth with a few less pains and anxieties than others is fine by me. I certainly don't wish the pain and death on anyone; but to ignore the reality of, as far as we can tell, millions of years of human history is folly.

Rooke: It's a new danger then?

Price: I think it's a terrible new danger. For one thing it's a danger to our greatest single problem in the world, which is overpopulation. One of the things that has always kept the population in check is the peril of having children.

Rooke: Could you talk a bit about what the specifically female heroism of the characters in *The Surface of Earth* might be? What kinds of actions and qualities occur in the women characters of that novel and are used by you in some sense to celebrate women?

Price: I think the chief heroism for all of them—and I think all of them succeed in greater or lesser degree—is in their having to deal with what seems to me the most difficult kind of life that a human being can lead: that is a life without what I would call external work. These were women whose work was home and family. Family did tend to stay around longer than it does now. You and I are aware that most women's children now are gone by the time the women are in their late thirties or early forties. In those days the children, if they moved at all, just tended to move down the street a few hundred yards and marry and have their own children but stay very much under the wings of the paternal/maternal family. So in that sense motherhood could be a lifetime career and turn into grandmother-hood, etc. That's obviously a rapidly vanishing reality for most American middle-class women and has led to many problems for them. I think that a large part of what I'd call the heroism—you know, the courage, the resourcefulness—of all the women in *The Surface of Earth* has been the way in which they've dealt with that extremely difficult vocation which was handed them. I mean a life based entirely upon love and duty, as opposed to anything more external to the body or to the mind and heart than that. Their husbands were at least able to leave the house and plow a field or sell electric stoves; they had to stay home and deal entirely in emotions—emotions and food.

Rooke: How would you compare Polly and Eva in their different responses to that kind of duty?

Price: Oh, it's hard to say. I wouldn't want to award prizes to either of them because I'm so fascinated by both and, in very different ways, so admiring of both. I suppose if I had to live with one of them, I'd choose Polly, though I'm not sure that means Polly is in any way a more resourceful human being. I think they both had the courage to do what they needed to do. Eva had the courage to do what a great number of women in history have needed to do, and used to have the courage to do—it was perfectly acceptable up until really the Second World War for a girl to spend the rest of her life living at home with either mother or father and not at all be unassuaged and looked upon as some denied old maid. She was just a girl whose career was her father, a girl whose career was her mother. Sometimes they were indeed people who longed to have family lives and had been denied that because no man invited them to have one; but in many cases they were women who simply decided "I love my father" or, very interestingly and frequently, "My brother, my bachelor brother." The South is full of those old-maid sisters and bachelor brothers who live with one another.

Rooke: And you would take that as an authentic choice?

Price: I think it's a perfectly authentic choice—the world hasn't lacked progenitors for many millenia now—and it was one of the ways in which I think the nineteenth and early twentieth century were much more emotionally tolerant than many of the situations into which we've backed ourselves now when we constantly laud our own tolerance and newfound freedom. It seems to me that nineteenth-century familial civilization was emotionally much more elastic and tolerant than it is now.

Rooke: Do you have any thoughts about the future of the family?

Price: They're all rather ominous thoughts, insofar as I have any. Perfectly clearly, the family is going to continue; but it doesn't seem to be working very well in America now. At least it doesn't seem to be working in its old terms, which were basically paleolithic terms—the family as defined by the earliest visible man, earliest visible social organization; father, the hunter; mother, the gatherer and nurse. That division no longer seems to be working. Especially children are telling us, if no one else. Husbands and wives are now telling us it doesn't work, and in *spades*; but first, the *children* in America told us "The family isn't working." If there was a central theme in the sixties, it was that children—it wasn't that they were talking about Vietnam so much or anything else; they were telling us that the American middle-class family no longer functioned. It didn't rear children who could in turn honor and love their parents.

Rooke: Would you describe yourself as a feminist?

Price: Very much so, yes. A lifelong one, I'd like to say, not one of recent stripe.

Rooke: Would you put any limits on that definition of yourself as a feminist?

Price: Only to remind feminists of what I've already suggested— that they might spend a great deal of their time attempting to understand *why* men have dealt with women in the ways that they have. They might also attempt to understand the enormous kinds of power that women have had over men. I think feminists denied themselves, in a very perverse way, a recognition of the enormous degrees of influence and power they have had over men. I think feminists have denied themselves the central fact which I've also just stated—all men were born, lived inside a woman's body for nine months and then came out.

Rooke: So did all women.

Price: So did all women, which is one of the big problems women have that men don't. Women's intense psychic knowledge tends to be only of female reality. Men, being reared by women, can also have an understanding of the other, which I think is in many ways denied to women.

Rooke: Do you mean that you are equally good at creating men and women characters?

Price: I never thought of it that way. I never felt any discomfort in trying to shift from one to the other. My first novel was centrally concerned with a young woman, and therefore I gave some people the notion that I was especially good at females. But then the next novel is basically concerned with a young man. *Love and Work* is basically concerned with a man. Most of the stories in *Permanent Errors* are basically concerned with men. I would say *The Surface of Earth* is six of one and half-dozen of the other.

Rooke: Would you be able to describe qualities that seem to you most commonly to belong to woman?

Price: I think I have. I think I only know that by reflection, however. I only know that because women have come up to me constantly and said, "How did you know that about women?" And they really look at me as though they thought I'd perhaps had some sort of sex change.

Rooke: What characteristics do you think they were referring to?

Price: Generally, it's the feelings of women about men. They say, "How did you know women feel that way?" I don't know. I just think you know it because you're a human being—if for no other reason, because you were reared by your mother and saw your mother's relations with your father. When you were young, it was the first love relationship you ever studied. Of course, girls also studied the relations of their mothers with their fathers. I think perhaps, on the face of it, they tend to know a little less about men than men may know about women. That may be—I've said this in many other places— one of the other reasons why most novels by women tend to be about women as opposed to being centrally about men, and why most of what we think of as the classical novels about women are by men: Tolstoy, Flaubert, etc.

Rooke: Again, could you put any abstract nouns to those qualities which you see as belonging to women? The kind of thing that people meant when they suggested that you knew the truth about women?

Price: I think they're qualities that relate to that one irreducible female fact, which is the commitment of women's physiology to childbearing—and therefore all the concomitant emotions and needs that follow from that, emotions which are readily describable in cliché terms: the emotions of stability, nest-building. Whereas man is seen as the wanderer, the buccaneer, the rogue, or the faithless one, woman is seen as the faithful passive waiter. I am amazed still to find how many women feel *that way*, no matter what feminist credentials they carry. If you really get them to tell you how they feel vis-à-vis men that they love, especially vis-à-vis their own fathers, they'll tell you they felt that way. And they're surprised that you know that because they've met very few men who will acknowledge they know. That's the kind of knowledge I think men have had to repress—

knowledge acquired from their mothers and too painful for men to deal with, too dangerous for many men to deal with.

Rooke: Do you think that the women in your books are much more centrally concerned with love than are the men?

Price: With erotic love, do you mean?

Rooke: With the relationship with their mates. You know, the old Byron thing: "Man's love is of man's life a thing apart. / 'Tis woman's whole existence."

Price: I think in the crudest terms I'd agree with Byron. Most human beings would, if they had to give a ten-word definition of what men *want* out of it and what women *want* out of it, basically say that man's love is of man's life a thing apart; it is woman's all. I'd suspect that's basically the structure of the male/female eros in my novels, though I haven't really gone back and thought through the relations of various characters to one another.

Rooke: Given that kind of structure, don't you feel that your books would be vulnerable to feminist assault? That is surely one of the things that feminists are most concerned with, i.e., the recognition that there are other things out in the world which can interest women.

Price: Well, it would seem to me irrelevant to attack them because they're not doctrinal books at all. They're not pieces of propaganda for a given way of life. They are descriptions of what seems to me the history of the human race, and an assault would seem as meaningless upon them as assault upon a beech tree. I think they might well lament that many women have had the kinds of lives many women have in my books; but I don't think I could be blamed for portraying that life, any more than the human race could be blamed for having produced it. I think in fact that *The Surface of Earth* ought to become a kind of feminist textbook.

Rooke: Would you care to talk any more about why you think that should be?

Price: Because, to be utterly modest about it, I can't think of a novel written for years that says more about women than *The Surface of Earth*—more different kinds of things about them. And about women in *America*, not women in the American South but women in America—because I think of the book as a very American book and not at all as a specifically Southern book.

Rooke: Would you be able to identify some other large area, in addition to the matter of childbirth, about which you feel *The Surface of Earth* has a good deal to say?

Price: Well, I think I have something to say about this whole problem of vocation in women—what women are going to do, what their career is going to be if it's not going to be cooking and diapering. There are three or four women in the novel who choose consciously to remain single, or to be married and then to surrender or retire from marriage: Eva, Polly, Eva's black maid Sylvie, Rena, and Alice—very centrally at the end of the novel—who becomes herself a kind of saint of art.

Rooke: But is there anybody else who has got a real *career?*

Price: I think Eva had a very successful career. Eva was a nurse. Eva nursed her father. She loved her father above all things in the world; her father loved her above all things in the world. I think they had a very happy life together. She didn't want to be married. She made a mistake. She thought she wanted to be married. She ran off, married, had a son, came home, and lived happily ever after. I've seen that happen in several cases.

Rooke: I have heard it suggested that Eva's permanent error was in leaving the marriage, and that all the pain of the novel for several generations follows from that separation.

Price: No, I think her mistake is to run away at all—with Forrest. I'm not saying that Eva couldn't have married anybody, but she certainly picked the wrong man to marry—this extremely needful young man with far too many holes in his own nature. She needed someone much more self-sufficient.

Rooke: Someone who would leave her room for her father?

Price: Someone who would leave her great room for all sorts of things in her life—for her own fiercely independent nature, for instance. And her father instinctively knows how to do that. She returns, I think, to a very happy life; I really do. It produces a great deal of unhappiness for her son, unfortunately. It produces great happiness for Forrest, by the way, because as soon as she leaves him, within a year, he has established a fruitful relationship with another woman, which gives him a very rewarding married life, though it's never a legal marriage.

Rooke: Wallace Kaufman says in an earlier interview with you that someone told him women have trouble reading *A Generous Man* because of "the all pervasive phallic symbol of the snake." [*Joint laughter*]. We can discount the snake, but what *about* the phallicism of the novel?

Price: Well, fifty percent of the human race has one. A portion at least of the other fifty percent seems to want one. It has been one of the central concerns of all the religions I can think of. It's a central concern of everybody's erotic life, everybody who isn't involved in some extremely exotic perversion.

Rooke: Such as lesbianism? [*Joint laughter*].

Price: Such as lesbianism—which is fairly exotic, since insofar as we can tell it involves five percent of the human race. So I don't think there'd be much more I'd want to say than that phallicism is an unavoidable component of all human discourse, including that of lesbians—they deal intensely with its *absence*. And it's an indispensable component of any complete picture of the adolescent male, which *A Generous Man* tries to be.

Rooke: I'd like to move on to another subject now. I know you often speak of how absurd it would be for you to write a sentence to sound like a Price sentence. Yet your style is obviously very strongly pronounced, and I wondered if you could define that in any way beyond perhaps saying that it is elaborate.

Price: Honestly, I can't. It always surprises and generally annoys me to hear myself thought of as a stylist. I simply think of myself as a mimeticist or mime of visible human realities which have crossed my own sight or imagination. I am aware in rereading the stories and the novels, or certainly in attempting to read the reflections of the stories and novels offered by other people, that most people find the texture of the prose elaborate and sometimes difficult. I've been conscious—I was certainly conscious in writing *The Surface of Earth*—of attempting to make the language as plain as I could make it and remain just to the complexity of the experience in the human situations being described, being mirrored.

Rooke: Is there anything perhaps about your material, as distinct in some sense from your vision, that requires an elaborate style?

Price: Beyond saying that it is complicated, I don't know what more could be said. Like most writers, I'm unsophisticated about what I'm doing while I'm doing it.

Rooke: Do you feel that your material is more complicated than the materials of writers in the plain style? That there is a correlation?

Price: No, not necessarily. I've been involved for the last several years, off and on, in translating a number of short narratives out of the Old and New Testaments for a small book I'm doing on the origins of narrative and on the major primitive narratives; it seems to me perfectly clear that the great stories of the Bible reveal that the most complex imaginable human situations and thoughts can be contained in sentences of the utmost syntactical simplicity and lucidity. So I don't claim that only a style like mine is responsive to the complexity of human experience. I'm just saying that it is the language my mind produces when brought in contact with particular kinds of human complexity that have passed in front of my mind.

Rooke: Do you feel that the origins of your style could be analyzed, if not by you?

Price: Oh, I don't know that they could. There are obvious gross attempts by reviewers to relate it to some previous writer, generally Faulkner—which I have spent more time than I should have denying.

Rooke: It's not fair he gets to have all the long sentences, is it?

Price: Exactly. As though he invented long sentences! My God, hasn't anybody ever read Conrad or Henry James or any novel written in the eighteenth century, any sentence in the seventeenth century? They all seem to forget, for instance, that I spent three years of my life as a young man, just before I began writing novels, reading seventeenth-century prose and poetry—which is infinitely more elaborate than William Faulkner ever dreamt of being. But that's something few reviewers could be suspected of being patient enough to have perceived. Also, I think childhood readings were much more formative upon my own view of the world than anything I read, say, after the age of fourteen or fifteen.

Rooke: Did you read good things at home?

Price: I read wonderful things, by sheer accident. No, not by sheer accident—by the fact that my father's sisters were very literate and gave me good books to read on all possible gift days.

Rooke: Can you give a few significant examples?

Price: Basically, the first things I read were children's Bible-story books, which were very close rewritings of the King James version.

Therefore, I was instantly immersed in one form of the paradoxically baroque plain-style. Maybe that's a definition of my style.

Rooke: Paradoxically baroque plain-style?

Price: Paradoxically baroque plain-style. I think I write the most Anglo-Saxon English currently being written in America, but it's also very baroque. [*Laughter*].

Rooke: Is your language sometimes too difficult, do you think on hindsight, too private or recalcitrant for the general intelligent reader?

Price: Probably. So was Shakespeare's. So was Milton's. So were all those other geniuses with whom I am constantly and brashly comparing myself. But actually, if one doesn't take those people as one's colleagues, one had better not start writing at all.

Rooke: To put what is perhaps the same question another way, does your work sometimes seem not to arrive at enough of an answer about what troubles it?

Price: That's an interesting-sounding question. It would probably take me weeks to think it out.

Rooke: It's based on my acceptance of what you have said about style being purely a matter of telling the truth. So my questions are analogous. If your language is sometimes too difficult, might that not really be a function of what themes or questions were troubling the work, a sign perhaps that your writing was not yielding an answer?

Price: Yes. Again, it sounds fascinating and I'm sure the answer must be yes. But I'm sure the answer would also be yes for any other writer—to make a self-defensive initial reply. On the other hand, the curiously polar response which my work has always aroused in readers and critics—almost more than any writer my age that I can think of, my work inspires either love or hatred, no middle ground—can be traced to the fact that my work does contain something outrageous. I'm never aware that it does while I'm doing it; but it seems to me that my work does frighten a number of people who read it and that they flee from it, hurling imprecations—hurling Parthian imprecations at it (they're a small minority but I treasure them). That's self-defensive too, but I honestly do think it's definitive of what the peculiar critical reputation of my work has been. I think it's a healthy reputation. I must say I'd hate to be a writer whom everyone admired. Jesus says that wonderful thing, "Woe unto you when all men praise you."

Rooke: Are there any labels from the marketplace with which you feel comfortable? Such as that you are basically a realistic novelist?

Price: Labels. Oh, I'd hate to be anything but a good novelist. I can't think of any other label which I would be satisfied with. Perhaps basically realist, with a very large admixture of the wild and the unreal—in quotes.

Rooke: Has your method of writing changed? Do you still aim at perfecting a single page a day?

Price: I tend to write about a page or a page and a half a day. It's not a matter of infinite sanding and polishing—if you looked at that page of manuscript, you'd find probably very little crossing out or changing—but it is a page which secretes itself slowly through the course of a day, a sentence or two at a time, over a period of four or five hours of daily work.

Rooke: But after you have four-hundred-and-ninety of these single pages, do you have to do very much shuffling around?

Price: Very, very little. It basically just tends to be the kind of gross correction that anyone has to do. You go back through to be sure that someone's eyes don't change color in the middle of the book, or someone's name doesn't change, or that someone's age doesn't change in the middle of a decade—those unavoidable errors that arise in working over something over a long period of time: the sort of errors that are in fact impossible ever to get completely out of a book.

Rooke: Have you written much—whole chunks of novels, say— that you haven't published?

Price: Never. I don't suppose I've written five pages that haven't been published—of narrative fiction, that is. I've written a number of poems which haven't been published, though there's nothing basically unpublishable about them, I trust. There are notebooks, which I've kept through the years. They're very much a craftsman's notebooks, not intensely personal journals, very much working plans for a given book under way. But those are the only unpublished work I have.

Rooke: Your critical comparisons tend to be with writers such as Tolstoy and Milton, rather than contemporaries such as Saul Bellow. Do you feel that it is a healthy thing for young writers to keep in mind the greatest writers who ever lived, rather than those close by?

Price: Certainly—if I could replace the word "greatest" by "biggest" and "most spacious": that is, those who contain the most knowledge about human existence. I'd certainly hope that young writers would resort to them. I find it a great recent failing of academic English study—that in whoring after popularity in a time of unpopularity, English departments have tended to seek students by offering them only what was "really happening now." Naturally you can loop in a number of kids if you offer your seminar on Kurt Vonnegut as opposed to Tolstoy, but I'm not sure you've given them bread, as opposed to stone, by the end of the semester.

Rooke: *The Surface of Earth* has been called old-fashioned. What do you think of that description?

Price: I think it's ignorant.

Rooke: What particular ignorances are contained in it?

Price: Ignorances of the intense freshness with which the novel confronts old-fashioned human problems such as family, eros, love and hate, need and giving. I don't know what other problems there are in the world. They're old-fashioned, but they're the only ones we've got. The novel as a form essentially has for its subject matter the past; it can't use the present, for all sorts of complex reasons. Insofar as we have one or two generations of Americans now who claim to be uninterested in anything that happened before last Wednesday—and I can only say that's *their* problem—the extraordinary thing is that there are still large numbers of readers in America who are interested in reading the sorts of novels I write.

Rooke: Is there anything about the originality of treatment that you could define, other than by answering with the sum of the book?

Price: Again, that's really the only answer; but it's not a very satisfactory answer for your purposes. I suppose just the stamina of the book, the intensity with which it looks at a number of human situations that perhaps, in America at least, have not been looked at with that kind of steady gaze for a while.

Rooke: A kind of formal relentlessness, perhaps?

Price: A kind of formal relentlessness, which I think has been one of the reasons that some of my more heroic friends have found it a hard book to read—though they have persevered and read it.

Rooke: Can you compare *The Surface of Earth* to the rest of your works, suggesting ways in which it is a continuation or a departure? That's an enormous question, I know.

Price: Well, certainly in the broadest sense, it seems to me a fruition of virtually all the concerns of the earlier books. I don't feel that it's a drawing of the line under anything; I don't feel that it's the end of anything. It doesn't seem to be a terminal book in any sense, in my career or my life or in its own life. I certainly hope it isn't. But it does seem to me a summary book, to that point. I think many human beings feel the necessity for some sort of summing up at roughly my age, the entrance to middle age—the early forties; I began that book when I was thirty-nine years old. It just seems to me the fullest examination of all the problems that perhaps, in your term, troubled the other books. I can't think of any problem which troubles it which it shuns or doesn't finally face—and in some cases, face down. I'm not sure that I can think of any concern which *The Surface of Earth* has that isn't present, in embryo at least, in the earlier books. There may be some—certainly in a book that long there might well be some—but I'd equally deny that it's in any sense a repetition of the themes of the earlier books.

Rooke: It has sometimes seemed to me that one could get a reasonably thorough sense of your work simply by pondering the titles, and I wonder in that connection if you could talk about the significance of the title of *The Surface of Earth.*

Price: Fred Chappell said that same thing in his own very interesting review of *The Surface of Earth.* I'd never thought of that, though I have been aware from book to book that the titles were important to me.

Rooke: But they seem to be filling something out.

Price: That's what Fred said. he didn't expand upon what he meant. You haven't either and I don't think I can. I just wrote the books. But I have talked before about the seriousness with which I've taken the problem of naming books. It's obviously as serious as naming a child; and it is a matter of extreme delicacy, it seems to me, to give a book a name which is both helpful to the reader as to the total reality of the book—the total being of the book—and also not too helpful. That is, I think it's dangerous to attempt to overdefine a book by its title. So I've tried hard to choose titles for my books which walk that narrow parapet between helping the reader and coddling the reader or bossing the reader to my own view of the book. *The Surface of Earth* was a very difficult title for me to arrive at because one of the many things that I discovered about the difference between a long novel and a shorter one is that a long novel is much harder to name—a long novel is about so many more things. Therefore your problem becomes to select a sufficiently neutral title—a title which somehow rides over, rides astride, as many as possible of the concerns of the book without minimizing or diminishing those concerns in any way, without oversimplifying. It's obvious—it becomes clear to me now, having finished *The Surface of Earth*—why so many great eighteenth- and nineteenth-century novels are simply named after a character in the novel. "My God, what are we going to call the monster? Well, let's call it *Tom Jones*." I seriously considered calling this novel *Mayfield*; and then late in my writing of it, I became aware—as I was gathering for the final scenes—that there was this echoing refrain throughout the book of the surface of earth, as opposed to the center of earth. Then I wrote that, for me, absolutely central scene in the book in which Hutch and Alice are on their sketching trip at the end, when Hutch remembers his childhood fantasy about the giant who is asleep in a cave in the middle of earth, dreaming the world. It's a fantasy I had as a child myself; and I've since discovered that it's apparently an archetype of almost all human beings, certainly found in almost all known societies.

Rooke: What psychological polarities would be involved in that distinction between the center and the surface?

Price: In my own mind—and again I wouldn't want to impose this too heavily on any reader's experience of the book—certainly that's the juncture at which the intensely religious concern of the book becomes visible for me: the sense, on my part as an observer of these multitudinous lives, that these people are perversely and tragically and comically insisting upon living on the surface of earth as opposed to anywhere near the center of what the earth might contain, the center of the possibilities of love both human and divine which the earth would seem to offer them.

Rooke: Is this in any way a justification for the length of the novel, do you think? It is necessary for the book to be so long in order to create a sufficiently extended *surface*?

Price: I think definitely so. After I'd finished the manuscript—and the total manuscript had come to some eight hundred typed pages—I very seriously scrutinized it to see if anything could go out. With the exception of the odd word here and there, I couldn't find a single *scene* which could go out without substantially altering the meaning of the book. And I still feel that over a year after finishing it, almost a year after publishing it. All the good novels we can think of—most of them are roughly that length, roughly five hundred pages long. I think *length* is an absolute function of the novel, the experience it uniquely promises to give.

Rooke: I have just a few questions about *A Long and Happy Life*. First, the obvious one. Does Rosacoke make a mistake in marrying Wesley?

Price: Oh, I don't think so. I think they're going to have as good a life as people have. I don't have a very clear sense of what their life has been. I haven't invented a little unwritten sequel to *A Long and Happy Life*, but I don't envision some bleak existence for them.

Rooke: What do you like about Wesley?

Price: I like his homogeneity. I like the fact that he's all one thing—which I think men generally are and which women find hard to accept in men. Wesley's like a loaf of bread. Any way you slice him you get bread. You're not going to suddenly turn up an apricot in the middle of the bread. He's Wesley all the way through. He actually says that, doesn't he? One of my favorite scenes in the book. She comes up and puts her hands over his eyes—no, wait: he puts his hands over her eyes and says "Who am I?" and she says "You are Wesley but that don't tell me why you act the way you do." He says: "Because I am Wesley." Wesley has that slightly godlike quality, you know—God tells Moses that His name is I AM. That's really all Wesley ever says to Rosacoke—"Look, I'm me. Take *me* or leave *me*." And she can't leave it.

Rooke: Could I record that you leered? [*Joint laughter*].

Price: Yes.

Rooke: I'm trying to remember something that Rosacoke thinks, about how she had hoped that Wesley would change, that he would learn how to talk to her, how to listen to her perhaps, and that they could get them some children, and maybe sometimes be happy. I am butchering your prose, but that is roughly the sense of it. There seems to be a kind of mourning in that thought. Are we to take it that he will not change? Or not for the better?

Price: Another thing Rosacoke says there, as I recall, is that he would "calm on down." Of course he will do a lot of that—he'd have done it in any case. Part of Rosacoke's problem is that she's trying to accelerate what would probably have been a perfectly natural evolution in Wesley. Wesley is just in the process of sowing the last of his rather sparse wild oats, and Rosacoke is doing that common thing women do—trying to slow a man down faster than the man himself wants to slow.

Rooke: So her vision of ironing shirts and eating strong pork liver and looking at the city people who hate each other, all that is not to be taken as a definitive vision of their future?

Price: No, not at all. And I think that there my own view of Rosacoke seems to be different from almost any other person's view that I've encountered. I don't accept Rosacoke's judgments on Wesley as being complete and accurate and just. It seems to me that she gives Wesley much too hard a time, that she takes much too righteous a line about Wesley. I think Rosacoke is very self-congratulatory. I like her a lot; I admire many things about her—but she does have a very typical kind of young Protestant self-righteousness and a very ready willingness to find anyone else's values lacking. I find Wesley, in short, a better man than Rosacoke finds him.

Rooke: That's interesting. Do you then not foresee a withering, such as Milo experiences, occurring for Rosacoke and Wesley?

Price: I don't really think I do. I think Milo withers to some extent because of the decisions he has to make at the end of *A Generous Man* and because of the kind of woman he chooses to marry. After all, Wesley is marrying a much more resourceful woman than Milo married; and Rosacoke is marrying a man who is at least as resourceful as Milo. So I think their marriage contains implicit promises which Milo's didn't.

Rooke: About this withering, a term you once applied to Milo, is that in your opinion an extremely common occurrence, more common than an increasing moral and emotional fineness? I'm talking about the movement out of early youth.

Price: I'm afraid it is. I wish I could say it weren't.

Rooke: Do you think this pattern is especially common to people of Milo's and Rosacoke's place, time, or class?

Price: Yes. I think, as is famous, that it is unfortunately common to laborers in any society. Their lives are in many cases severely limited and, in many other cases, strangled by the sheer laboriousness of their lives.

Rooke: Have you liked each of your books in succession better than the ones before?

Price: If you would let me take them in the order in which they were written, as opposed to the order in which they were published, I think the answer would be yes. I'd say that because most of *The Names and Faces of Heroes* was written before *A Long and Happy Life*. Yes, I'd say that would be true. I think most writers feel that. There is the odd writer who's neurotically self-hating; but most writers I know, most of the writers I admire, tend to be excited about their most recent work—and as a matter of fact quickly lose interest in it: not *care* but *interest*.

Rooke: I am asking beyond that whether now, at the distance you have from the books before *The Surface of Earth*, they still seem to you of ascending merit?

Price: They seem to me of growing size. I'd say that much—in their concerns, in their breadth of attempt, certainly in their breadth of effort. I wouldn't want to speak about their degree of achievement. I honestly don't think I could speak about that. That's for the world to decide, if it wishes. Or any piece of the world.

The Spy that Stayed: A Conversation with Reynolds Price

Daniel Voll/1983

From *Tobacco Road* (April 1983), 4–6. Reprinted by permission of Reynolds Price.

Since 1954, except for three years taken to study at Oxford on a Rhodes scholarship, Reynolds Price has spent his academic career studying, writing and teaching at Duke.

Price lives on the banks of a pond in eastern Orange County, North Carolina, living in a tiny house trailer while he wrote his first three novels, and then later, in 1965, moving to a spacious ranch house where he has since completed twelve books: five novels, many short stories, essays, a play and a volume of poetry.

Price's fictional work is anchored in the land and among the people he knows best here in North Carolina. He illuminates through his characters the universal relationship between the family and the individual, the discordant tension between imagination and actuality, and something he likes to call the Quest—that perpetual striving for self-understanding, acceptance, love.

Eudora Welty, a close friend and admirer of Price, said that through Price's fresh style, "We can enter, by yet another turning, into his reverence for the mysteries and comedies of people and place."

The following conversation took place at Price's home among his collected memorabilia—his books, skulls and art.

Tobacco Road: Is it really true that for the past 32 years you have been going through Dempster Dumpsters looking for illicit letters that Duke students have been sending each other?

Price: The fact that I once admitted in your presence to having occasionally glanced into the Dempster Dumpster has led to the myth that I'm a sort of bag man who searches the Duke garbage on a regular schedule. I don't, though I share the human race's fascination with other peoples' mail. I also have a writer's fascination with what people say to one another when they think they aren't being watched.

Tobacco Road: Do you remember the first letter you found?

162

Price: The first letter I remember finding was when I was a Phi Delt in 1954. It was a sensational letter—from a man in Pennsylvania to one of my fraternity brothers. It was one of the great, funny confessional letters of all time.

Tobacco Road: With all this watching of Duke students, what are the major changes you've seen in the last 32 years?

Price: There have probably been four distinct "generations" here since my time as a freshman. We as freshmen in 1951—people who were born in 1933, the year of Roosevelt's inauguration—were very much a post-Second War, post-Depression generation. And in a peculiar way the tone of our lives, the tone of our assumptions survived into the mid-1960s. The first great break that I perceive, the first seismic change in the Duke psyche begins around 1966–67. Of course, there had been some pretty shattering events in the 1950s— Korea, all the anxieties surrounding Berlin, the serious likelihood that any male of my generation would get drafted; but the real psychic change occurred in the late 1960s and was heralded by the arrival of drugs on campus, drugs other than alcohol and nicotine.

Tobacco Road: How did teaching in the '70s differ from teaching the '60s?

Price: The '60s were both the most perplexing and most exciting time in the years I've been at Duke, the most exciting and baffling in which to try to teach and to deal with students. The '60s ended the day we withdrew from Vietnam. They just came to an absolute scalding halt the moment we flew out of Saigon with all those people hanging onto helicopter skids, and the halt was a little disheartening to the elders who'd been watching, disheartening to realize how crucial the simple dread of being drafted had been to the after all very valuable and grandiose claims and rhetoric of the 1960s. They were dreading for their lives, to be sure—their lives in an unjust war—but so many of their other hopes and aims were abandoned at the moment of Nixon's capitulation.

Then the '70s—the great nadir in my own experience of Duke. The '70s people seemed to suffer a failure of imagination, a failure to try to extend into a world beyond themselves. There were serious, gifted, admirable people here in that period; but the general tone was depressed, self-absorbed, career-oriented in a narrow and airless way.

By the end of the '70s, I was really beginning to think, "I don't need to take this much annual repulsion and depression. I'm going to give this up." Then around 1979-80-81, I began to sense a sort of upswing. The economic situation, paradoxically, was getting worse; but I think a number of the best students had decided, "Well, the situation is so awful that we might as well give up this dumb quest for security and simply dedicate ourselves to what we're interested in and might want to spend our whole lives doing." So a number of our best students have again abandoned the more "practical" majors and are coming back to the old lovable mind-expanding majors—the liberal arts. I'm getting much better students in my writing and literature classes; and believe me, the relief is enormous.

Tobacco Road: What kinds of students have interested you most in your years of teaching writing?

Price: Students who have the gift of curiosity, who for whatever blessed reason were not totally absorbed in their own stereotypical adolescent agonies. Occasionally there comes a sort of miraculous student who just is more interested in other people than in him or herself. The first class I ever taught at Duke contained a 16-year-old girl named Anne Tyler from Raleigh, who was almost as good a writer at age 16 as she is now; and she's now one of the best novelists alive in the world. She had an absolutely innate curiosity about the outside world, which is one of the two major pieces of equipment a novelist must possess—the other being a built-in mastery of language. That's the other main thing that has attracted me to particular students, the marvelous ability to manipulate language in a magical way; and it's the rarest skill of all.

Tobacco Road: How much does the University prepare students for the larger "real world"?

Price: For students, the university is, to a large extent, a holding pattern. It's a place in which society has agreed to detain them before they're permitted to land at Newark and unload and get on with the activities at their destinations—their destination being, we assume, adulthood. An enormous number of the perennial complaints in the *Chronicle* are simply the complaints of students in all generations from the middle ages to now. "We're dangling in midair, our feet are not touching ground, no one cares what we think or feel." The general answer to that is, "Right, nobody does much care what you think or feel yet because this society has not really agreed to admit that you are functioning adults. It is holding you in place until its schedule says you're ready to become 'real' people." And students—appallingly—agree to accept this status.

Tobacco Road: What about the current generation of Duke students?

Price: Numerous people here have been through profound and maturing experiences of the major dilemmas of adult life. But we're also now dealing with a generation who, economically and emotionally, have been more sheltered and more fortunate than prior Duke generations. The fact has produced an interesting paradox. I'd say that present Duke students have a degree of *surface* sophistication considerably beyond that of my own student contemporaries. But also an internal innocence which is often startling—the number of things that 18- to 22-year-olds still don't seem to know.

Tobacco Road: How would you define that innocence?

Price: Innocence of the dangers and burdens of normal human life. I'm not talking about the possibility of nuclear holocaust or starvation and massacre in Biafra. I'm talking about the normal bafflements and compromises and terrible settlements that adults must make in their daily lives—the things that people of my generation saw their parents having to accept in the awful burnt-out end of the Depression. I saw my father lose the only house he ever built because he was unable to borrow 50 dollars.

Tobacco Road: Given the chance, would you trade places with a college student in the 1980s?

Price: Absolutely not. I think we were much freer, especially in terms of emotional freedom. In our social naivete—in the absence of the presently prescribed sophistications like drink and drugs and more or less universal sexual freedoms—we were far freer to develop at our own private rates and not to be tyrannized by a societal norm in the way students are today. There was a refreshing and scary freedom to develop on one's own particular line, one's own particular graph.

Tobacco Road: Henry Miller remarked in the movie *Reds* that there was just as much sex going on back then as now, but people enjoyed it more.

Price: We enjoyed it more because we didn't talk about it as much, I suspect.

Tobacco Road: So you don't think our alleged sexual liberation is a liberation after all?

Price: There are, though fragile, degrees of tolerance which seem to be a fallout from a higher percentage of sexual experience among undergraduates. There are also a lot of disasters and regrets that come with that experience. The main disaster I would point to again is the degree of compulsion involved, the greater degree of tyranny to which the undergraduate who really does not need an active sexual life during his college years has been subjected—the sense that there's something wrong with him, that he or she is ludicrously out of step. That's not simply a Duke phenomenon but a phenomenon of the entire culture—every television commercial is dedicated to making us feel that if we haven't had sex three times today we're un-American.

Tobacco Road: Did your very serious academic interests preclude you from having fun as an undergraduate?

Price: Are you asking if I was a wimp? No, I loved being in college. It was the first time in my life when the things I was good at were prized by the place I was in. So I worked like a dog. I was also in a hell-raising fraternity and greatly enjoyed that. It was new and strange to me—like being an honorary member of a zoo for three years.

Tobacco Road: Parochialism and privilege—words used to talk about Duke students. Are they dangers?

Price: There is much less a sense in the European universities of college as an irrelevant holding-pattern, much more a sense that it's a real place. And there's still room for plenty of absurdity and fun. But the very absence of an intellectual tradition at most American universities is a terrific self-engendered blight on the energy and the financial investment of young Americans. Though perennial efforts are made to improve the tone at Duke and Harvard and Yale and everywhere else, I see very little advancement in the last 32 years. Every day I park by the gym; I walk to the post office and then to my office. If I hear five student conversations, three to four of them are about how drunk X was last night.

Tobacco Road: If literature alone could get us out of that holding pattern before we end up at Newark, which books would you require every student to read, to put them more in touch with your ideal of life?

Price: If I assumed they'd already done a good deal of reading, I'd probably give them *Anna Karenina, Madame Bovary,* and *Wuthering Heights*—simply because those are my three favorite novels. They're each enormously instructive and endlessly rich portraits of human nature and human destiny.

Tobacco Road: What keeps you as a writer here at Duke University?

Price: I teach one semester a year. I'm here most of the rest of the time. I come in every day to get the mail. I might have lunch on campus. Everyone has to live in some sort of community, so Duke is literally my village. It's the place where I buy my legal pads and pens and where most of my local friends live and operate. Since I don't have children of my own, I'm able to come into contact with young people and thereby come into very direct contact with what a given younger generation is feeling and thinking. Otherwise, I'd lose touch fast. I've had the added advantage of having a sort of 25-year perpetual parenthood of 18-22 year olds. And Duke has been a benevolent employer. Working for a corporation is of enormous interest to a writer. I'm glad that I'm not some solitary Robinson Crusoe who has no boss, who doesn't have to keep any hours. I enjoy departmental meetings and the inner-workings of the corporation itself—to a certain degree. I wouldn't want to drown in it all.

Tobacco Road: Have any of your students or colleagues appeared as characters in your fiction?

Price: I've written one novel in which the hero was a college teacher. I've written another where the hero had taught for two years in a prep school, which is not quite the same thing. No, I can't think of any direct ways in which I've made use of my particular experiences here as a teacher. Though, I think my students have been important contributors to my work—in their vitality, in their constant ironical questioning of the pretty solemn assumptions I make about my own importance and dedication. They've been important challenges to me in that sense, though they haven't often known it. Or cared to.

Tobacco Road: Have you ever allowed your writing classes to criticize first drafts of your fiction or poetry?

Price: Quite often. I think it's useful for me, and I hope it's useful for them. If they're showing me their work, why shouldn't I show them mine? The fact that I'm x number of decades older doesn't mean I don't value their criticism.

Tobacco Road: In your lifetime, movies have superseded the novel as the popular form of entertainment and instruction. Have films influenced your writing?

Price: Films were enormously influential in the formation of my own imagination, my particular sense of the world. I grew up on films. I began going to movies alone when I was eight years old, in the 1940s, in the age of Bette Davis melodramas, Spencer Tracy and Katherine Hepburn comedies, Roy Rogers westerns. I was taken to see *Gone With the Wind* when I was in first grade. Movies were a big part of my curiosity about the visible world. After all, they provide us with yet another form of visible life. They remain the most immediately exciting art we have. There are other forms, such as the novel, which may turn out to be more profoundly exciting than films; but in the short run, it's very hard to beat a good two-hour movie. I watch an enormous number of films; and in the age of the video-recorder, I'm able to study them in a way that I've never been able to before. One can now study a film like a poem, with instant replay and a text. You could never do that at South Square.

Tobacco Road: What is a successful day of writing?

Price: The completion of 300-500 polished words, which will take me the best part of the day. That's about one to one and a half typed pages a day for a novel. I try to write every day except Sunday.

Tobacco Road: Looking back at your own undergraduate years, how important were teachers in your intellectual development?

Price: Teachers were absolutely crucial to me. When I got to Duke, I landed by luck on some of the very best teachers. I never had more than two or three bad teachers in my life; I had one or two sadists—that's always a danger for teachers, that they can become sadists. But I only encountered two, I think.

Tobacco Road: You began writing your first novel—which sold over one million copies—soon after you graduated from Duke. Was that novel, *A Long and Happy Life,* inspired by any experiences you had here as an undergraduate?

Price: On a Sunday afternoon when I was a senior, I went with a Brazilian friend to Howard Johnson's for lunch. I had to write a short story for William Blackburn, and I couldn't think of a subject. I was sitting there, and suddenly this lovely girl walked in with her boyfriend and sat at the ice-cream counter. She was still in her church dress, and she just immediately threw me back into my own adolescence in rural North Carolina. I instantly knew a whole story about her and who she was. And I began writing the story, which I completed that semester. It was called "A Chain of Love," and it was published in my first volume of stories. I called her Rosacoke Mustian, and she became the central figure not only of that story but of my first novel *A Long and Happy Life.*

Tobacco Road: Is it true that you were a tyrant as editor of *The Archive* your senior year?

Price: Well, yes, but a *benevolent* despot, I hope. In those days *The Archive* was run in a much more practical way than now. It was run by a single editor. There were no committees who voted democratically as to what would be in each issue. No trustworthy magazine has ever been run in so cumbersome a way; all the good magazines have been run by a strong-willed editor who made his own choices. And that's the way I ran *The Archive.* People made their submissions, and I decided what would be in. For better or worse, that was it!

Tobacco Road: That same year you made a trip to the Durham train station to pick up a writer who has become your very good friend, Eudora Welty. What do you remember about that evening?

Price: It was in February 1955. Eudora had been invited to give a lecture at the Women's College on East Campus. I had never met her before, but I'd known her works since I was in junior high. I knew she was arriving in town very late at night in the downtown train station, which was immediately behind the courthouse and the jail. I thought, "My God, if you're going to arrive in Durham at three o'clock in the morning, you're in terrible trouble." There'd be no taxis at the station; and she had to get to the old Washington Duke Hotel, which no longer exists. So I just decided that I would go down in the dead of night and meet this great writer and convey her safely through darkest central Durham to the hotel. She seemed pleased and grateful. Our friendship began at that point. We corresponded after that, met whenever we could, and have gone on doing so for the last 28 years. She remembers that I wore a snow-white suit that night; but since it was February, I seriously doubt it. I owned a light gray suit at the time, and I think that's what I must have had on—at least I hope so!

Tobacco Road: Beyond the formation of a long friendship, how important was this meeting to you?

Price: It was crucial. I knew that she was a great writer. The fact that, the next day, she read and praised as professional the only short story I'd yet written—that constituted a final kind of validation for me. If someone that good said *I* was good, then I was right to devote the rest of my life to proving her correct. Such a license is the last best thing a teacher can give a serious student.

Love and Work: The Art of Reynolds Price

Terry Roberts/1983

From *The Arts Journal*, 8 (September 1983), 6–10.
Reprinted by permission of *The Arts Journal* and Reynolds Price.

Reynolds Price's career began in 1962 when the then unknown Southerner published a first novel with the misleadingly simple title of *A Long and Happy Life*. Price's germinal book, it is the story of an adolescent girl named Rosacoke Mustian who is mired in the social rituals of rural North Carolina. She is, of course, in love, a very personal, very painful love, trying to attract and hold the enigmatic boy-man she is sure she belongs with. Their single sexual adventure brings pregnancy and further conflict, but the story is essentially a simple one. Because of its beautiful clarity, it drew the kind of unrestrained rave reviews that are seldom awarded first novels. William Barrett even compared it favorably with Joyce's "The Dead," and words like "poignant," "mature," and "beautifully flowing" gave Atheneum, Price's publisher, something alluring with which to decorate his next cover.

And four years later it appeared, wrapped around *A Generous Man,* which brought a second volley of praise nearly as lush as the first. Its hero is Rosacoke's brother, Milo, a fifteen-year-old sexual dynamo whose energy stuns those fortunate women around him for the few hours before his grace begins to fade. Only a single shadow marred the brilliant surface of Price's reviews to this point. He is a Southerner who occasionally lets slip an elaborate sentence, and in doing so, becomes fair game for Faulkner baiters. Sentences like this description of a supposedly rabid dog in *A Generous Man* attracted too much attention:

> His awe was not curiosity, *justice,* and he knelt on, losing this vital moment, dazed by the eyes to his own natural aim—restoration of

his ruined pride: he tan-haired, torn-eared, welted, called *mad* and
thus doomed and desperate but held, fixed.

It is obvious from this why Price was damned for rewriting Faulkner,
but it was then, and remains, a near-sighted criticism. There are
much clearer antecedents to Price than Faulkner (why not James
Agee for instance), and Price has, by his own admission, spent too
much breath denying old Sound and Fury's influence.

Price's next novel, *Love and Work* (1968), went directly to his
point. Its protagonist, a young college professor and writer named
Thomas Eborn, is stuck in a self-consciously painful, modern marriage and is having trouble with his writing. In an uninspired essay
written for the college paper, Eborn maintains that the two joys of life
are the love of others and enjoyable work, and, of the two, only work
lasts. He is unable to move on his own writing, however, until he
begins to make sense of his dead parents' love, of his own origin in
love. This brief novel (143 pages) ends in a stunning appearance by
the ghosts of Eborn's parents. We are left to wonder about the
writer's own life and marriage after this visitation. Has Eborn learned
enough to salvage his own marriage, nurture it into lasting?

Love and Work is markedly different in setting than the previous
books. Its characters are well-educated and relatively cosmopolitan,
perhaps one whole generation removed from the lonely dirt roads
and tobacco barns of the Mustians. And with it the reviewers began
to sense a difference they had trouble articulating. R. F. Clayton (in
Library Journal, 1968) wrote that *Love and Work* was "flawed by the
lack of the lyrical style and exquisite mosaic structure which were
basic components of Mr. Price's two previous novels."

The style of *Love and Work* is simpler, more direct and well suited
to its task. What is more significant than its style, however, is that
the novel is quite different in tone. One feels with Price that Eborn is
much less loving and lovable than either Rosacoke or Milo Mustian.
And his dilemma is not one of choosing between attractive options
but rather the much more modern one of being trapped by a slowly
closing net of frustration and unnamed fear. Rosa must choose how
to love; Milo, whom to love. Eborn, in comparing his own marriage
to that of his parents, discovers that he is nearly incapable of love.
Love and Work is a more frightening book than its predecessors

because it portrays the bleakness of a loveless life that they had only hinted at and anticipated.

In *The Surface of Earth* (1975), Price expanded on the vision sketched in *Love and Work*. Victorian in length, it is as broad a book as its title suggests, tracing the lives of three generations of the Mayfield-Hutchins clan with all their employees, cousins, friends, and hangers-on. Price has said that it took twelve years of planning as well as three years of composition to produce. Reviewers complained that it lacked focus and structure, or more simply, that it was just too long.

Price needed the vast *Surface of Earth* to provide a catalogue of situations involving all types of human love. Its structure is like that of a nineteenth century novel, say *Middlemarch,* though it is not at all old-fashioned in its concerns or viewpoints. Its scenes focus not on a single character or even a concentrated set of characters but rather on a single theme. That theme is human love, its presence and absence: filial love, fraternal love, conjugal love, parental love, brotherly love, hetero- and homo-sexual passion. And all of this struggling *eros* is caught in the web of family relations. It is not quite so gothic as this might suggest because its characters balance what is painful in their lives with healthy doses of self-deprecating humor. But still the primary ingredients of *Surface of Earth* are love and family, and Price attempts to show how our ability to love is almost genetically shaped by our forebears.

With *The Source of Light* (1982), Price provided a more modern structure for his now characteristic concerns. He traces ten months from the life of Hutchins Mayfield, a character who both in name and body provides the culmination of the two families portrayed in *The Surface of Earth*. There is more bisexuality in *The Source of Light* and fewer family knots, but all in all, there is the same pattern of seriously frustrated need coupled with tragically frustrated giving.

As in the earlier *Love and Work,* there is one central failure of love which marks and disturbs the entire book. The dying Rob Mayfield and his son, Hutch, do succeed in reaching a loving understanding before Rob's death. But far more important for his future is Hutch's failure to answer fully the near selfless love of his fiancée, Ann Gatlin.

Ann and Hutch meet in Rome during the Christmas break of Hutch's Oxford school year. There, almost mystically stripped of their armor of contraceptives, they conceive a child. Physically, they connect briefly, but in every other way they misfire, partially due to the death of Rob which pulls Hutch away from Ann and back to America. Ann aborts the child because she senses, quite rightly, that there is no lasting, shared desire between them, not for complete union, complete intimacy, complete commitment.

It is a far more dramatic failure than that of the Eborns in *Love and Work* (the abortion scenes are chillingly real), and for that, Price must be commended. What gives *The Source of Light* its tragic weight is that Ann Gatlin is a sweet, intelligent woman who, in effect, takes over the last chapters of the book from the more apathetic-seeming Hutch. She, unlike Hutch, knows exactly what she wants and is willing to pay dearly to get it. But she pays and pays with no reward. As Hutch is much like the earlier Milo Mustian, so is Ann Gatlin like his sister, Rosa, in her sacrificial waiting and her solitary pain.

Perhaps the key to Price's novels can be found in this statement he made in 1966 (*Red Clay Reader 3*), just after the publication of *A Generous Man*:

> I think there is a good deal of *harshness* in my work toward various kinds of people, relationships, events. This is something which very few people comment on. . . . Those things in human experience which are most appalling to me are dealt with, it seems to me, truthfully and therefore harshly in the books.

This is important and has been generally forgotten in the sixteen years since, inundated in the flood of words both by and about Price. Nevertheless, it is still true and, I believe, holds the key to the eventual success or failure of Price's work. Human love is more often than not tragic, ending not with a bang but a whimper.

And yet, human love of all kinds is occasionally triumphant, overcoming odds that would dilute and destroy any other human force. Rosacoke's patient abstinence and Milo's hungry excess were triumphs of this sort, even measured as they were against a dark background. Those characters had a willing innocence about them that caused the reader to desire their success and dread their failure. Of the later characters, Ann Gatlin is like this. Her pain stuns like electricity, burning in the emotions of a reader. But the selflessness of these few has largely been missing from Price's characters; recently he has focused on the more worldly but perhaps less worthy. Price is an unquestionably talented writer, and I hope that the spirituality which is a force in his work will eventually shed a more *comic* light in his world. I hope this because characters like Ann Gatlin and Hutch-ins Mayfield are too real and too deserving to fail consistently when success is possible . . . and when the emotional price is so great.

Reynolds Price offered the following views on the sexuality and spirituality of his work at Duke University in Durham, North Carolina, on April 15, 1983.

TR: Is it fair to say that writing is an act of love for you?

RP: I think it's a fair statement, but it's a partial statement, and I think it's grown increasingly partial the longer I have written. I was a very personal kind of writer in the earlier parts of my career. I felt strongly that the individual works were specific communications to specific other people in my life, and that feeling still survives as a powerful source of pleasure and reward. But it now seems to me that one of the luckiest things that can happen to a writer—and one of the things that doesn't happen to a great many wonderful writers—is the gradual acquisition of the sense that one is doing it just for the sake of doing it, that it's become a kind of lonely long-distance running which nonetheless has its own huge rewards. I'd hate to think, though, that writing for me would ever reach the point where it would become an entirely hermetic and solitary activity. I'm still very conscious of a general audience in that I desire to be as lucid and comprehensible as the material permits me to be.

TR: Have you ever felt about your writing that it is a way of answering a need in terms of your relationships with others that you couldn't answer in other ways? Does it help you say things you could not say otherwise, and could that be partially why you began to write?

RP: I'm not sure that it was. I come from two enormously articu-late families, so I don't think that writing for me has ever had an important role as saying the unsayable, but it just has been the chief way in which I've chosen to preserve and record certain extremely important things which might have already been said in private but which I wished to make permanent in some way.

TR: In a 1978 interview with Constance Rooke, you said that your books were about human freedom at one point, and at another point, you said they were about "Eros and Aphrodite, the rewards and terrors of love." Are these two ideas related in your mind? Are we somehow at the mercy of the rewards and terrors of love?

RP: It's a theme I'm intensely interested in—the continuing sense that my work is largely a dialogue with the idea of freedom and liberty. The whole concept of various kinds of love—eros, *agape,* friendship, family relations—obviously relates to and impinges on our own abilities to be free and to shape the limitations of our freedom. But I suppose that love in the sense of eros, the sense of being "in love," has been the main lens through which I've looked at human freedom. Perhaps that kind of love has been most important to me and has *remained* more important to me than it has to a great many of my contemporaries. As I look at my friends who are now roughly my age, which is 50, I begin to sense that eros has not been important for many of them since they were in their mid- to late-20s. It's remained perilously important to me!

TR: Is Hutchins Mayfield's vacillation over his relationship with Ann Gatlin in *The Source of Light* an example of these forces working themselves out in two characters' lives? Does he feel that he is resisting the force of eros in his own life by separating himself from Ann?

RP: I don't think he's resisting it. I think he's responding to an extremely powerful dose of eros which he's got. If anyone has gone back and read the prior history of his family, which is related in *The Surface of Earth*, one sees that Hutchins almost *genetically* acquired a powerful sexuality. So his relations with Ann and various male friends are symptoms of both a tremendous hunger *for* love and a tremendous need *to* love, not only to fill a hunger but also to vent a kind of fullness that he has.

TR: Like Milo in *A Generous Man*?

RP: He's a rather intellectualized version of Milo, yes.

TR: He has an erotic *genetic* inheritance?

RP: I wouldn't claim it was literally locatable on a particular gene, but I would say that it runs in his family quite clearly—that the Mayfields and the Kendals, especially the Mayfields, are erotically intense people.

TR: In a recent review of a novel you praised the author for writing about "the possibility for adult love." The things we've been saying seem to point in this direction. Is adult love possible over time in our world, in the twentieth century?

RP: I know it's possible.

TR: Is it probable?

RP: No, it's not probable, because it's too difficult, but it's *possible*, and I could look through the files of my friendships and my own relationships and think of perhaps several dozen examples of people who seem to me to have maintained steady and valid brands of love over long periods of time. I would include all kinds of love—parental, erotic, fraternal, and many others.

TR: What makes it difficult, or is that too broad a question?

RP: The chief thing that makes adult love difficult is the human animal's desire for freedom, some innate rebelliousness in the creature itself, probably springing from a claustrophobic relation to our mothers which is inescapable so long as we are mostly born from within our mother's bodies, an experience that gave us this terrific and sometimes satanic need to be *ourselves alone.*

TR: Part of the sadness of *A Generous Man* is the loss of intimacy between Milo and Rosa, brother and sister. You don't seem to suggest there that either of them will ever have quite that intimacy again, such a twinning again. Could we read that as a statement that only children are capable of the kind of devotion and trust that this sort of intimacy requires? That we somehow lose that ability as we grow older?

RP: Puberty itself becomes a major problem for the members of a family who've grown up with intimate relations between them: brothers and sisters, brothers and brothers, sometimes even parents and children. The incest taboos simply do become a matter of great importance once both parties are aware of themselves as functioning reproductive organisms. Rosa and Milo never consciously define it that way to themselves, but it becomes one of the unconscious barriers between them. Also the fact that Milo simply reaches puberty sooner than Rosa, and therefore seeks his own sexual expression in relationships with girls his age, becomes a further rapid means of distancing this innocent sister from him.

TR: Do you mean that becoming sexual creatures necessarily complicates our relations?

RP: I'm not sure that we aren't sexual creatures from the time we're born. Our erotic lives are obviously intense long before we are functional reproductive animals. But when we become fully conscious of ourselves as the carriers of the race, as genetic vessels of homo sapiens as a race, then the problems do become actively different.

TR: No one in *The Source of Light* bears children successfully although many of the characters desire them dearly . . .

RP: There's no conscious statement being made by that, though I certainly wouldn't want to guarantee that there's no unconscious one. And I wouldn't guarantee that Hutch didn't grow up to have a child. But he's only 26 and that wasn't an unusual age for a man to have not had children in the 1950s. I certainly don't think of Hutch or Ann or anyone else in the novel as being beyond the point of procreation, though I think they are dealing with dilemmas in their own struggles with the idea of freedom which basically, for them at that point, preclude children. Ann of course goes through with an abortion—a pretty titanic decision for a woman of her background to make in the mid-1950s—and she makes the decision on her own and goes through with it in a way that is agonizing but which also reveals the strength of her own drive toward freedom.

TR: How will that lost child haunt them? Isn't it something quite tragic between them?

RP: I think it is. I think they're both serious, moral human beings who will always find that a disaster lies in the past as well as in the continuing present of their lives. I'm not being cagey in saying that I literally haven't speculated about their lives beyond the point at which the novel ends. I might someday write another novel about Hutch. Whether Ann would figure in his life then, I quite literally don't know.

TR: Then Hutch is the more interesting of the two characters for you?

RP: Finally, yes, because I've been involved with his family—more than fifty years of his family—for nearly ten years of my own life. So he's the bearer of the particular genetic message that I've been dealing with in his two families.

TR: The sexual encounters in *The Source of Light* are almost invariably successful. Yet none of these encounters lead to any permanent peace or permanent binding between the characters involved.

RP: I think that's an accurate analysis. I think their sexual relations are generally successful in providing pleasurable interludes of reward and tranquility and in generating new kinds of energy in their lives. The relationships in *The Source of Light* are temporal largely because Hutch at this time in his life is a vagabond. He's an American who's living in England, traveling in Europe, forced to make a trip back home unexpectedly because of his father's death. So there's this particular kind of vagabond light thrown over sexuality in the book by the nature of Hutch's itinerary. If you look at the sexual activity in *The Surface of Earth,* you'll find that there's enough bad sex to satisfy any puritan! But Hutch is just at a stage in his life in which he's not set up to have tedious, mechanical sex. I don't mean to say that Hutch will be an erotic vagabond all his life, though that might not be bad if one were set up to make a good and responsible thing of it.

TR: Considering Hutch's background in the more fundamentalist and more conservative South, is it realistic for him to feel no guilt, particularly over the homosexual encounters and the abortion? Granted, he has this genetically sexual inheritance, but still wouldn't guilt be a factor in . . .

RP: I believe it is a factor in his life but not an obsessive one; and I think that is realistic, yes—of him and of me, as his author. He comes from a sexually robust family as I do. Both my proud old families were sexually robust without being sleazy about it. Sex caused them plenty of problems, but they didn't sit around picking at festering guilts. Certain members of the family were more interested in and open about sexuality than others. But sex seemed largely a matter— insofar as family *talk* was concerned—of fun, of delight rather than of repression and guilt. Also in Hutch's case, it can be said that he's quite naturally less guilty having come from a similar family. Certainly the Mayfields were highly sexed people and proud of it. The South's full of such people, thank God. One of the things that we don't really remember about the Victorians is that they were quite aware of their sexuality and talked about it *at length*, as I know from my own childhood memories of Victorians. I recall certain people who were born in the 1860s and who talked freely about sexuality in family situations. The difference was that they would never have written the talk down and we will. Therefore, it will be remembered that we were obsessed with sex!

TR: In your recorded conversations with William Ray, Ray brought up the ideas of *need* and *giving* and how they are, at best, complementary forces. Is it part of your experience and perhaps part of your message that one of the most difficult and frustrating experiences we have is in somehow coordinating these forces in our relations with others, the need to give of ourselves with the need to be succored by others?

RP: I've certainly experienced the frustration in my own life. It's also a dilemma that most of my characters confront. I'd have to race back quickly through the large file of characters to see if there are any real exceptions, but none come immediately to mind. No, I think it's one of the great dilemmas of robust people—in all senses of the word—that they quickly discover once they pass into adulthood. They discover that most human beings are not emotionally robust and find it difficult to engage in another human being's life on an intense continuous basis. Most human beings are not set up for that.

TR: Do we, like Milo who lost his generosity, lose that energy, that intensity?

RP: Most do, as quickly as they can. They're eager to because such generous vulnerability is dangerous and painful. It gets them in trouble constantly. They give up that energy as soon as society honorably permits them—as soon as they're married and have a child or two and can admit to being bored with their lives. Then things are vastly simpler.

TR: Then those couples who schedule love once a week are happier with their "normal" lives?

RP: Sure, but I don't mean it just in the sexual sense. That's one of the evil illusions—that the impulse can only take sexual form. But one sees old couples together and suspects that there's little sexual energy left, yet there's a wonderful creaturely care and courtesy which is a beautiful achievement in itself. So I'm not pounding the drum for geriatric sex necessarily—though God bless them if they have the energy and inclination. But I do think that most people are not set up for intensity of any kind for very long, and I'm not blaming them for that. That *is* the difficulty, though, that the more intense human beings encounter when they confront other people. Because of the perverse laws of human nature, they tend to be attracted to their own opposites—an intense person tends to be attracted to a more serene person—and trouble begins.

TR: You spoke of Hutch and Ann Gatlin as very moral, conscientious characters. Could you say a little bit about the moral code of their universe? Does the power of *eros* as portrayed in your books exist within a moral framework?

RP: Yes, their ethic is basically *Christian* as opposed to *Pauline*. Hutch and Rob are specific about this in an exchange of letters. They rely for their ethic on the actual red-letter teachings of Jesus far more than on the more puritanical and tormented teachings of Paul, who as a matter of fact never knew Jesus.

TR: Are you a red-letter Christian in the same sense?

RP: I think of myself in that way. I don't think of Paul as a great enemy or evil force. I think of him as a genius, but I also think it's one of the misfortunes of institutionalized Christianity that Paul is the author of about a fourth of the New Testament. I wish we had more, say, than the one probably authentic letter of Saint Peter. Peter seems to have been a much more healthy, broadly-based human being than Paul.

TR: In the introductory statement accompanying your selected poems, you mentioned "realities which lie invisibly but overwhelmingly behind the visible and tangible." Could you speak to that? Is there a way for you to talk constructively about those "realities."

RP: I believe in God—which is to say that I believe the world was created by a non-human intelligence which continues to monitor that creation with great interest and love. I believe that a particular man called Jesus of Nazareth is the nearest access that our culture has to knowledge of that mystery, that creator. I'm technically a member of the Methodist Church but haven't attended with any regularity for thirty years, a matter of which I'm not proud but about which I don't feel guilty because my religious concerns are still seriously dealt with in my daily life—though by no means perfectly or even adequately dealt with. That's about as much as I would know how to say without becoming more proselytizing than I would ever be comfortable being. I have a tremendous resistance to overt missionaries.

TR: Are the dreams and ghosts that play such a dramatic role in your fiction an effort to capture or suggest the existence and power of those realities without becoming proselytizing?

RP: Yes. They're also candid confessions on my part that I really suspect there are such things as ghosts.

TR: Having never seen one?

RP: Having never seen one myself, though my mother saw one which is recorded at the end of *Love and Work*—a literal record of something my mother told a friend the day she died.

TR: Do you believe in the prophetic or communicative power of dreams? I know that you've said that we shouldn't spend too much time crouched behind your character's beds with notebooks in hand. But are dreams metaphysical events?

RP: Some are and some aren't. The dreams, especially in *The Surface of Earth*, are arranged with a kind of order and meaning which was secret to me when I was doing them. Someone wrote a master's thesis on the dreams in *The Surface of Earth* and discovered things about them which I hadn't at all been conscious of but which I'd obviously *unconsciously* intended and planned. Dreams are primarily interesting to me, in my life and work, as the acts I perform during that third of my life in which I'm asleep. A hell of a lot of one's life is spent in a state which is not really unconsciousness but another kind of consciousness. In my daily activities, I go around speaking to people, touching people, being alone, watching television, eating meals. I write about those things. Why should fiction not be able to comprise also those acts which I commit when I am *in the dark*? Those acts are dreams, and I've tried in the novels to indicate what the continuing lives of characters are like during that very crucial third of their lives. Also, I'm enough of an old-fashioned "Egyptian Book of Dreams" fan to suspect that dreams are constant attempts on our part to communicate with ourselves, with other people, and with God. I understand dreams primarily as *actions,* interesting things we do.

TR: In your essay on the origins of narrative, you wrote that "we are satisfied only by the one short tale we feel to be true: History is the will of a just God who knows us." Have you ever tried consciously in your novels or in your poetry to suggest just that?

RP: I hope all my work suggests that—but implicitly and almost invisibly. Not so invisibly you can't see it but so nearly invisibly that the reader is neither manipulated nor proselytized. There are some lovely secret things going on, especially in *The Surface of Earth* and *The Source of Light*, which to the best of my knowledge no reader has ever perceived but which are secret messages that "history is the will of a just God who knows us."

TR: Can you give us an example?

RP: I'll give you just one to put you on the trail of others. The woman who performs the abortion on Ann tells us in two hints— without knowing it herself—that she is, in fact, the direct descendant of the old black man who nearly murdered Hutch's grandfather Forrest fifty years before in an old abandoned hotel in Virginia. You only guess it by her name and where she comes from.

TR: Thesis writers take note!

RP: Yes.

TR: Would you call the poems included in "Nine Mysteries," a section of *Vital Provisions* (selected poems) religious poems?

RP: They're religious poems in a traditional sense of the word— but very strange religious poems, hardly "devotional."

TR: In what way are they strange?

RP: They look at erotic aspects of the lives of New Testament characters, which Christianity has never really permitted itself officially to think about. With the triumph of Pauline Christianity, we were not allowed to imagine the sex life of Joseph, for instance—as we *are* allowed to imagine the sex lives of Moses or Abraham in the Old Testament.

TR: Do you think part of the modern dilemma is a kind of hyperactive ignorance of things spiritual? Do we tend to be perhaps willfully ignorant of "those realities which lie behind . . ."

RP: "We" doesn't include me. I don't think I'm ignorant of them, though I don't behave the way those realities might wish I'd behave most of the time. Certainly if I were to limit myself to speaking about my students, the students I now teach at Duke are more intelligent and better prepared than those of the past; but they do appear on the whole upper-middle-class Americans for whom traditional religion has little value.

TR: If in fact that's representative, is it a dangerous loss?

RP: I obviously think it's a dangerous loss, though most of the available alternatives are things that frighten me as much as they

frighten the students—things like the Moral Majority, the new funda-
mentalism.

TR: You once wrote about Ernest Hemingway that whatever other
faults or virtues his writing might have had, it did get him through
his life, a long and many times unhappy life. Has writing done that
for you? Has it been—not a crutch—but a vehicle that has carried
you through otherwise barren and unhappy times?

RP: It's been a vehicle, though definitely not a crutch—it's important not to think of it that way. I think of myself, at least so far in my
life, as a psychically and physically robust person—as my ancestors
were. But the writing has been one of the two major vehicles that has
gotten me through my life. And of the two—love and work—I'd
certainly say that it has been the more reliable of the two, provided I
take good care of the vehicle, the talent itself and its maintenance.

Reynolds Price on Writing

Ashby Bland Crowder/1986

From *The Southern Review*, 22 (April 1986), 329–41 and *Writing in the Southern Tradition: Interviews with Five Contemporary Authors* by Ashby Bland Crowder (Atlanta: Rodopi USA/ Canada, 1989). Reprinted by permission of *The Southern Review*, Ashby Bland Crowder, and Reynolds Price.

During the fall term of 1982 Reynolds Price visited Hendrix College, Conway, Arkansas, for a week. His primary reason for being on this campus was to participate in a course in modern southern literature, which also included visits by Cleanth Brooks, William Humphrey, Andrew Lytle, Harry Crews, David Madden, and Robert Drake. In this class Reynolds Price discussed his own fiction as well as the state of southern writing in general.

Mr. Price also participated in a writing class where he answered questions about how he works as a writer on a daily basis; about the sources for his writing; and about the attitudes, circumstances, and writers that have influenced him as a novelist, short story writer, playwright, essayist, and poet. In addition, he was prompted to give his opinion about the future of writing in the United States and to give some advice for aspiring writers.

Before the interview, Mr. Price made the following introductory remarks.

RP: I thought I would talk very briefly about a matter that's little talked about, especially by and to young writers, which is the terrific, I would say overriding, importance of *routine* in the work of writing, especially of writing extended narrative prose. I had many good teachers when I was in high school and college and certainly grade school. I had one quite famous teacher of writing in my last year of undergraduate school at Duke University. He himself did not write, so he was unable to make any specific suggestions about the process of writing, and it took me years to learn for myself the fact that I think could have been conveyed to me economically and simply by someone who understood the importance of routine in work.

I would say that the most important thing you can arrange to do if you wish to be a writer is to be born gifted. That would be number one, literally indispensable. But number two would be—once you're

185

an adult, once you're more or less in command of your own time, time not dictated by parents or college courses—that you work out what your particular creative metabolism is in relation to the amount of available time. My own life for the last twenty years has basically offered me eight months each year in which I'm free to write and four months in which I teach.

My own metabolism has been quite constant since I was, say, twenty-two years old. It has dictated that I work best if I work Monday through Saturday, in the morning after a good breakfast, and until such time in that day as I have completed a predetermined quota of words. I don't recommend that particular routine to anyone but myself, though I know quite a lot of good prose writers who work at some version of that routine. My own quota is a minimum of three hundred prose words a day, which is a typed page (though I don't compose on the typewriter; I compose by hand). I often do more but I don't let myself do much more—even if my hand tries to race away with me—because I know that if I write twelve hundred words today, I probably won't be able to do anything for the next two or three days. I will have used up the work for the next two or three days.

Why is that? I think it's simply one more proof of perhaps my firmest belief about writing of all sorts, which is that artistic creation is done in the unconscious mind. It is to a very large extent an unconscious faculty. And one has to arrange one's life so that the unconscious mind will cooperate with one. I don't mean to sound occult; it's no more occult than the fact that the brain is a physical organ and has to be given the right conditions of courtesy and nourishment under which it can do its work. A friend of mine who is a well-known novelist says that the unconscious is like children and dogs; it loves routine and hates surprises. I think that's terribly true. If I surprise my unconscious mind by suddenly having a friend arrive who will take up two or three days of my life while I'm in the midst of an important chapter in a novel, then I won't be able to work for a number of days after the friend has left.

Question: When and to what extent do you rewrite?

RP: I rewrite while I'm doing that day's stint. I try to get that day's page the way it ought to be. Then at the end of a week, I'll type up those handwritten pages while I can still read my own writing. Then when the whole book is finished—which can often be as much as two years later—I will type the whole thing up one more time. So it gets written by hand once, with a lot of revision in the process of that day's work. It gets a certain amount of revision when I'm typing it the first time. It gets another certain amount of revision when I'm typing it the second time. Then it might get very minor revisions while I'm reading the galley proofs. But I would say that ninety-five percent of all the revision is done the day I write the first draft.

I would say a majority of writers don't work that way. The majority of writers work in drafts. They write a whole first draft, then a whole second draft, then a whole third. It's just my temperament—the wish not to involve myself in the amount of waste that's involved if one works in a draft situation. Maybe it's because I grew up in the Second World War and was always told to eat up the food and wear out my clothes. I hate waste. I know friends who can perfectly cheerfully throw away the fifty pages they wrote in the last two weeks. I've never thrown away two pages I ever wrote—I don't think. You may say it sounds like it or it looks like it, but I really don't think I have. I work at a deliberate enough pace that I get it the way I want it; whether you like it or not is another, and to me irrelevant, question.

Question: How do you maintain a steady enough level of inspiration to write your daily amount?

RP: You try to be as careful as possible about where you cut off at the end of Monday because sometimes you can write yourself through all that you know. You can come to the point at which you have absolutely used up all your knowledge; and you have to start cold the next morning if your subconscious doesn't invent something else during the night, which in fact it usually does. Every now and then you wake up the next morning and your engine is just totally cold. It's like a Michigan February morning, and you've got to get the thing cranked—and that's hard. So I always try to stop—in fact I discovered this for myself before I read an interview in which Hemingway said one of the most important things is to stop at a point at which you know what happens next. I will often, myself, write out the last line for that day; and then in the margin I will sort of cheat and say, "He said, 'Shut up.' " That will give me the first line for the next morning's work, to prime the pump. But as I said, you can't always arrange it. Sometimes you get into the end of your knowledge, your inspiration.

Question: Do you encounter any special problems when writing short stories instead of novels?

RP: One of the most difficult things about writing short stories as opposed to writing novels is that stories are short. It's possible to write a good short story in an afternoon or a day or two, depending on the length of the story. Great classics of the form have been written in very short periods of time—so that the engine warms up, runs, and stops and goes cold very fast—whereas one of the joys for me of writing a novel is that you can start the engine; and with careful maintenance, you can keep it going. In my case, the longest I've ever kept a novel going is three years. But it was a great joy to wake up, six mornings a week, and to hear the engine still running; it had been working all night.

Graham Greene talks about this in the preface to his collected short stories. He said if he's ever having a problem with a piece of writing, he always reads through the problematic part just before he goes to sleep that night, and he says the next morning he always finds—he uses the French noun—he always finds that the *nègre* in the cellar has solved the problem. I thought, with my college French, that he meant the Negro, the slave, the black in the cellar. But I looked it up to check and, interestingly enough, *nègre* in French does mean black; but it also means ghostwriter. The ghostwriter in the cellar is the unconscious mind.

I don't for a moment mean to imply that I do some sort of automatic writing like Mrs. W. B. Yeats. I don't take dictation from the spirits, although sometimes that's fun to do—just don't ever try to publish it. No, there's an enormous amount of conscious discipline and shaping involved in writing fiction; but the impulse is unconscious.

I think of all those wonderful patterns that critics and scholars find in one's work after the work has been published. The scholars always think you're pulling their leg when you say, "I really didn't know they were there." But you're almost always telling the truth. Your unconscious mind knew they were there but not your conscious mind. Someone recently did a thesis on the dreams in a novel of mine called *The Surface of Earth*. There are important dreams in there, and he carefully laid out all the dreams. I've forgotten how many there are; but let's say there are seven dreams about this theme, and another seven dreams about that; and in the middle is a pivotal dream which is about both themes. He definitely demonstrates in the thesis that this is the way the novel is built. I had absolutely no conscious intention of structuring the novel on these dreams, but I'm sure that some sort of unconscious architectural faculty in my brain was choosing to do that.

Question: Do you ever find that you can't restrain yourself, so that you just keep on writing beyond your ordinary limit?

RP: I do sometimes. Very often, the last two or three days of a book, I'm galloping because I know I'm finishing it. But galloping for me is three pages a day. That's just flat-out-down-the-track, a sizzling pace.

Question: When you finish a work, where do you get your idea for the next one?

RP: Well, that's when you just ask Baby Jesus to help you. I'm serious. There's always a kind of postpartum depression after finishing a big work. If, indeed, my theory is true that the subconscious mind is doing this, then it follows that your most uncontrollable faculties are harnessed to a powerful load; and when you suddenly stop, it's hard to keep the horse from dying right there in the traces, just totally collapsing on you. It's well known that women tend to have bouts of depression after the birth of a baby. Every serious creative artist I've ever known tends to have a big down at the end of an extended piece of work—so much so that a number of wonderful writers like Virginia Woolf and Scott Fitzgerald and Ernest Hemingway have had periods of serious insanity or extreme disturbance at the end of long periods of work. There are probably biochemical explanations for this—there seem to be biochemical explanations for an awful lot of things these days—but it's something you have to watch. I always try to have some alternative activity planned, something to do as soon as I finish, and turn to another form completely. If I finish a novel, then I arrange to take a month off or a couple of weeks off and then write a play or start working on poems or translations, to start using some other muscles, related but different. And then you just hope that the same unconscious beast that you've got down in there will eventually offer you something new that it's been working on—processing.

I mean, I have some extremely vague ideas for a novel right now. I'm not forcing them at all. I'm not making any notes about them. I wouldn't tell you about them. I just feel my mind sending me up these occasional little flashes of light. There may not be anything down there. But if the past is any indication, my mind is making up a story; and when it's ready for me to have it, I'll know. Again, that sounds a little kooky, doesn't it? But it's accurate.

Question: Is it harder or easier to write a play than a novel?

RP: It's easier in the simple sense that a play takes a lot fewer pages than a novel. *The Surface of Earth* was a manuscript of 800 pages; *Early Dark* is probably 120 pages. It's plainly a lot easier to write 120 pages than 800. So yes, plays require less overall effort, though the moment to moment intensity while you're actually doing it is as great—these things don't admit of quantification very well. Also there are just a lot more things you have to do in a novel than in a play. Nothing can happen in a play that can't be totally visualized and articulated or at least portrayed in human gesture. All sorts of other things have to happen in novels—physical descriptions, interior monologues, thoughts, dreams, feelings. The drama is a simple form. That doesn't mean it's less good; it's just simpler. *King Lear* is a simpler work than *War and Peace*. That doesn't mean it's less good.

Question: As a young aspiring writer, how did you support yourself?

RP: I had a scholarship when I finished undergraduate college to go to graduate school. I had a handsome scholarship that paid all my tuition and living expenses in Europe. Europe at that time was a great deal cheaper to live in than America; so for three years there, from age twenty-two to twenty-five, I was really the guest of a munificent foundation. I didn't much like that, as a matter of fact. I was enough of a Depression child not to like being a kept man. And by the time I was twenty-five I was getting very nervous at taking somebody else's money. So I got a job teaching back at my old alma mater, and I came straight back from graduate school to do that. I had to because my father had recently died, and I had to support my mother and my younger brother. I came back and taught at Duke University for three years beginning at forty-eight hundred dollars a year, which was something you were glad to get in 1958, probably the equivalent of sixty-five hundred now or maybe a little more. Still I remember those months when I would wind up with fourteen cents on payday.

And all that while I was writing my first short stories and my first novel. But I *was* teaching, and teaching has one enormous advantage. As an old friend of mine, who taught in the county schools, likes to say, "Name three good reasons for teaching—June, July, and August." You get these fantastic vacations. It's actually shameful what college teachers get away with, when you think about it. Nobody else in the whole work force gets these great vacations. For that reason alone, if for no other, teaching has been a very hospitable occupation for writers—though I must say that the teaching nine months of the year are about as demanding as coal mining. Teaching, when you're doing it flat out, is a terrifically draining enterprise, an awkward combination of psychotherapy and acting, two of the more demanding trades—at least in emotional terms.

That's the way I lived as a young writer. And then my first novel was published in 1962, made a certain amount of money; and I was able to go to the university and say, "May I go on part-time salary because I have a little money of my own now?" And they said, "Yes." So for twenty years I've been teaching four months a year and writing the rest, which is a marvelous arrangement. I've been very lucky and very blessed. Other people haven't had such good luck, and it's been harder for them. Writing is a very difficult business. People who go gaily trooping off to MFA programs, I think, seldom have an idea what a torturous road they are laying out for themselves. If nothing else, it's a solitary job; and almost nobody wants to work alone, though it's the only way to write.

Question: Then you would never find it possible to collaborate with anyone in a writing project?

RP: I collaborated with someone on a screenplay, which was never produced. I don't think it's because it was bad; most screenplays are never produced simply because most people don't have three or four million dollars to make a movie. I enjoyed it. It was a screenplay of a novel that I'd written. I worked with someone who had a lot of prior experience. I wouldn't object to doing that again; but I think writing, like most forms of creation, is an individual activity—you want to do it all yourself. I can't bear to have anybody tell me how to do something in my writing. I won't hear it! If you say I've got the color of somebody's hair wrong on page thirteen, I'm liable to leave it wrong just because it's mine—satanic willful error. No, actually, I will change things like that. Madame Bovary's eyes change color in the middle of *Madame Bovary*—supposed to be the most careful novel ever written, and it really is—but her eyes are two different colors in the book. No one ever caught it, to tell Flaubert. I will willingly change things like that. But if someone says, I don't really like what she says on page thirteen, then I just go and make it even worse for them. I'm terrifically willful about creation, obviously.

Question: Any general advice for would-be writers?

RP: What things are you good at? What things are you bad at? I think you should examine your own skills. If you're not a very attentive person, you ought to make yourself do a lot of sensory exercises. A walk from your dorm to the library—what do you see? what do you hear? what do you do? Write a little five-hundred-word sketch of that. People really don't ever see anything, and that's a great secret about life—that most people literally never see anything. The most graphic demonstration of that I ever had was that once I was on a committee with Clint Eastwood, and we had to go to a big meeting in Washington together. We had to walk from the hotel about five blocks to where we had a luncheon and then five blocks back. On the walk back it was a beautiful sunny spring day in Washington; it was the end of lunch hour, and the streets were filled with people going back to their offices. I was walking along beside Clint Eastwood, and we walked for five blocks—and Clint Eastwood looks exactly like Clint Eastwood (he looks even better in the flesh than on screen, and he's commercially the most successful actor in the world)—and not one single person in those five blocks in our nation's capital recognized him. They just didn't *see* him.

I think I see a lot more than most people because I'm trained to; I've trained myself—which I think is one reason writers often make people nervous; they have a feeling you're casing the joint. That has an obverse, which is that people are enormously trusting of writers. People will almost immediately, if they find out that you're a writer, tell you their darkest secrets within ten minutes, especially if you've given them a drink. They have a sense that writers are father-confessors. It's fun sometimes, and other times, it's very boring.

Question: Do you use people that you know as sources in your novels?

RP: Well, you know, an arm here, a leg there. Literally. I mean you can't use more; otherwise, you get sued. I made the mistake of using the name of a real person in my first novel, someone who lived in my hometown. I had subliminally picked his name out of the newspaper without knowing him—he was a local real-estate dealer; I'd never laid eyes on him. His name was Wesley Beavers, and I had this whole character called Wesley Beavers. I finished the novel, and a friend of mine in town read the typescript and said, "I hope you got Mr. Wesley Beavers' permission." I said, "What?" It's a very long story; but my publisher (the book had already been set in type) said, "Oh, my God, you'll be sued. You'll have to change the name." I said, "I can't change the name; that's his name. It's been his name since 1955 when I invented him in a short story." "Sorry, you've got to change the name, *or* you've got to prove there're other people with that name."

I looked in every telephone book in America, which you can do in a big library. No other Wesley Beavers in America. So then the only alternative was to get Mr. Beavers to sign a release, saying that he would sell me the use of his name for one dollar for all perpetuity. I was young enough and brave enough to go downtown to this sixty-five-year-old real-estate agent's office and ask him to sign a paper saying I could use his name in a novel. He ultimately agreed; but it's a very tricky business because most states have invasion of privacy laws. And if I use your name and you can even remotely prove that I had actually used *your* name as opposed to coincidentally inventing your name, then you would have a serious case against me.

Question: Why do you write?

RP: Because it's what I know how to do.

Question: Do you like it?

RP: Yeah. It's hard, but I love it. It's the only thing in the world I was *ever* any good at. I wasn't any good at all the things children are supposed to be good at. But I guess it was in the seventh or eighth grade, teachers began to say, "Hey, you're good at this." Children do what they're praised for—right?—unless they're psychotic. So I just kept on doing it. Then I found out how hard it was after I signed aboard—like joining the Marines for life.

It's the loneliness that's the hardest part. I don't want to sound like the pope or the president—the loneliness here at the top, the Oval Office. I don't mean that. But you are alone; you just sit in your room, all day for two years, and you work. At night you get to go out (you're not locked up at sunset). Most other people do get to stand around the water cooler and pinch the secretaries or get pinched by the secretaries. But you don't get to do that if you're a writer.

Pascal said something that I think is the truest thing ever written about the human race. He said (I can't quote it exactly), most of the troubles of the human race are attributable to one thing: we cannot sit in our room and do our work. You can just tattoo that on your palm.

Question: Do you keep a journal?

RP: I keep a notebook in which I write down things to do with my writing. But I don't keep a journal about my life. It's hard enough to get through a whole day, without having to live it all over again on paper before I go to bed. Also, I don't like the extremely self-conscious quality that journal keeping imposes upon life. About three years ago, I did keep a journal for a year. I absolutely forced myself to do it. It's interesting to have it to look back at now, but during the year I realized that I was beginning to live for my journal. I'd be having a conversation; I'd think, "This is really going to be great for my journal." Or "This is going to be boring in my journal tonight; what can I do to make this a little more exciting for my journal?" The great journal keepers, like André Gide, must have been monsters in the real world. Who would ever have said a word to them? You knew that everything you did or said would be immediately embalmed in their journal. I have one or two friends who are absolutely obsessive journal keepers, and I find that it very much becomes a factor in my relations with them. There are certain things I wouldn't dream of telling them, certain things I wouldn't dream of doing in their presence. So it's not an activity without its own severe repercussions on one's life.

Question: What writers have particularly influenced you?

RP: Tolstoy, Milton, Chekhov, and all sorts of books I was reading as a child: *The Boy's King Arthur* by Sidney Lanier, *The Arabian*

Nights, Grimm's Fairy Tales, Toby Tyler; or, Ten Weeks with a Circus.
I think when scholars are trying to find out what influences writers,
they invariably go wrong because they leave out childhood reading.
Childhood reading is obviously the most influential of all in forming
the fantasy life and impressing the unconscious. There are lots of
living writers or recent writers that I admire enormously and love to
read, but the ones I've named for you are the names I feel most
influenced by because they are what I was reading when I was
adolescent and being instructed and informed. I had good taste,
didn't I? Well, *I* didn't have good taste—people were just telling me
who to read; those wonderful teachers were saying, "Here, go read
Anna Karenina." When I was fourteen someone said, "Here go read
Anna." I was just an obedient boy, and I went off and read it.

I don't know whether you have it now or not, but I remember the
terrific pride in being able to say, "Hey, I just read a six-hundred-, a
sixteen-hundred-page novel." It was like running a marathon, a great
feat that you'd accomplished—the longer the book, the better.

Question: I'm wondering if you think that someone in his early
twenties can suddenly decide "I want to be a writer" and then go on
and become a good writer.

RP: I don't think you can unless you have some sort of deep
innate linguistic skills; they tend to go back to earliest childhood. I
think enormous amounts of improvement can be made—discipline
can be worked, training can be instituted—but I think the way one
recognizes someone who is likely to be a writer is really by some sort
of flair for language.

That's the way you can see the boy on the sandlot who is likely to
become a basketball player. The kid who is fumbling and stumbling
around, the way I was—unable to dribble a ball—is certainly not
going to go into pro basketball years later. But I was the little guy
who was writing poems in the first grade, long before poems were
ever fashionable to write in school—they write poems a mile a
minute now.

Question: Do you feel confident that books will always be
around?

RP: Books are always in peril, especially in America. They always
have been. Although it's alleged to be the freest country in the world,
America is extremely paranoid about the idea of freedom of speech.

We're all uncomfortable with certain aspects of it. I mean, who could
have objected to the Supreme Court saying the other day that you
are not allowed to make child pornography and sell it? Yet clearly the
first amendment to the Constitution says that you can. Go and read
the Bill of Rights. It says Congress shall make no bill abridging the
freedom of speech. The Supreme Court has just announced that
they will abridge freedom of speech, communication in the form of
pornography starring children. So the whole society has agreed that
we will breech the Constitution in that way.

But I think, insofar as all of you are going to leave this place to
become functioning citizens of the community, it's something you
need to be enormously sensitive to—the fear of words. In the last
three or four years there's been a brand new, miserable new, on-
slaught on novels and poems and books of all sorts in schools and
public libraries. That's always been the case, but there's been a
whole new vicious round of it.

Question: Have any of *your* books been banned anywhere?

RP: I've had little dustups occasionally. I don't know that one has
ever been banned. But I know of a couple of cases where colleges
have assigned them in courses, and then irate mothers and fathers
have written in and said, "How can you ask my unblemished son or
daughter to read this garbage?" What's the women's college in
Atlanta?—Agnes Scott. They had a great dustup over a novel of mine
called *A Generous Man* about fifteen years ago. They asked the
whole freshman class to read it in the summer before they came up,
and I was supposed to go down during orientation week and talk to
the freshmen about it. Then a lot of mamas in Georgia—a lot of
blue-haired mamas—read the book, and it really hit the fan all over
Georgia. The college had to cancel the plan, and it was fifteen years
before I was invited back to discuss *A Generous Man* at that particular college. It helped the sales of the book, of course; all the girls
bought three more copies.

Question: Has any of your work actually been censored?

RP: *A Long and Happy Life* has been translated into Russian, and
I have never been able to get a copy. It's listed in all sorts of
bibliographies with the Russian title, but when I learned that they had
pirated it and published it, I wrote to the publisher (I didn't care: I
was flattered they wanted it). So I asked if I could have a copy to add

to my shelf of publications, and they wrote back and said, "No copies are available." They obviously didn't want me to have one; maybe they were scared I was going to create an international incident. That was in about 1965 and then, in 1975, amazingly enough, I got a letter from them saying (they had signed a copyright convention in the meanwhile), "We offer you this *large* sum of money for the rights to *The Surface of Earth*." I was flabbergasted. I thought, "Well, this'll be fun but they won't send me the rubles; I'll have to go to Russia to spend the rubles." It turned out, in fact, that they sent me a large number of dollars right through the mail.

But the point I was making has to do with a letter I received about six months after we'd signed the contract. The letter said, "Dear Mr. Price" (you know, Russians, however well they learn English, seldom learn how to use English articles; they often omit *a, an* and *the*. They say things like: "Russian language does not contain"). So "Dear Mr. Price: Russian language does not allow for scenes descriptive of sexual behavior, nor does Russian language contain words describing sex. Do we have your permission to omit such scenes from our translation of your novel, *The Surface of Earth*?" Well, *The Surface of Earth* is hardly a red hot sexual novel. There are maybe three or four scenes that might give your grandmother a bad afternoon. But I talked to my agent; and she said, "Look, they're going to do it anyway, whether you like it or not." So we wrote and said, "Sure." Interestingly enough, I talked with a Russian scholar-friend of mine not long ago, and he said they weren't really kidding. The Russian language has an extremely small vocabulary for dealing with anything related to physical love. Classical Russian language does not contain words for dealing with these activities.

Question: Have your American publishers ever tried to alter what you wrote?

RP: They never change the words—never, just the occasional misspelling.

Question: Do you ever want to revise your works after they've been published?

RP: Oh, sure! I'm not a self-hater; I'm not especially neurotic about my own work, but I don't really like to read my own work again, and I almost never do after I've read the final proofs. By the time you've published a book, you have read it so many times, you can recite it; it's getting to be like the Twenty-Third Psalm. You've read the typescript three or four times, you've read the proofs at least twice, and you're going bananas reading the thing.

But after a few years, you glance back. My own experience is not that I hate it or say, "Oh, how could I have been so bad?" I just think, "That's me, the way I was then." Don't you ever go back and look at snapshots of yourself and say, "Oh, God, I had a haircut like that! Why did I ever wear that horrible suit or that dumb-looking sweater!" That's the kind of problem I have looking back at my own work—looking back at the old me. I respect all the work I've published, and I'm glad I did it; I stand behind it but I stand behind it the way I stand behind my cousins and my nieces. I don't feel that it's a series of little me's out there anymore; a lot of the stuff is rather distant from me.

Question: Which of your contemporaries do you most respect?

RP: Robert Stone, Eudora Welty, Bernard Malamud, Toni Morrison, Anne Tyler, James Welch. They would be my favorites. I probably omitted one or two of my absolute favorites. They would be six of my top ten.

Once you've written a lot, you get to know a lot of writers; and it becomes hard to judge your friends' work. You're so implicated in their lives, and you bring to their work so much special knowledge. Often I read a book by a friend of mine and think, "That's marvelous." And then a very intelligent person, who doesn't know the author, will read it and say, "Yes, well, but it lacks X, Y, and Z." And I'll suddenly realize it does lack X, Y, and Z, but I'd subliminally put them in there because I knew what the intention was.

Question: How did you gain confidence in yourself as a writer?

RP: I don't think I became really self-judging, confident in my self-judgments, until I had published a couple of books—by which time I was thirty years old. By the time I was about twenty-two, I'd had enough really professional people—who were not in love with me, who had no great stake in telling me lies—assuring me that my work was good. Then I began to think, "Hey, there must *be* something here." Eudora Welty came to Duke when I was a senior in college. I didn't know her; I'd read her work ever since I was in the eighth grade and very much admired her. She read the only story I had written at that point, which was nine pages long, and she said, "This is a thoroughly professional story." And I thought, "Hey, Eudora Welty would know what a professional story is, and she has no stake in telling me a lie." That story, "Michael Egerton," was published in a volume called *The Names and Faces of Heroes.*

You distrust your teachers because you know what a stake your teachers have in you as their students and your parents in loving you personally. So I think one of the many things going on in young artists' careers is the search for credible judges. You begin to realize, "Hey, I can't believe Mom and Dad because they love *me*; they have certain kinds of ambitions for me that prevent their looking at me objectively." Then you begin to trust your schoolteachers, and then you begin to realize, "Hey, they can't be leaned on too hard either because they've got a big stake in me." And then, if you are mentally healthy—by which I mean not really paranoid or schizophrenic—there comes a point at which you become your own judge; and you say, "This is the way I want it to be, and I don't give a damn whether anybody likes it or not." I very much want to be lucid; I want to be clear and unobscure to the intelligent reader—a reader let's say at least as intelligent as I am. But beyond that, I'm not really interested in whether anybody likes it or not. I've got it the way I want it, as nearly as I can. And that's a sort of deal between me and God. If anybody else wants to buy the book or look in or send me a pound of fudge, that's fine. I love it. I love to be liked and praised and read and bought and invited places and whatnot. But that's not what *I* do it for.

Let me say at the end, as the last thing, that everything I've said I believe to be true—as true as I can make it today for me. But I'm not in the business of offering commandments to other people, since I'm a relatively sane human being, more or less. It's by no means any sort of decalogue that I'm passing down.

Feast Thy Heart: An Interview
Jefferson Humphries/1986

Transcript of taped interview conducted on 4, 5, and 6 April 1986. Printed by permission of Reynolds Price.

These discussions took place at Reynolds Price's home just outside Durham, North Carolina on 4, 5, and 6 April 1986. They were recorded on tape but have not appeared in print before. This was just prior to the publication of *Kate Vaiden,* so I began by asking him about that novel.

JH: Is *Kate Vaiden* related in any thematic way to *The Surface of Earth* and *The Source of Light*?

RP: No, it isn't related; it's a completely separate stream. I had thought when I finished *The Source of Light* that I might well eventually write a third panel to what seemed probably a triptych, but the third panel didn't insist upon itself, and I didn't try to push it. I'd been working with the Mayfield family story since about 1972 and was not eager to force myself onward if it wasn't urgently demanding to come.

Something else in the early eighties did seem to be demanding to come, or slowly insisting upon coming. That was my growing sense that what I wanted to do was write an autobiographical memoir, not of myself but of an imagined character, and I wanted to write it in the first person.

I don't know why that was such an important impulse—because that is what I remember as the initial impulse, somehow to deal with a strongly individual imaginary voice talking about its life. In both the Mayfield novels, *The Surface of Earth* and *The Source of Light,* I had written numerous monologues in which various imaginary characters told the stories of their lives, or important segments of their life stories. I think I became fascinated by the shape of a life, the shape that an individual narrator can give it in narration. It's obviously one of the most ancient forms of fiction, especially in the English language

200

with the early first-person novels which are generally great first-person accounts of my-story-according-to-whomever.

So as I recall it, I thought of a first-person male—this was going to be a man who recounted an outrageous and adventurous boyhood merging on into middle and perhaps old age, a modern picaresque rogue novel. I thought of it as having a lot of erotic comedy built into the texture. I don't know why I wanted to do that; perhaps I thought it might be fun.

I had greatly enjoyed working on *The Surface of Earth* and *The Source of Light,* but in a lot of ways, they had also brought a lot of heavy weather with them, a lot of heavy emotional weather in my involvement in those imaginary situations. Also insofar as both novels allegorized, at some considerable imaginary distance, the history of my own two families (my father's and my mother's), I had thought of a new novel as in a sense giving myself a vacation, a time off.

But as I advanced on into 1982–83, the impulse began to change in my mind to a woman's voice. I can only begin to understand the reason for that when I remember that at the same time I was beginning to do a great deal of thinking about my own mother's life.

My mother had died in 1965, shortly after her sixtieth birthday. I had been close to my mother all my life and had especially seen a good deal of her in her last years when she was living close by in Raleigh and was pretty much under the weather with what finally killed her. She was very heroic and very adventurous and continued to be up until she just suddenly died one afternoon of a cerebral hemorrhage.

For years after her death, certain protective mechanisms prevented my thinking about her life very much. I had spent a lot of time thinking about, and allegorizing in fiction, my father's life and my questions about it. (He lies to a large extent behind several of the male characters in the Mayfield story.) But Mother had really, aside from making an imaginary appearance in *Love and Work* shortly after her own death, swept out of my fiction till now, eighteen years or so later, I began to find her stepping forward again out of my unconscious and demanding to be dealt with.

JH: How much of her is in the mother in *Love and Work?*

RP: A great deal—though the mother's dead, technically, within the first ten pages of the novel. Nonetheless her remembered personality and force hang very much over *Love and Work*. She's not an active character in there except in memory.

JH: Does *Kate Vaiden* represent, then, any kind of return to things that you were concerned with in *Love and Work*?

RP: No, not really. *Love and Work* focuses on Thomas Eborn and his own kind of hyper-intellectualized approach to something as complex as family emotion and filial response to a parental death. The remembered mother in *Love and Work* is very much like my mother, or my memories of my mother.

Thomas Eborn, I am glad to say, is a character whom I like a good deal less than I like myself! Someone recently asked me if I wasn't obviously behind the character of Hutch Mayfield in *The Surface of Earth* and *The Source of Light*. I said that I was to some extent but that Hutch was a much nicer person than me, which I meant quite fervently and sincerely; but I think that I'm a nicer person than Thomas Eborn, at least more approachable. He's a very dried and balked man.

Just before the impulse for the novels switched from the male first person to the female, I had found myself suddenly writing a longish poem about my mother. It was called "A Heaven for Elizabeth Rodwell," my mother's maiden name, and it consisted of three climactic catastrophes in my mother's life—the death of her mother when she was about eleven, the death of my father when she was forty-nine, and her own death when she was sixty. Each panel of the triptych begins with a straightforward narrative description of the actual event (or what I know of the actual event) and then awards her—the poet awards Elizabeth Rodwell—an imaginary rescue in which the worst doesn't happen—her mother doesn't die; her husband doesn't die; she does die at the end of the poem but in some way happily transformed.

So the poem became an imaginary reversal of the actual tragedies of my mother's life. I think that was the liberating impulse which then set me free, not only to begin to ask other unanswered questions about my mother's life but to explore a lot of the questions that I had for Mother and could no longer ask her—nor ask anyone else who ever knew the answers because all her contemporaries were by then dead.

My mother had in many ways an exemplary and fascinating life for a woman of her generation. She was born in 1905, her mother died in about 1916, her father died three or four years after that. She was reared by an elder sister in her elder sister's family. The elder sister and her husband and three sons came back to the small town— Macon, North Carolina—moved into the family home, which my mother never had to leave, and reared her there. So she was in the peculiar position of being an orphan and yet never having to move out of the house she was born in. The rest of her life she remained extremely close to that sister and the sister's husband and the nephews. She had a very ambiguous sense of her own past. She very much felt that she had been an orphan. There was a certain amount of hostility to the relatives who were felt to be interlopers, who had moved into her life, and yet a great deal of gratitude to them for having made it possible for her not to have to go to an orphanage or not to be thrown to the mercy of a strange place.

So all her life she had that slight outlaw quality to her, someone born out on the edge and kept out there. She was a very unself-pitying person, but one who nonetheless didn't want to forget, didn't want you to forget, that she had a much more adventurous life than almost all her contemporaries.

The impulse for what later became *Kate Vaiden* really arose out of a desire to write a particular person's autobiography and then slowly homing-in for whatever complex personal reasons on the idea that, at whatever imaginative remove, I wanted to write an *emotional* autobiography of my mother. The actual story that Kate tells in over three hundred pages is by no means the story of the actual events of my mother's life, but it still seems to me emotionally true to the interior voice of my mother, as I remember it anyway.

JH: Well, the fact that it was written in the first person means that you pretty substantially shifted gears from what you were doing in the previous two novels, doesn't it?

RP: Oh, yes. It's very unlike them.

JH: What's the difference in writing the third person kind of narrative that is in *The Surface of Earth* and *The Source of Light* and this kind of first-person story?

RP: Well, one of the things I discovered was the truth of something that Hemingway said more than half-jokingly but that turns out to be rather true. He said, "Anybody can write a novel in the first per-

son"—if you are imaginative by mental construct and if you are a
born mimic, which certainly most fiction writers are and which
everyone in my own family was (writer or not). So it's not terribly
difficult to say, "I am not Reynolds Price but someone called Kate
Vaiden, and I was born not in 1933 but in 1927, and my parents
died violently when I was eleven years old." You just take it from
there. Almost any creative mind could do it.

JH: Is this novel as long as the previous two?

RP: No. It's about as long as *The Source of Light*; it's not so long
as *The Surface of Earth*.

JH: That's somewhat lengthy though.

RP: Oh, *The Surface of Earth* is a normal Victorian-length novel. I
remember a number of the reviewers raving either praisefully or
blamefully that I had written such a long novel!

JH: Which you seemed to get blamed for while other writers
didn't.

RP: No one seemed to notice that every novel of Dickens or
George Eliot is at least that long, though someone else did point out
in a review that it was a real pleasure to be able to sink back in a
book that took at least two weeks to read and was not, as the
reviewer said, one of those novels that can be read in two waits on
the supermarket line.

JH: Which seem to be becoming extremely prevalent, such short
novels.

RP: They're very prevalent now, and they were even more prevalent when things like *Jaws* were so commercially popular. Oh, I think
they were popular because people don't want to do the kind of eye-
work and brain-and-soul work that's involved in immersing themselves into a many-streamed and complex work of narrative. I think
we're beginning again now in the '80s to get a large population of
intelligent, trained fiction readers who are indeed prepared to do that
sort of work.

JH: A friend of mine in book-marketing told me recently that book
sales, particularly fiction and hardcover fiction, are way up for the
first time in quite a long time. What do you think of that?

RP: I think it's wonderful, and I suspect the answer is rather
obvious. It's simply that the baby boom is now old enough to wish
no longer to buy its four thousandth rock-and-roll album but to invest

in the reading of fiction. Those unimaginable mountains that they were forced to climb in high school and college, they now find that they rather enjoy climbing again—that they possess the skills for it and like to use the skills.

JH: Do you think that they feel guilty because they maybe haven't pursued the careers they would have liked to, but rather careers that were more lucrative?

RP: One never wants to underestimate the guilt motivation of any American, but I'm not terribly aware that it's largely produced by guilt. I think probably it's produced by boredom. They've grown up to the point where they simply can no longer watch their four millionth hour of mindless television, and they try to think of something more interesting to do.

JH: Well, to get back to this novel, *Kate Vaiden,* I wanted to ask you if maybe it isn't inevitable, when you're writing in the first person, that the length of the narrative be limited. Can a first-person novel be as long as *The Surface of Earth*?

RP: There must be novels of Defoe's or somebody's which are. Certainly, Richardson, insofar as *Clarissa* and *Pamela* contain a lot of first-person narration in their various epistles, is very lengthy. But I think you're right—one doesn't expect a fifty-seven-year-old woman to tell us the story of her life in much more than four hundred pages. So there is to that extent a kind of limitation set upon length.

I was appalled about two or three months into the writing of *The Surface of Earth* to find out that I wasn't writing a tidy narrative that could be comprehended in the summer of 1944 as I had originally thought but in fact had to go back to 1903 and cover all the time thereafter. So that's why it took me many hundreds of pages, nearly five hundred as the book finally printed up, to cover the time.

Kate covers 1927 to 1983 or '84 in considerably fewer pages, but she also points out that for effective narrative purposes the first seventeen or eighteen years of her life are the only interesting portions, so she concentrates heavily for the first two hundred pages on those first seventeen years. Then she summarizes in a matter of, say, twenty-odd pages the remaining years until the 1980s when various events bring her back out of a kind of hibernation she's been in for so long and set her off again on interesting action.

JH: I may be wrong, correct me if I am, but I think this is the first time since *A Long and Happy Life* that you've gone back to a female protagonist?

RP: It is, in the sense of having the absolute central figure of the work be female. Certainly Eva Kendal is an enormously important emotional pole in *The Surface of Earth* and *The Source of Light* and Ann Gatlin, who's Hutch's girlfriend in *The Source of Light,* is a very important female pole there. But yes, Kate is the first unquestionably central female since Rosacoke Mustian more than twenty years before. I've just written an essay for the *New York Times Book Review* in which I talk about the phenomenon in my own work and in American fiction, which has increasingly led to the ghettoization of the genders in American fiction. The men only write about men; the women only write about women. [Editor's note: the essay referred to is "A Vast Common Room," in *A Common Room: Essays 1954–1987.*]

JH: Why is that?

RP: The essay goes into it in more than three thousand words of detail, but basically even the rare great female novelists of the nineteenth and twentieth centuries have specialized in the portrayal of female characters because women were deprived as children. Because of the way the western family has been constructed, they were deprived of intimate contact with the male personality until they themselves were of marital age. They were reared by women and since they were women anyway, they had their own innate mental and spiritual structures simply doubled for them by their nurses. Boys happened to be male and possessed whatever innate male structures there are in their brains, but they grew up in the very intimate company of women until they were old enough to leave home and go off to college, prep school if not college. So boys have the added advantage in western culture of an immersion in female sensibility, and therefore, I think, both a powerful curiosity about female sensibility and also a great fund of acquired knowledge that they get from watching their mothers, their grandmothers, their aunts, their mother's friends, and the maid in the kitchen.

This is something girls have almost never possessed. Plus I think that the great female novelists who've existed—who've brought themselves by force of will out of the strong ban against women doing any sort of work outside the kitchen or the nursery—have tended to obey, regretfully again, the even stronger cultural ban on a woman's really profoundly investigating the internal life of a man, the secret life of a man. The one thing you never get from the great women novelists who portray men—women like Emily Brontë and George Eliot and occasionally Jane Austen—is any real investigation of the sexual life of men, which is really to omit something like 60 percent of male sensibility in whatever century. Men didn't just discover sex in the twentieth century.

Emily Brontë in Heathcliff is about the only great female novelist who even begins to investigate male sexuality, and that's only as an elemental force. There's no real attempt to understand what drives Heathcliff. He's simply portrayed and portrayed very memorably. I think he is the most memorable male figure created by a woman, but he's comprehended no more than one comprehends a cyclone. He's simply there and he blows down trees and buildings, but we don't know why.

JH: I know that's still true. For instance my own wife often says things to me that corroborate what you say, implying that all men are children—which is to say incomprehensible, mysteriously and primally innocent and irresponsible—that men are often this kind of cyclone and that they are almost never comprehensible, whereas my own experience of female sexuality, and I think most men's experience of it, is not that way at all. It somehow is very comforting and very familiar.

RP: Yes. I think this view of men must be one that we have wished women to have. It increases our power over them, but I think it's also again part of a deception that has been worked upon your wife and upon all women reared in traditional western families—that they were simply told that men were exotic creatures who were not to be understood but only appeased.

JH: Don't we need to get past that?

RP: That's the whole final point of my essay. The title of it is "A Vast Common Room," and I think our knowledge of one another is simply there, waiting. It's a common room which we inhabit, and it's waiting to be used by each of the genders.

I think it's fascinating that almost the earliest invention of the novel in English is the female first-person memoir written by a man—*Moll Flanders* by Defoe, *Clarissa* and *Pamela* by Richardson.

There are *almost* no good male first-person novels by women. The earliest I can find that's of any continuing value and fame is *Franken-stein* by Mary Shelley, written about 1818; but since then the examples, the distinguished examples, are rare—frequently written by women who happened also to be lesbian. Willa Cather's *My Antonia* for instance inhabits the male sensibility in fascinating ways. Extremely rare now also is the reverse—the male impersonation of the female voice. Really the last great writer in English to make a specialty of the female sensibility was Henry James. Tennessee Williams is the last great writer, I think, to come close with his long gallery of intensely portrayed heroines—horrific, most of them, but very instructive and very convincing.

JH: And very true.

RP: And very true. But if you think of the great novelists who've succeeded them and the distinguished novelists who are writing now, male and female, you're faced generally with writers who have accepted the ghettoization of the genders and who simply march right along it.

I obviously assume that my impersonation of *Kate Vaiden* is convincing, and I'm glad to say that a number of honest women agree. I think that, to a large extent, the liberation from this ghettoization is a matter of saying "nonsense" and going back and carefully excavating the mutual knowledge that we all possess as heirs of our parents and older people in our own generation.

I do think, for the reasons I've already stated, that women have the harder job of it; but I think also that they have accepted the myth that they know nothing about men. Right now we've accepted a terrible media-obsession with father-daughter incest, which has obviously had tragic consequences in a relatively small number of cases. But I think most women, if they will really go back and deal with their own knowledge of their fathers and not simply accept the suppression of it which has been forced upon them, will find that men are not mysterious at all but are creatures very very much like themselves, and painfully ready to be investigated. Certainly men *want* to be investigated. It's only the rare terrified macho mask which is afraid of penetration. Most men are longing to be unveiled!

JH: Well, my own father, and my wife's father for that matter, and most—all I can think of, of the men their age I've known—are extremely private, reserved men who may be vulnerable underneath, but I'm not sure I would know how to go about beginning to get past their reserve, even though I'm male.

RP: Well, I have discovered in my own life that the shyness is very largely self-generated. My own parents are, alas, dead; but all my aunts and uncles proved in their late years to be simply open doors waiting for me to walk through. I had only to say, "Aunt Louise, what really happened back then when Mother and Father separated for two weeks?" And she'd just tell me. I had just been afraid to ask.

JH: Do you think that's maybe because she wasn't part of your immediate family or because she was a woman?

RP: No, I think it's because nobody had ever asked. I think also I was now an obvious adult myself. I was a middle-aged man thoroughly ready to be in possession of the family secrets insofar as they were secrets. My family had very few secrets; they were very confessional people and glad to be so. No, I think that what's largely at issue is the monumental self-absorption of American adolescence and early youth. Once we proceed into middle age and are really old enough to begin to notice that our parents were human beings like ourselves, we are then balked by a convenient shyness in assuming that our parents wouldn't tell us.

I have never yet had a friend who's gone to a parent and said, "Mother, tell me what really happened when you had that miscarriage," or "Dad, tell me about that time you seemed to have an affair with your secretary twenty years ago." They just tell you, that's all—if you choose the right setting.

JH: So you think most people just don't ask the question?

RP: They don't ask because, a) they don't want to think about the question—it involves being really interested in another person's existence; and b) because they're really afraid of possessing the knowledge.

I have found that once people know I'm a writer, they assume that—like a priest—I have a right to their secrets and that all I have to do is ask the questions.

I don't know that it's some terrifically secret power that I possess, but sometimes I have to stop people from telling me their innermost secrets. They seem to turn on like automatic faucets. I sit down in an airplane, and five minutes later some stranger's telling about his adulterous love affair that his wife is on the verge of discovering. I think people are more or less secretly yearning to talk. After all, if you talk with them about their secrets or what they've been trained to believe are their secrets, you have indicated to them for one of the first times in their lives that someone else is really interested in them, that someone is really watching them, and I think that most people are delighted to know that.

JH: Do you think people are more inclined to reveal themselves to disinterested third parties?

RP: I don't know about how disinterested you have to be. Often I have been quite interested in the lives of people who've told me a great deal.

JH: But you had no personal stake in them.

RP: I think what's very true in what you just said is that people are still sufficiently self-absorbed and sufficiently narcissistic to prefer talking about themselves to listening to you. Perhaps what's different and exotic in me, eccentric in me is that I'm really much more interested in hearing other people's secrets than in telling my own. I don't mind telling my own. I'm a tremendously confessional person, if a friend asks me, but I don't tend to volunteer and marinate you in my secrets unless you ask. And very few people have ever asked me.

JH: Does *Kate Vaiden* represent a departure from what you've done before toward more "confessional" fiction?

RP: I don't think it's a radical departure. It's a very thorough exploration of the sensibility of a particular human being. I don't think Kate's going to seem, to anyone who's read my other work, like a revolutionary different sort of human being. She resembles, at least genetically, certain other figures in my work—people like Rosacoke, people like Eva in the Mayfield family—but she's also very original and very adventurous. In all my central female characters, I can look back now and see that I've always been interested in the kind of revolutionary woman that my mother was, the woman who would absolutely not buy the harem-wife-mother stereotype that was forced upon all women in my early life. They simply said "nonsense" and accepted those portions of the stereotype which they themselves wished to accept, but otherwise they went about being radically independent, at least for their own time—the early twentieth century. But Kate's brand of radical freedom is more intense than any other

woman's I've ever created in that she does indeed literally abandon
the only child she ever bore; and for a mother to abandon a son—a
white middle-class woman—in the late 1930s, early '40s was an
almost unheard of event and one that Kate ultimately comes to
regret, though not in a punitive but in a realistic way.

And she's interested in why she abandoned this son; she's interested in trying to find out, now that he's almost forty years old
and she hasn't seen him since he was under a year old, whether he's
alive and whether or not she has the right to reveal her identity and
her existence to him. That becomes her real reason for telling her life
story. She's writing it down for herself, now that he's alive and she
knows where she can find him. She's writing the story down, a) to
find out if she has the right to tell it to him and, b) to have something
to tell him once she does indeed decide whether she's going to locate
him or not. So the story becomes her credentials, her apologia for
her particular existence. She doesn't ask for pity; she doesn't ask for
pardon; she just asks to be heard and understood.

JH: I know in many previous interviews, in more than one way,
you have talked about the family as maybe the most powerful force
in an individual's life and as a positive force. Reading you, the family
emerges as sometimes a very destructive force in individual's lives.

RP: Oh, I think it's unquestionably the most destructive force there
is, except for tornadoes. I said somewhere else that if Freud taught
us nothing else, he taught us what Sophocles had at first thought—
that the family is the hothouse of neurosis and psychosis. In the
Reagan era's saccharine stereotypes of family togetherness, we are
led to think that it's the greatest thing that exists.

Well, what it is, is the only way that civilization has worked out for
the procreation and the more or less successful rearing of children,
though the history of the human race wouldn't lead us to suggest
that the family is especially successful in rearing civilized children,
nonviolent children. I think that the family is the only way that's
offered to most of us for protection and rearing and for our ultimate
education in such matters as love and emotional navigation. But if
one looks at the people one knows, reads about, or watches on the
evening news, one realizes that people haven't learned anything very
useful or very successful about love or hate.

JH: I have observed that women are extremely loyal to extended family structures even when those families have exacted tremendous emotional and psychic tolls and continue to do so.

RP: I suspect you're right. I can certainly say that in the case of my own family, you're right. But in the case of *Kate Vaiden,* I'd have to say that part of what's truly remarkable in Kate is that she turns on her family, who of course had previously turned on her in a major way. She is extraordinary, but she's by no means unique in that.

Far more than we know, there were these renegade women around the landscape in the 1920s, '30s, '40s, '50s, who had left behind some home situation which was inhospitable to them for whatever reasons, of their making or someone else's making, and had struck off on their own. There were many female bachelor secretaries and school teachers, women who worked in draft boards and whatever else, who were just quietly permitted to be creatures of considerable mystery. No one ever asked who they were, where they came from, why they lived fifty miles away from their birthplace—they seldom lived farther away than that.

Kate vanishes when she leaves her child and becomes one of those people. She's a responsible citizen always. She never becomes an outlaw in any legal sense. But she is, by her own definition, a moral outlaw for forty years of her life in which she's abandoned her family and her only child, for what she ultimately suspects were adequate reasons; and she asks the reader and finally her son to believe that the reasons were adequate.

So I've imagined, for my mother, a life and a situation in which she refused to accept the humiliations which fate and other human beings subjected her to and a life in which she went off and made her own alternate fate.

JH: This is a woman who, many years later, would not have changed what she did? Or doesn't feel overwhelmed by guilt for what she did?

RP: No, she doesn't.

JH: That's extremely radical.

RP: As I said, I think you—like a number of southerners—think a lot more about guilt than I do or than my family does. No, I think Kate is far more concerned with having people understand the context in which she committed certain actions. As I look back on my parents' lives, I realize that I resented and blamed my parents for decisions which they made when they were far younger and far less experienced or educated than I am now. I am the age at which my father died, and I'm within six years of the age at which my mother died, and it certainly doesn't become me to blame them for any shortcomings that I might perceive in their rearing of me or my brother, when I now realize that I would have made similar if not greater mistakes had I come along with my own problems and tried to rear children simultaneously. So I think that one of the things that *Kate Vaiden* is, is a way of imagining and forgiving my mother, as it were, for her life.

JH: It sounds like a pretty radical response and a very effective one to what at least one critic has said, that the female characters that you've depicted are very negative images of what a woman is.

RP: The fact that a number of male reviewers, at least, have seen women characters such as Rosacoke Mustian or Eva Kendal as being destructive says to me a lot more about male reviewers' ideas of what women should be like. I've found that female critics and students of my work have been far more sympathetic to the kinds of women I portray than most male reviewers have been.

I think I frighten the socks off of a lot of male reviewers, both in my portrayal of women and in my portrayal of modern American marriage and of the severe deficiencies of the official modern American male way of education and life, especially the official approach to romance and marriage and fatherhood.

JH: Could you talk a little more about that? What is there about the way you have depicted women that scares men so badly?

RP: That I've portrayed women who had severe reservations about men; that I portrayed women who have a strong passion and appetite for independent life, for power of their own, for their own particular kind of eros. That I've portrayed women who often had highly unorthodox views of their children, who didn't simply accept the great mother stereotype, lie back and accept the praise of their children and the Mother's Day presents from them; who think that they may have hatched a couple of little sons-of-bitches in the lot and wish to get rid of them or get them out of their lives as soon as possible.

I think Kate says as much about herself. She says the one thing in the world that terrifies any man is the idea of a mother who doesn't want to be a mother. She says we can forgive almost anything except a mother who doesn't want her children.

I know that's really true—even in a society which tends, in divorce actions, always to give the child to the mother however much of a hound dog the mother may be. We are still horrified by the mother who really says, "I don't want these children."

JH: Do you think that it's possible for marriage to work in a positive way for the two people who are involved in it? The kinds of depictions of marriage in your work are not terribly optimistic.

RP: I wouldn't think anybody could honestly look at American marriage in the twentieth century, insofar as I've watched it, and come away with a terribly hopeful prognosis. I think that a marriage is one of the most difficult of balancing acts to bring off. I remember E. M. Forster saying in an interview twenty-five years ago that he thought the silver wedding anniversary was one of the greatest achievements of civilization.

I'd just say that the picture of marriage in my novels is not very different from the picture of marriage in middle Tolstoy or D. H. Lawrence or any of the other serious fictional students of the institution. Marriage basically doesn't work very well. I've never married; almost all my friends, 99 percent of my friends have married. One of the saddest things I'd have to say is that it would be my observation at fifty-three that I have never watched closely more than two marriages that I envied.

JH: Why did you envy them? What was different about them?

RP: There was a level of mutual tolerance, mutual reward and compensation for the individual efforts invested.

JH: Was there something structurally different about those marriages or was it just because of the two individuals involved?

RP: It was basically because of the two individuals involved. They each had a high level of intelligence, of emotional discipline and control, a realism of expectance, and an ability to gauge emotion and action for the long-term journey, the long haul-as opposed to the short trip, the short joy ride as so many marriages seem gauged to.

JH: You've just written a trilogy of plays in a very short time. Why do you think you first wrote a play? How long ago was it?

RP: I wrote plays in the eighth grade and in high school which hardly count, but they were in fact the first things I wrote of any serious length and ambition. The first play that I published is *Early Dark*, a play that I completed in 1976 or '77. It was based on a screenplay that I'd written of *A Long and Happy Life*. It's a different look at the same characters and story by a person who was nearly twenty years older than the person who had first invented the story and characters in a novel. So I wrote that play in '76; it had its first professional production in '78 in New York at the WPA Theatre; and it's had several other good productions.

I then wrote nothing else dramatic until the early '80s when I was commissioned by public television to write an independent original screenplay for production in their American Playhouse Series. I generated and completed a play called *Private Contentment* which was produced for television by PBS and then on stage in 1985. Both plays have since been published.

I then was commissioned in 1984 to write a play for the drama students at Hendrix College in Conway, Arkansas—a college which I had earlier visited as a writer-in-residence. I had been going through a personal health crisis and had been in a period of frozen-up energy so far as my writing was concerned. I was eager to get back to work, so I took the commission as a kind of act of the Holy Spirit. I began in November 1984 writing a play which would be entirely new and which would be written for a cast of characters who could be portrayed by college juniors and seniors. This play was based on an idea that I had conceived shortly after finishing *Private Contentment* and that was, again, a situation arising out of my own curiosity about the married life of my parents before I was born. They were married for six years before I arrived in their lives, and I was their first child. I'd hoped to write this as a second screenplay for American Playhouse and ultimately didn't do so, but survived to write it for Hendrix College.

It's called *August Snow* and concerns the first big crisis in the married life of a young couple. When I completed it in January of 1985, I sent it off to Hendrix. I had so successfully cranked up the writing apparatus in me that I quickly turned back to *Kate Vaiden* and was able to resume work on that and finish it. But when I went out to Arkansas for the rehearsals and first production of the play, in October and November 1985, I was so intrigued and ignited by the excellence of the direction and acting that the Hendrix staff and students gave my play that I came home and quickly wrote two other plays about the same characters, which view them in later years of their lives so that we see this couple in the 1930s, the '40s, and the '70s. We see them just before the second war begins, at the end of the second war, and at the end of the Vietnam War. We see them in the first crisis at the end of the first year of their marriage; we see them during the second crisis of their marriage which has to do with the question of whether or not they're going to have a child; and we see them in one of the late crises of their lives which centers around the return of their son from Vietnam.

The final two plays in the trilogy have not yet been produced; and therefore, in my own mind, are not yet ready for publication. Once they've had their initial productions, and I have had the opportunity to revise them in rehearsal and performance, then I do plan to publish the trilogy. The individual titles are *August Snow, New Music*, and *Better Days*; the name of the entire trilogy is *New Music*. It was great fun to do and was written with a kind of speed which I had never managed to achieve in any previous work.

JH: Why do you think you suddenly were able to write so quickly? You wrote the second two plays in a week apiece. Is that right?

RP: About a week or ten days apiece, not much more than that.

JH: Why, do you think, you were able to write so fast?

RP: I really don't know. I've often wondered if all the radiation I went through after my spinal surgery didn't somehow speed up my epizootic. Certainly by that time I had become something of a local master of the word processor which I had acquired in the summer of 1983 and was able actually to generate the marks on the page at a much faster rate, though I had always previously resisted the temptation to compose on the typewriter.

I'm such a bad typist that I hated all the noise and the mess of typewriting. I would always write my prose and poetry out in long hand on lined yellow pages and then type it up at the end of the day or the end of the week when I had relatively fresh copy to type from. Once I acquired the word processor and discovered the beautiful ease of correction and the possibility of producing a clean manuscript from moment to moment, I was greatly freed up to write at a more rapid speed. I finally composed all of *Kate Vaiden* by hand. The final two plays of the trilogy were the first two things that I'd ever entirely composed on the processor. Thereafter I composed two or three long poems on the processor. I probably shouldn't reveal the titles thereof, since reviewers will say, "Mr. Price has now learned to write speedily on the processor and is writing all the worse."

JH: Some writers have suggested that the advent of the word processor was going to bastardize the writing process and that it was a real detriment in disguise. You don't feel that way?

RP: Oh, I think that's absurd. I think that the same people would have thought the invention of the fountain pen was probably the end of all good writing. I think it is fascinating, for instance, to look back at the origins of typewriting as a means of composition. We're told by Leon Edel that Henry James dictated his last novels to a typist who sat in the room typing directly from his dictation and that James's friends and greatest admirers felt that his late work was lamentably mannered and difficult as the result of the luxuriant rhetorical freedom that the process of dictation gave him. I'm not one who happens to think that the later work is all that awful, so I don't share their regret.

Someone recently told me—I don't know how true it is—that *The Tragedy of Pudd'nhead Wilson* by Mark Twain was the first novel composed on a typewriter. Well, I'm not sure that anyone could prove that *Pudd'nhead Wilson* is a less good work than anything else of Mark Twain's. I think it's a fascinating question though. I certainly don't suspect that the processor represents any decline in the difficulty of, or the possibility of, good writing. I think it just slightly alters the technology by which we proceed and perhaps greatly speeds up the process.

JH: Well, the notion that it must take a long time to write anything of quality, that it must be painful and slow has always been an excuse that you hear, if you do happen to be someone who produces steadily and with relative ease—and it's something you tend to hear from people who produce one book or two books and that's it.

RP: Oh, the agony of it all! That's so boring to hear. One of the great joys of my professional and personal life has been a friendship for almost twenty-five years now with Leontyne Price, the great soprano. Leontyne and I were once driving back to the hotel from a recital that she'd given with the Florida Symphony Orchestra, and she had sung the great soprano aria from Puccini's *Turandot, In* *questa reggia.* I said, "Gosh, Leontyne, that really does have to be one of the most difficult things ever written for your voice." And she said, "Shoot, Reynolds, you can either do it or you can't. If you can, you just stand up and do it." She could and did, and I think you can either write or you can't.

It is hard but it's no harder than being a marvelous gymnast or a great singer or a marvelous anything else. If you have the ability and you perfect the discipline, the work can be done; it's simply a matter of sitting down every day and doing it. It's by no means unimaginably difficult; and I've had an extremely happy work life with very few days in which I haven't written, very few days in which the writing didn't produce a lot more pleasure than pain. So I would absolutely argue against those people who see it as so difficult. I would just say that those people are either under-talented or under-energized.

JH: You have been referring to a physical ordeal that you've been through. How has that affected your work?

RP: Oh, I think that it'll be years before I or anyone else will know what the effect has been. In late May of 1984, I was diagnosed as having a malignant tumor of the spinal cord, a ten-inch tumor extending from my neck downward. It had begun to affect my ability to walk. In early June 1984, I underwent ten hours of radical spinal surgery and five-and-a-half weeks of daily radiation to my spine after that. Soon afterward—following the surgery and the radiation—I lost the ability to walk. I have gradually lost some other physical abilities and may be losing more. I am entirely confined to a wheelchair. I am approaching the second anniversary of the discovery of that condition and of the surgery and treatment to combat it. I have done, however—once I recovered from the initial five months of shock and depression—done more writing in the past two years than I've done in any other two-year period of my life. I've essentially finished four books—*Kate Vaiden,* the novel which I had written a third of before the surgery, two-thirds afterwards; most of a new volume of poems which is due to be published next fall and is called *The Laws of Ice*; the three plays in the trilogy *New Music*; and a volume of new and selected essays which will probably be published sometime in 1987.

JH: So it's energized you, in a way.

RP: Certainly in the short term, the term of two years which is a

long time in a writing life. It seems indeed to have energized me. I
have yet, except in a few brief lyric poems, to deal with the condition
and the ordeal itself in any work of mine. But then it's been my
general schedule in life to find that it takes ten years or thereabouts
before an event in my real life becomes any sort of event in my work.
So I'd be surprised if the condition itself or the resulting paraplegia
was a feature of my work for a while to come.

JH: Could you talk about why you call this trilogy of plays *New Music* and why the poems are called *The Laws of Ice*?

RP: I'm not sure I could tell you, not because I want to be
mysterious about it or because I don't think I know. *New Music* is a
phrase that occurs in the second play a couple of times with connota-
tions that are, within context, rather complicated. Also I felt that the
trilogy itself was new music in my own life insofar as I've been a lyric-
dramatic artist, which I think I have, and also because the characters
in the three plays continually renew their marriage and their own grip
on existence by inventing new kinds of music for confronting given
situations, new kinds of emotional and spiritual music.

The Laws of Ice is the title of one of the poems in the new volume;
it's also a phrase from yet another poem in the volume. It just struck
me, I suppose, as giving out the appropriate kind of emotional chime
for the particular kind of poem that I thought was characteristic of the
book. The poem *The Laws of Ice* begins, "Ice has its own laws, just
as other things in the universe, fire, gravity, etc. have their laws." And
ice in the sense of death, trouble, reversal of whatever hope there is
in our expectations.

Titles have been a very important part of what I think I've made in
my work, and I'm proud of the titles of most of my works. Fred
Chappell said once that you could almost look at my titles on a page
and see the progression of my career, the growth and the different
principles that seem to go into the formation of the titles. I've always
taken the titling of a book or any given work seriously, as being a
means whereby the author can help the reader read the book, give
him some sense of what the book's about, and give him some
help without trying to give him the author's interpretation of the
book, which I always think is a great mistake.

JH: You've always taken epigraphs seriously too.

RP: I take epigraphs seriously, though the new novel doesn't have

an epigraph. *Kate Vaiden* wouldn't give herself an epigraph, so I
didn't give her one. *The Laws of Ice* has no epigraph as my first
volume of poems *Vital Provisions* did not; it has a little epigraphic
poem of my own as it has a little epilogue in the end.

JH: Do the plays have epigraphs?

RP: No they don't, come to think of it.

JH: That's highly coincidental, that everything you've written in
the last few years suddenly doesn't have an epigraph, and I think
everything before does.

RP: I think all the fiction does—does *Permanent Errors*? I can't
remember.

JH: Yes it does—your adaption of Rilke's "The Alchemist."

RP: Certainly all the fiction does, and I would never say that
something else won't again down the road, but it just hasn't been
appropriate lately for the particular kinds of things that I've been
publishing in the last few years.

JH: In the last few years there has been a kind of renaissance in
southern writing which a lot of older scholars said could not happen.
Why do you think that's come about?

RP: Most of the scholars, as you've described them, who've said
that have been people who've wished themselves to be southern
writers and have proved unable to write. I think the renaissance that's
occurring now is very real. I think young southern writers like Josephine Humphreys and Charlie Smith and Michael Brondoli and Dave
Smith the poet—young writers of your age and generation—are
distinctly talented. They represent a clear genetic declension from the
first great generation of southern writers of the 1920s and '30s, from
my generation of the 1950s and '60s and going on. Yet while clearly
in the same genetic line, the new writers are very different in tone
and angle and vision, and I for one am delighted that there are
wonderful younger writers.

I know that some southern writers slightly older than I have a
vested interest in denying that there is anything new or interesting or
certainly that there is anything that matches the unquestioned high
quality of Faulkner or Welty or Katherine Anne Porter. I disagree. I
think a novel like Josephine Humphreys's *Dreams of Sleep* is as good
as anything we can point to in the older tradition, and I think we
deprive ourselves of a great new resource and pleasure if we fail to

see that a writer like Josephine Humphreys is as good as anybody who precedes her and that she has sprung full-grown into her ability at the age of forty by her own doing. She's nobody else's creature. She didn't have to get an MFA degree from anywhere. She simply lived her life and did her work and here it is.

JH: One of the really astonishing, I think positive, things about that generation of younger writers and critics who are interested in southern literature is that they don't owe anything to that southern literary establishment that has had a hammerlock on what was conceived as the canon of southern literature and what could be said about it.

RP: Oh, I think that control by a small group was nearly disastrous. If you look at writers of my age, one of the terrible things we've had to contend with is a sort of death grip of a generation of scholars and critics ten to fifteen years older than ourselves, almost all of whom are, in their own careers, sadly disappointed would-be novelists and poets—men who achieved almost nothing in their chosen trade, because art selects her own priests and doesn't permit them to volunteer. So they've gone out and they've papered such small landscape as was available to them with billboards denouncing writers younger than themselves and idolizing far beyond what I think was appropriate large figures such as Faulkner or Flannery O'Connor, an interesting and eccentric but not very large writer.

It hasn't, I think, damaged my own ability to do my own work and it hasn't seriously damaged the commercial fate of my works because luckily those scholars and critics have had extremely small audiences for their work—only a few Ph.D. students in southern universities and the readers of a few literary journals of extremely limited circulation.

JH: They still control, however, at least two of the major literary quarterlies in the south that I can think of, maybe two and a half.

RP: And they have great influence in one or two of the major southern university presses.

JH: Now you have the younger generation of the age of Michael Kreyling, Skip Gates, Randy Runyon, Houston Baker and Bill Andrews who are doing really, I think, the most interesting work on southern literature at the moment, and don't owe anything to that older generation.

RP: Yes.

JH: What's going to be the outcome of this kind of renewed and more open-minded interest in southern literature?

RP: I think it only has to be good. Again, critics like Kreyling and Andrews have a very small audience for their work, but I think their effect is already being felt—their work and that of other good critics like Noel Polk. It's beginning to be felt within such small circles of southern academic literary criticism as exist, and the effect can only be good insofar as it means that we begin to get serious attention paid to work of writers of my generation and of younger generations like that of Anne Tyler and now Josephine Humphreys and Dave Smith.

Time wounds all heels—the bad old generation are simply retiring and dying off. The younger writers are continuing to be born; and the younger critics, thank God, are continuing to be born to take care of them. But when you consider that writers of Faulkner's and Welty's and Katherine Anne Porter's generations had critics of the quality of Robert Penn Warren and Cleanth Brooks to fertilize the ground for their work, you realize how unfortunate the writers of my generation were in having absolutely nobody, in having only older southern critics who were attempting, if possible, to stamp out their existence.

JH: Yes. Well, that's certainly part of the difference between your situation when you were starting out and the situation of any writer, southern or otherwise, who's starting out right now. Do you see the situation as different in other ways?

RP: I think it's better in some other ways. One of the important facts that I contended with as a young southern writer coming into view in the late '50s and early '60s was that my debut was coinciding with the South's worst hour in the public eye since the Civil War, which was the South's absurd and criminally wicked response to integration. And all southern writers were tarred in the rest of the nation's eyes with the brush of George Wallace and southern segregationists in general, so that even writers of the withdrawn nature of Eudora Welty were blamed for being southern in the 1960s. There was no national critical establishment which had our defense at heart.

The distinguished national critics of fiction in the 1960s and '70s were those who were quite understandably involved in the promotion of American Jewish literature which was coming into its own

prominence at the time. One of the interesting critical stories that
remains to be told is the degree to which American fiction and the
American critical response to fiction of the last 30 years has really
been a contest—the southerners versus the Jews. *The Partisan
Review* versus the *Kenyon Review* or the *Southern Review* versus the
Partisan. It is a match that I find far more interesting to watch than
the southerners versus the southerners. A sad story indeed is southern writers versus southern critics. But in the last thirty years, a very
amusing and enriching story is southern novelists versus Jewish
novelists because we two brands have been by far the best. And it's
been a wonderful time for American fiction. I would say that, on
balance, it's been the best time for American fiction in the last two
centuries.

JH: You talk about a conflict between southern writers and Jewish
writers, but I know you've been on very friendly terms with some of
those Jewish writers.

RP: I certainly thought extremely highly of Bernard Malamud,
who's just died. He was always very kind to my work, publicly as well
as privately. I'm friends with and a great admirer of Philip Roth. He's
been a great help to me at various times in my own career. No, I
have absolutely no personal sense of conflict whatever with Jewish
writers. On the contrary, I see far more resemblance between the
concerns and methods of modern Jewish fiction and the concerns of
southern writers of the same period than I do with any other schools
of American fiction.

JH: I wanted to ask you about the fact that you and another
Jewish-American writer, Isaac Singer, are the only two serious
contemporary writers that I know of, in America, who depict supernatural presences as really perfectly natural and very real things.

RP: You may be right in saying we are the only ones. Certainly in
some short stories of Malamud's there are presences that could be
looked upon as supernatural. But I'm trying to think of exceptions to
your observation, and I can't come up with any immediately. I've
talked elsewhere about the presence of ghosts and the workings of
coincidence in my fiction as being, I think, signs of the supernatural in
our lives. I suspect that coincidence, or synchronicity as Jung calls it,
is indeed that, and I very much believe in the reality of ghosts in all
sorts of forms in our lives. I hadn't really thought of Singer as the

other major proponent thereof; and he can hardly be thought of as
an American novelist in any case, being such a product of the
nineteenth-century eastern European ghetto. But given his grounding
in ultra-orthodox Judaism, it's hardly surprising that he would be
another example.

I've delighted in having in several of my novels, especially the
Mayfield novels, various instances of coincidence and supernatural
intervention which very few if any readers have picked up—little
moments in *The Surface of Earth* and *The Source of Light* in which a
particular character or members of a particular family will turn up in
strange beneficent situations over the periods of generations. There's
a situation in *The Surface of Earth* where Forrest Mayfield is assisted
by a mysterious old black tramp in something like 1906; and then in
The Source of Light, in about 1956, Forrest Mayfield's grandson's
girlfriend aborts a child (Forrest Mayfield's great-grandchild). She
aborts the child at the home of a Negro woman in Richmond,
Virginia, where Forrest had died many years before. When that black
woman tells the girl her name and birthplace, she also tells the
knowing reader that in fact she's a direct descendent of that old black
man who had helped the great-grandfather years before. So that's a
little example—of secret operation of the supernatural in human
life, and it's a kind that I enjoy tucking into the text and hoping,
probably futilely, that some readers will pick up.

JH: I've always been acutely aware of it in your work. Do you
believe in the supernatural as that kind of presence in people's lives?

RP: Well, I don't think it's mathematical chance. Two of the very
dearest friends of my life are people whom I met when they were
students of mine at Duke, and they had, long before they knew me,
the same post-office box that I had as a freshman at Duke. When I
discovered that, years after we had known one another closely and
been good to one another for so long, I thought, that's a lovely little
joke that God was playing on us. It's very plainly an example of what
Jung calls synchronicity: very peculiar chronological jokes that are
being played on us by Something. I don't think it's just chance that's
playing the jokes; and they're not always jokes, by any means.

JH: And they're not always fun.

RP: No, exactly.

JH: What do you think it is?

RP: Oh, I think it's God, whatever God is. Sir James Jeans says in one of his great popular works of cosmology in the early twentieth century, "God tends to think in a manner which would be called mathematical."

JH: What does He mean for us to learn from those instances of synchronicity?

RP: God or Sir James Jeans?

JH: God. Or does He mean us to learn anything?

RP: I'm not sure He does. They may be tricks that He's playing with himself.

JH: Yes.

RP: Or with numbers or with some other aspect of the Godhead, the Trinity, or the Hexagonity or whatever ultimate reality is super-divided into. No, my own particular theological beliefs have always fit rather comfortably within the tenets of orthodox traditional Christianity, but I don't for a moment think that the Apostles' Creed or orthodox Christianity, as embodied in any particular institution at the present, are by any means adequate descriptions of the complexity of the reality of the universe.

Was it Einstein or some other great physicist of the twentieth century who said that reality is not only more complex than we understand? It is more complex than we will ever be capable of understanding. We simply don't possess the organs of sensibility or of observation that would permit us to comprehend whatever God is.

Milton says in his theological treatise concerning Christian doctrine that he describes God in the way in which God has chosen to describe himself to man in the Bible. Milton says that we don't think for a moment that God has eyes or hands or arms or legs or any of the other organs which are attributed to him in scripture, only that this is the way in which God has chosen to accommodate his illimitable reality to our extremely limited organs of perception and understanding.

JH: How do you feel about organized religion?

RP: I don't feel very good about it. I spent my childhood being reared by parents who were fitful communicants of the Methodist Church, in my mother's case, and the Baptist in the case of my father. So my brother and I were pulled back and forth in the family loyalty battles between Mother's church and Father's. I tried for some

years of my fervent adolescence to think of myself as an Episcopalian, which my father's family had been. Ultimately I joined, as an
adolescent, my mother's church, the Methodist Church in Raleigh. It,
however, didn't really serve me for long. I know that that's not what
a church is for; I don't think it's the prime duty of a church to serve
its communicants. However, my own great disgust as a young man in
the South with the stance white Protestantism took in relation to the
integration battles really was the final fact which made it impossible
for me to get any profound spiritual nourishment out of orthodox
church attendance. So it's really been thirty years since churchgoing
has meant much to me.

There are certainly sacraments of the church, especially the holy
sacrament of communion itself in which I intensely believe and upon
which I certainly lean at difficult moments of my life. But at the
times in recent years when I have tried to reinstitute churchgoing, I've
found that within a month I'm being asked to teach the Wednesday
night men's bible class and coach the boys' soccer team on Thursday
afternoons and come to the bake sale on Saturday. I'd join a country
club if I'd wanted those services.

JH: It seems that organized religion does have much more to do
with those kinds of, what to me are very secular social activities, than
it does with our real needs for communion with the supernatural.

RP: And the fact that the churches had to move into those
functions in our lives is one more testimony to the death of the
American family. In the lives of my parents the family served every
need imaginable for food and entertainment. You certainly didn't
need to go to the church to get dinner or to play bingo or to coach a
basketball team.

JH: Or to see and be seen.

RP: Or to see and be seen, exactly.

JH: Yes. Well, what would you say, if anything, to people who do
feel compelled to participate in that kind of outward pseudo-religion?

RP: I have absolutely no desire or even temptation to condemn
anyone who goes. I have friends whom I love and profoundly admire
who go every Sunday of their lives and often more than once a
week. I respect them and I admire their discipline. There's still a little
part of me that, more than once a month, wakes up or comes to at

about eleven on Sunday morning and says, "Why aren't you in church?"

JH: What do you say to yourself then?

RP: I say to myself that I spend a good deal of my week in prayer or in other kinds of activity which I know are distinctly religious or are distinctly identifiable as negotiations with the supernatural and that I don't feel the need for conducting them in the presence of similar minded folk in their best bibs and tuckers.

JH: Yes. And that in fact this kind of experience of the supernatural doesn't have anything to do with the social experience that is involved. What about the eruption, and maybe it hasn't really happened only in the past decade, but it seems to have become much more visible, of evangelism and an increased popularity of television evangelism?

RP: All that's very frightening and on the whole has been very bad for America as a republic. I'm not a great student of the effects of that kind of debased evangelism in the life of the nation, spiritual or political; but insofar as I understand at all what Jerry Falwell and his breed have meant to America, it's almost all been on the side of intolerance and ill-will amongst human beings rather than the reverse—which is what we're taught by Christ and by the whole Judeo-Christian tradition.

JH: Exactly. Well Jerry Falwell, in fact, is quite moderate compared to someone like Jimmy Swaggart.

RP: Jimmy Swaggart?

JH: He lives in Baton Rouge. And he openly preaches a gospel of repression and hatred of people who are different, who live and amuse themselves differently from the norm. He also openly condemns the Catholic Church. What do you make of the popularity of someone like this, who's built an immense fascist temple to himself in Baton Rouge? Has built a Bible College, an immense complex which looks like a backdrop Albert Speer would have raised for Hitler, and who packs this facility several times a week with thousands of people. I've even met a couple of them, and they seem like perfectly normal people. Swaggart, for instance, condemns women who wear shorts.

RP: Well, I don't make anything more of it than I would have made of the fact that some silly Florentines in the early Renaissance listened to religious fanatics and burned up their secular paintings.

There are always enough people in any given society who are featherbrained and guilt-ridden enough to listen to the latest religious charlatan who's on hand. So I don't think it's terrifying about the life of America as a nation. I think it's just one more testimony to the spiritual superficiality of most nations of people that these kinds of charlatans can always get together a huge audience and a large treasury for themselves.

JH: I have a friend who explains the success of such individuals by saying that it's simply that people are bored and want to be entertained in some way.

RP: Certainly it's a form of entertainment, and that's another thing that Protestantism and Catholicism have always been in the lives of southerners—church was their main form of dramatic entertainment and certainly of emotional aesthetic catharsis. I mean, even a Presbyterian can go to one of those scrubbed-down whitewashed pineboard tabernacles of theirs and come away feeling spiritually and aesthetically uplifted. I can certainly go to a black church and hear the shouting and the backtalk and come away feeling spiritually energized. But again the church is not the place that I want to go to or need to go to for either cheap theatrics or high drama in my life. Though I must say attendance at something like Christmas Eve Mass in the Basilica of the Nativity in Bethlehem which I attended some five years ago was certainly one of the high dramatic moments of my life.

So I think Christianity and numerous other of the respectable religions of the world are still capable of being, aesthetically, enormously transforming and transfiguring, but none of the churches that I attended as a child or that are available to me within an hour's drive of my home today seems capable of giving me that sort of self-transformation, self-enlargement. That very likely says at least as much about me as about the churches.

JH: Do you think being a serious writer involves a kind of awareness of a supernatural presence or a sense of drawing on the supernatural?

RP: It certainly does for me. I couldn't imagine being a writer or an artist of any sort if I weren't also a person whose bedrock beliefs are founded upon a powerful and traditionally Christian sense of the structure of reality. I would have to say that all of the great writers

whom I've personally known in my life—from Stephen Spender to
W. H. Auden to Eudora Welty to John Updike, Bernard Malamud,
Toni Morrison—have all been people who had personal profound
relationships with something that, for better or worse, could only be
called God. But very few of them were actual faithful communicants
of a particular church. All of them, I think, were people for whom
religion—in all those cases, either traditional Christianity or Judaism—is or was a powerful continuing, fertilizing force in their lives
and work.

JH: Do you think that is true also of the younger generation of
southern writers that's coming of age—the generation of, for instance, Jo Humphreys? Do they have that same sense of a spiritual
presence?

RP: I've never, I think, actually talked with people like Jo Humphreys or Dave Smith about it. It's my strong suspicion that they may
not have quite so orthodox or traditional a relationship with it as
people my age and older have, but I don't know any one of them
who, I think, would flat describe him or herself as an atheist. I think
they are all in some sense or other believers, in the sense of a fairly
straightforward belief or enlistment in the notion that we are ourselves creatures and not creators and that creaturehood implies a
relationship with visible and invisible reality which it's incumbent
upon us to attempt to understand and to accept and adhere to.

JH: Is it possible to write serious fiction without believing that? Is it
possible to be an atheist and write serious fiction?

RP: I wonder. I don't know. I'm trying to think of a serious atheist
who was ever a good writer, certainly not Tolstoy, certainly not
Dostoevski. You might look now at a great writer like Garcia Màrquez
who is indeed a Marxist, though there are Marxists who are capable
also of being believers. It's very hard to read the work of Garcia
Màrquez and imagine that he has absolutely no personal adherence
to some idea of the supernatural.

JH: I would say it is impossible for him not to believe in some sort
of supernatural. He depicts it as existing very palpably among us,
whether he admits it or not.

RP: And he may indeed have spoken to this in some essays or
interviews. I don't know but it would be very difficult to see how he
could have produced the work he's done and have told himself that

he was utterly inventing a universe as made and remade by the supernatural as his visible universe is.

JH: Do you see an affinity between southern writers and Latin American writers?

RP: No. I think, if anything, it tends to run the other way. People like Garcia Màrquez have talked about the influence of Faulkner on their own world view and how they, when they were young and reading Faulkner, felt a tremendous resemblance between their own brand of small-town provincial life and the kind of life portrayed in Faulkner. I think it's far more likely that they were reading southerners first than that southerners were reading them. But certainly when I read *A Hundred Years of Solitude,* I can see tremendous and lovable resemblances between his village life and my village life.

He's a marvelous writer. I know very little about other currently fashionable Latin American writers. I've read very little in the magical realists who are having such a rich reception right now. I think that *A Hundred Years of Solitude* is certainly a great novel, but I'm not someone who wants to sign aboard the current bandwagon which thinks it's the greatest novel ever written. I think if one stands it up beside *Anna Karenina* and *War and Peace,* one begins to get a slightly better sense of what the nature of its ambition and its achievement is, but I think it's a wonderful book and I wouldn't contest an atom of its power or energy.

JH: What other books that have been written in the past twenty-five years would you classify as outstanding?

RP: Novels, let's say, since the mid '60s, early '60s, that I would think of as really deserving a very big place in world literature? I would certainly place *A Hundred Years of Solitude.* I would place *Losing Battles* by Eudora Welty. I would have to place my own novels *The Surface of Earth* and its mate *The Source of Light.* I think perhaps that Anthony Powell's *Dance to the Music of Time* has been completed since 1960. I admire certainly the work of a number of other living writers. Toni Morrison is a great favorite of mine; Malamud was. Some of Updike's work, especially his early work I greatly admire; some of Philip Roth's.

JH: Which of Philip Roth's?

RP: I tremendously admire the early stories, which everyone loves. I think *Portnoy* is one of the great comic classics. It doesn't end very satisfactorily, but very few comedies manage to end very satisfactorily. It's not in the nature of comedy to end well.

The American novelist presently engaged in publishing whom I admire most is a novelist very different from me, Robert Stone. He's just published a new novel that I haven't read, but his *A Flag for Sunrise* and *Dog Soldiers* and *A Hall of Mirrors* strike me as being three marvelous novels of an imaginative and moral grandeur that I think sets his whole work very much in that elite company I was trying to enumerate a few minutes ago. I'm not sure he's yet done a single work which quite rises into that category, though *A Flag for Sunrise* comes very close, if not actually landing there. For me his great deficit lies in the unmitigated blackness, ghastliness, of his vision. If there's a milkcow in Robert Stone's world, be sure it's a three-legged cow. Thomas McGuane is a writer whom I tremendously admire as a comic novelist—a very serious one who, I think, has only got better and better as he's kept going; and he's now only in his mid-40s and writing better than ever.

JH: Is there something that all those writers have in common that you could describe, even the ones who are very different from you or from, say, Eudora Welty?

RP: Two things, I think, right off hand—one of which is a tremendous appetite for the world. They have a voracious susceptibility, a hunger for vulnerability to the whole world, to everything in it. They try not to leave anything out—some things more successfully than others, obviously depending upon the proclivities and skills of the writer. Secondly, some kind of innate and trained genius for architecture: the ability to build large and durably useful structures out of that appetite for life and that long and carefully acquired testimony to life.

JH: I remember you always used to say that writing really was a matter of getting your unconscious to work for you.

RP: I still say that, say it all the time; I say it this semester very hard to a class of fifteen Duke University seniors, all of whom are quite skillful writers of the well-made sketch and the well-made sensitive short story, but all of whom I'm trying to get to write a longish story or a novella. I'm finding that they are approaching it in an intense and constipated way, and they're trying to make every page perfect with its own wonderful little Joycean epiphany, and I'm trying to get them to relax and let a large story begin to manufacture itself in their own unconscious and to come out as an interesting and entertaining and useful piece of architecture. I'm not having much success so far in convincing them, but at least I can't say that they finished college without having someone who mentioned the existence of such a possibility anyway.

JH: You used to say that the unconscious is like dogs and children, it loves routine and hates surprises.

RP: I've repeated that until people can recite it with me in the audience now.

JH: One thing you taught me, and I've always been grateful to you for it, and have tried to spread the lesson, is that writing anything is simply a matter of making yourself go in and do it, even if you look at a blank page for two hours.

RP: Your "simply" is breathtaking. But yes, it's first of all a matter of making yourself available for X number of minutes a day until your mind finally gives up and says, "Okay, I quit; here it is." It's a matter of outstaring the page to a very large extent. And of being careful of your brain cells, as I keep having to point out to students who think of their bodies and brains as immortal and inexhaustible. When you're twenty-two years old, you've lived nearly a third of your life expectancy, and you've put some wear on the mechanism. The mechanism can only stand so much more abuse in the way of what are now called controlled substances and recreational drugs—all of which, of course, include liquor, my generation's often disastrous recreational drug.

JH: It's the present generation's recreational drug too.

RP: Beginning to be—though at a place that's as wealthy as Duke, there's a lot of cocaine around.

JH: Yes. Well, of course that's the expensive alternative. Very often people associate the vocation of writing with a kind of dissolution and self-destructiveness, a kind of self-immolation in alcohol, and you don't believe that is true at all?

RP: Absolutely not. I think that one can, especially in American literature, make up a long list of the burnt-out, the self-burnt-out, the big novelists of the 1920s and '30s, Fitzgerald, Hemingway, Faulkner, and Wolfe, who were all alcoholics far too early in their lives. Their great work is over by the time they're forty, which is a shameful disaster inflicted on them by their own inability to understand what they were doing to a very fragile gift that was given them, the human brain and the human body.

American poetry is filled with examples of wonderfully gifted burnt-out men, not so many women—women have been much better caretakers of their own organisms—from John Berryman to Robert Lowell to Randall Jarrell and Hart Crane. The list is near infinite of poets who have blown themselves out of the water by the time they were forty. In the case of several of them, they were contending with powerful neurotic or psychotic syndromes which were to some extent wished on them by their own metabolic organisms and not by personal abuse, but I think there are very few cases of the profligate dissolute writer in America which can't be chalked up to bad stewardship, bad behavior.

JH: It's funny that in Europe, I think, writers tend to be much less associated with this kind of dissolution.

RP: Oh, exactly. European literature and music is filled with geniuses that are doing their best work when they're seventy or eighty years old. One of the great spectacles of the last couple of years has been the tricentennials of Handel and Bach and to realize that these two vast geniuses were doing their best work as very old and ill and afflicted men, Handel blind and Bach blind and greatly suffering; Verdi writing his greatest operas when he's 70 and 80; Yeats writing some of his greatest poems in his old age; Mann writing some of his greatest fiction when he's in his 70s. It's one of the great joys of European literature to see the triumph of the carefully lived life in art.

JH: Do you think American writers have tended to dissolution because American culture has somehow viewed this as an outlandish and somehow unacceptable vocation and made them feel guilty for pursuing it?

RP: I never felt that. I think Hart Crane felt it because he did grow up in a very repressive upper mid-western puritan background. I was certainly never made to feel that I had done anything bizarre in choosing to be an artist, though I grew up in resolutely southern Protestant middle-class surroundings. I can believe that some people were, Bill Styron says he was, but I never was. I don't know what produced the reaction.

Certainly all the novelists whom I named in the '20s and '30s were themselves victims or veterans of the First World War, which God knows was a catastrophic experience to have had to survive as a young man—though Faulkner's First World War was hardly so intense a matter as Hemingway's and Fitzgerald's, involved no actual combat; and I would guess that Wolfe never went at all. A number of the writers of the generation just before mine were victims of the Second World War and Korean War experience; and lots of younger writers now are victims of Vietnam, though so few upper middle-class white males ever had to go. I don't really know where the necessity for drink comes from in American art; but certainly insofar as it comes from anywhere, it comes from French writers like Baudelaire and Rimbaud or Verlaine who might well have warned anybody away.

JH: There are in France poets like René Char who've been active in this century and have not followed that example.

RP: Not at all. Nor Valéry who might just as well have been a banker as far as the regularity and care with which he lived. We have a few older ones in America. We've got the beautiful spectacle of Wallace Stevens going to the insurance company every morning; we've got the beautiful spectacle of William Carlos Williams going to the doctor's office every day for all those decades; T. S. Eliot going to Faber & Faber every day to put in a day at the publisher's desk. So we're not without wonderful specimens of the enduring writer. Certainly Eudora Welty amongst living writers now, or Malamud who's just died, are wonderful testimonies to care and persistence and respect for the human organism.

JH: Is there a particular reason why there have been so many extraordinarily gifted southern *women* writers like Eudora Welty, Flannery O'Connor, Katherine Anne Porter and a whole new generation, Jo Humphreys, Gail Godwin, Anne Tyler, Bobbie Ann Mason, Ellen Gilchrist?

RP: I don't really know except to say that I think the South preserved a respected notch right through my early manhood for the smart woman who wanted to drop out of the baby and kitchen world and just do what she knew how to do. Many of those women were single, of course, because no one ever asked them to be anything else; they didn't get asked to be married. But the ones who did drop out and go on to become writers provide us with some of the great names in American fiction—Flannery O'Connor, Katherine Anne Porter (who though she had three or four husbands and numbers of lovers, was to a very large extent the sort of prototypical unmarried woman genius).

I think I mentioned O'Connor and Welty of the single women who took all that time and energy and put it into art. Jo Humphreys, of course, Anne Tyler, and Gail Godwin are women who have seemed to have good long-term marriages; but I think the South kept alive always the possibility of that sort of life for that occasional woman.

One of my most important teachers, when I was in elementary school, was a woman called Crichton Davis in Warrenton, North Carolina, in 1947, who taught me in the eighth grade. She had herself written good fiction, some of which had been published in the O. Henry anthology. This excited me greatly when I was fourteen years old, to be able to work with a woman who had had an early sad marriage and sort of dropped out of that old particular battle and put the rest of her life into thoughtful and aesthetic pursuits. She was a very early model for me of the possibility that one could live a life in art in the best sense of the word.

So there were always these emblematic women around the southern landscape, many of whom got not much further than being wonderful ninth-grade English teachers, but that was a tremendously important and fruitful thing to be.

JH: When you refer to the numerous lovers and husbands Katherine Anne Porter had, do you think there's a relationship between literary or artistic activity and erotic energy?

RP: Oh, I think there is to the extent that almost all, not all by any means, but almost all of the really good writers I've known have been erotically very intensely energetic people. There does seem to be, as a sort of general rule, a high level of appetite and energy of all sorts but certainly of the sexual sort in great creative artists. Great creators and performing artists are rather famously passionate in their approach to the visible world, and it's fuel for their work.

JH: Well, in that case how do you explain the prominence of celibate, or I guess I should say unattached, women in the history of southern literature?

RP: It's a fascinating question which so far—because some of the

women are very much alive and with us still, thank God—hasn't
been publicly asked. I think the whole subject of celibate women in
the arts in general has yet to be investigated very profoundly. I know
that some feminist critics are beginning to discuss the matter; but it's
far from having a really widely-gauged study, I mean, from Sappho
down through Jane Austen and Emily Dickinson, Emily Brontë,
through Flannery O'Connor to now—the secular nun who has gone
on generating out of her loneliness, bypassed as it were by the
mainline of western tradition and culture, who has nonetheless
woven a richly central artistic response to a world which has for all
intents and purposes declared her useless to itself. I don't know how
they did it. I don't know how those wonderful old English and math
teachers kept us all going through years and years of elementary and
high school in the 1930s and '40s when they reigned supreme as
the shapers of intellect and civilization in the South and in a good
deal of the rest of the country.

   JH: Yes, an awful lot of those women have been very influential
teachers. You had a very influential teacher at Duke whose name was
William Blackburn. Could you talk about what was so extraordinary
about him—because he taught, not only you, but William Styron and
Fred Chappell, Jo Humphreys and a great number of people.

   RP: Jo Humphreys and I were discussing it just last week, and
Blackburn's been dead now a little over ten years and his second
wife, who herself was a marvelous person, just died last month. It's
only now that we're beginning to be able to look back at the rather
seismic phenomenon of Bill Blackburn and try to understand what
fueled him and what produced the quite considerable and unquestioned impact that he had upon so many good writers. Bill Styron
and Jo and I, I think at separate times, have talked and agreed that
by measurable pedagogical standards Blackburn really wasn't a
teacher at all—at least insofar as a teacher of writing is concerned.
Anyone who's ever read the few little attempts that Blackburn published in the way of essays or critical articles knows that he could
barely write two consecutive sentences.

   There was a peculiar muscle-bound awkwardness to his written
work. He wrote wonderful letters but they've yet to be published. I
hope someone will quite soon pull together a volume at least of his

letters to young writers whom he shepherded along through college and in the years thereafter.

He taught by a kind of incommunicable and unrepeatable sort of magic, which was the magic of so many great teachers of that older generation. It was a magic that was based upon their miraculous rarity in the culture itself.

What was extraordinary—most extraordinary for me about Blackburn, as I think it was for Styron and Jo Humphreys and a number of other people like Fred Chappell—was the fact that we encountered in him, for the first time, a quite obviously adult and sane, if rather fragile, man, of unquestioned virility, for whom works of art, literary art, were of supreme importance in the enjoyment and understanding of life and in the navigation of life's most dangerous rapids.

Though I had had wonderful, as I say, women teachers in elementary and high school, this was the first time I had really encountered a man who was capable of communicating that sense of urgency and excitement. He was a marvelous reader, for one thing. He was a great theatrical reader who had one of the great bass-baritone voices. Without affectation or theatricality, Blackburn could read you a Shakespearean sonnet or a Spenserian epithalamion and take twenty minutes of class doing it and leave you as moved or shaken as you might have been by, or even more so than by a reading by Gielgud or Laurence Olivier, who were alive and flourishing at the same time.

It just was of tremendous importance to young southerners like us who had grown up in a society where those skills were by no means common nor praised by the society. My own parents were literate but certainly not literary; their own education had stopped with the eleventh grade which was as far as high school went in North Carolina in their time. They encouraged my own literary interests; they never for a moment tried to discourage or ridicule them, but the excitement of someone like Blackburn would have been inconceivable to them.

It was also very important for me that I started writing with Blackburn the year after my father died. Oddly enough Blackburn was very much the same size and, in his general demeanor, very like my father. He was nearly the same age as my father, a year or two older; so that likeness was important for his particular impact in my life, in my early twenties.

And he invested passionate amounts of energy in us. His own first marriage had broken up shortly before I came to study with him, and he was basically alone. He lived alone for twenty years before meeting his second wife. A wonderful woman who gave him nearly a decade of very happy years at the end of his life. And very dangerously and often very frustratingly, he invested huge amounts of emotional energy in his students—especially his male students. He once said to me twenty-five years ago, when I came to teach at Duke, "Be very careful of investing much in female writing-students; they never go on to write." Well, since that time two Duke women have—Anne Tyler and Jo Humphreys—and others are in the process of beginning now. But at the time of which he was speaking, at the time of his own career, he was basically correct. Bright young women who were interested in writing tended to go off and vanish into domesticity.

I think his betting on his male students was not so much a key to any psychic erotic need of his own but simply a realistic estimate of what was in fact likely to be a good investment. So he really taught by magic and by a kind of restrained and disciplined and entirely genuine form of theatrics.

Good teaching is at best always a form of performing, and the great teachers whom I've had in my American and English lives and whom I've observed amongst my colleagues at Duke have almost always been in some sense or other great actors, and Blackburn was certainly supreme in that respect.

JH: How did he actually go about teaching writing? How did he do it on a day to day basis?

RP: As I've gone on teaching myself and watching certain other quite competent poets and novelists and playwrights teach writing, I've realized that Blackburn wasn't really a very good teacher of writing. He wasn't very skillful; he himself didn't know how to write. He did, however, have a very good built-in radar for what was good and what was bad, what was promising, in amateur fiction and never tried to deal much in the criticism of student poetry. He said he didn't know about that. But he had read an enormous amount of fiction in his life, and he knew a good story when he saw one, at least if it was good in a particular kind of way that touched him—a sort of basic nineteenth century realism, early twentieth century realism (his favorite novelist was Conrad).

We would read other people's short stories in the two semesters in which I started writing with him. In the only writing class I ever took, in the first semester we read the stories in Brooks and Warren's *Understanding Fiction*; and in the second semester we read Forster's *A Passage to India* and Eudora Welty's *Collected Short Stories* because she was coming to campus to pay a visit late that winter. We would on alternate days discuss the fiction of masters and then our own fiction. We started out writing short sketches from various angles—a sketch in which we explored the problem of point of view, a sketch in which we discussed people and related places. I remember those as two of the earlier assignments, and we gradually built from there into the writing of one large short story each semester. In my first semester, I wrote a story called "Michael Egerton" which remains the most anthologized story I ever wrote.

JH: Does that surprise you?

RP: Oh, I think anthologies are always surprising in what they pick. In the case of "Michael Egerton," I think it's so anthologized because it's one of those rare stories about pre-adolescent children which is both serious and good and in which nobody says "fuck" so that you get to put it in all kinds of junior high-school anthologies without offending any parents or schoolboards.

JH: That leads me to another question. I know that the matter of explicit sex, sexual content or language in fiction is something that you have addressed before in an essay that appeared in *Esquire,* I think. How do you feel about that? You think there is a place for it in serious fiction?

RP: Very much so and I think it's the only serious advantage, new advantage, that's been handed to fiction writers and poets in the second half of the twentieth century. We can now basically say anything we want about Eros in a novel and not be arrested or banned in Boston, though the state of North Carolina has recently passed a deplorable censorship law that now affects almost entirely pornographic movies but may soon affect God knows what else before the Supreme Court gets around to striking it down.

JH: That law has to do with community standards.

RP: Community standards which are themselves horrendously shaky matters on which to base anything—I mean, who's gauging the standards? But I do think that our freedom now to explore the secret and public sexual needs and expressions of literary characters is one of the great new freedoms that we have.

I certainly, from *The Surface of Earth* on, have tried to use that freedom richly and responsibly in both fiction and in the more personal poems that I've written simultaneously. *Kate Vaiden,* herself, though to a large extent a woman of her time in what she will and will not describe, is rather free in her description of what sexual contact has meant to her in her life. She's funny about it, but I think she is also very honest about it.

I think we would be greatly enriched in our understanding of Madame Bovary or Anna Karenina or Tess of the D'Urbervilles, for instance, had we been able to know more of their sexuality. As it is we know a great deal about it by implication from the sort of buried hints that Tolstoy and Hardy and Flaubert have managed to secrete into the texture of the fiction within the standards of their time; but we could fruitfully have been told a good deal more since all three books are to a large extent about the collision of personal sexuality with societal standards. We really know very little about what Emma Bovary thought sex consisted of. We do know much more about Anna, as a matter of fact; but with Tess again we have a hard time imagining what this force which so distorts and ultimately wrecks her life means to her.

JH: Would you say that the prohibition against any kind of explicit discussion in fiction of characters' sexual habits has cramped the style of fiction writers more recently?

RP: Oh, very much so. I can think of wonderful novels that would have been considerably richer had their writer felt personally or publicly free to do or say more. The work of E. M. Forster, as wonderful as it is, suffers badly from his inability to discuss what it was in the world that erotically fascinated him. I think even a writer like Hemingway suffers, free as he seemed to be for his time, from an inability to be sexually candid in his work.

JH: I've heard it said that editors tend to be more prudish than the general public. Do you believe that?

RP: I think in general that's very true.

JH: Why do you think that is?

RP: I've no idea, but I have noticed that editors in general, and my editor with whom I have as happy a relationship as I know of in the history of American fiction, tend to be more nervous about sexual matters than most of my readers are. Though I must say my editor's never vetoed me in anything that I wished to publish that had any sort of sexual content. I know that nonetheless he has at times seemed uncomfortable with aspects of the work that didn't strike me as discomforting at all.

But I think one can very quickly overestimate the real degree of sexual freedom that exists among intelligent and literate Americans. We are told and we officially believe that there's a great deal of new freedom in the land; but the minute we try to employ that freedom, we quickly find out that a number of people are rapidly and shame-facedly rushing for the fire doors.

JH: On the subject of editors, a lot of writers don't get along at all well with editors or think well of them. You think your editor is an exception to that?

RP: My editor is a miraculous exception. He's little talked about when editors are mentioned in articles or essays nowadays, but Harry Ford, at Knopf and at Atheneum, has gone from being unquestionably the best and most elegant of designers to also quietly and quite unobtrusively one of the very best editors in modern history. The number of poets whom he's assembled at Atheneum is unquestionably the finest set of poets that any American publisher has had in a single stable. The two or three novelists whom he's edited, I think, are an especially elegant and resourceful group. And he's operated very much in the way that Bill Blackburn operated as a teacher—by a kind of personal radar, a kind of personal magic. He sees his function as basically that of an encourager and an excellent valet, someone who lets the artist make the art and then sees his purpose to be the correction of minor errors or typographical mistakes and the presentation of the book in as attractive and as readable a fashion as possible.

You can't imagine how rare a set of gifts that is in American publishing unless you yourself have gone far into the matter. I find so often when I've dealt with other editors or heard my friends describe their battles with editors that again what one is so frequently faced with is men, and occasionally women, who themselves badly wished to be novelists or poets, who failed in the attempt and are now attempting to write by proxy, as it were, through other more fortunate and more disciplined creatures. Someone said to me the other day, "My editor's just had a nervous breakdown." He added, "I always thought the writers were the people who were supposed to be flaky, and the editors and the agents were supposed to be the rocks of Gibraltar." I really couldn't agree more; one does tend to notice that editors are tremendously fickle in their job affiliations. If you start following an editor around American publishing houses, you're going to have a very gypsy career, as my first agent pointed out to me twenty-three years ago when my first editor left Atheneum and asked me to follow him elsewhere. He said, "Hiram Haydn's been to five places in ten years; how many jumps are you prepared to make with him?" I realized I wasn't prepared to make any, and so I had a very unhappy break with Hiram Haydn, a fine man.

I think one of the interesting little sidelights that could be investigated in contemporary fiction is the situation which has been created when a given writer has tried to follow a beloved editor from house to house to house.

JH: You have had an extraordinary relationship with Atheneum. They've published all your books.

RP: They've published all my major titles since 1962, which has got to be one of the longest unbroken careers of any presently active American novelist. John Updike has been at Knopf for about as long; but if I think of those writers who are my own contemporaries, then we're about the only two I can think of.

JH: Has your relationship with Atheneum changed since they were acquired by Scribner's?

RP: Macmillan. No, it hasn't at all. I've gone on dealing almost entirely with Harry Ford and some of the younger people who've come into the firm, whom I've found sympathetic and encouraging to my continuing work there. I go on publishing with them and feeling happy with them, and I have at least three or four other manuscripts waiting in line to be published by them.

JH: You mentioned Eudora Welty a few minutes ago. Is she the single most important contemporary influence on your work?

RP: Eudora is one of my two or three oldest and dearest friends in the world; and she's certainly, as I've already made clear, one of the

four or five writers that I most revere of those now living and
working, but I wouldn't say that Eudora has been a powerful influence on my work for many years now.

I don't mean to imply that I've moved on to better things. I think
that once a writer becomes *himself*, rather early in his career, if he is
a serious ongoing creative artist, then he is basically his own influence. It is indeed really the case, if academic critics could only get it
through their beans, that writers have continually been influenced
more by the observable external world than they have been by other
literary objects. I tremendously disagree with some presently fashionable theorists on that question. Literature continues almost always to
be made out of the visible world and not out of the cannibalizing of
other works of literature.

JH: So you would say that Eudora Welty has served you more in
the way of an example when you were young?

RP: An example of excellence and of a writer who took the
properties of the world that I grew up in and had already made great
works of art of them. I as a teenager could look at her work and say,
it can be done; my world is a world which can fuel the creation of
great works of art.

JH: I can't remember what Mississippi Delta writer it was, maybe
Shelby Foote, who said that there've been so many writers who
came out of the Delta because when they were children, growing up
in the Delta, living writers were around to serve as examples, so
that it seemed possible to become one.

RP: That's very likely true. The fact, as I mentioned, that my
eighth grade teacher herself had published a short story in the O.
Henry volume in the 1920s or '30s was for me an extremely important example of "It can be done" by the lady who lives down the
street and who grades your homework every night. That was in
a small town in eastern North Carolina of no more than two thousand souls, 70 percent of them black. So it was a very important act
of literal pedagogy for me that Crichton Davis existed when I needed
her.

JH: Do you think it's harder or easier at the present moment for a
young writer to get his or her first work published?

RP: I think it's getting a little easier again. In the late seventies and
early eighties there was an alarming cutback by the good serious

publishers in the number of first volumes of fiction, first novels and short stories, that were being published. When I was on the National Endowment for the Arts Literature panel, we did a survey which showed a really alarming cutback in the numbers of first novels being published. But now with the arrival of a large new population of early thirtyish readers, we're getting again a nice new crop of good first novels and short stories.

JH: To go back to what you were saying about criticism earlier, is criticism necessarily a kind of parasitical thing or can it be creative in its own right?

RP: I know that this is an assertion that critics are in the rather desperate process of trying to advance now, the suggestion that their own work is itself a legitimate art object. Certainly there've been times in my life when for years on end I functioned basically as a critic, but I've never for a moment thought that criticism was a primary skill, a primary literary activity. I tremendously distrust those graduate students who would prefer to read an essay about *Paradise Lost* to reading *Paradise Lost*.

I find it very difficult when I teach Milton to senior English majors to make them realize that the paper I want from them is not a research paper but is a critical paper in which they themselves respond directly to a great poem. Very simply, they're trained and ready to go back and cannibalize the shelves one more time, and I tell them that just bores me. They're such timorous souls; they've been trained to be, and the good ones know exactly how to write a nifty little research paper by disemboweling *PMLA* on the subject of Milton. They know I'm asking them to grow up and to stand on their own two feet in public, and this terrifies anybody the first few times they're asked to do it in their lives.

But to get back to the question of criticism as a prime art. I can think of three or four volumes of criticism that were very important in the formation of my own love of poetry and my understanding of it. They're all famous and by now looked upon as rather old-fashioned works, but Bradley's *Shakespeare* and H.D.F. Kitto's *Greek Tragedy* were true revelations for me. But they were revelations, I must say—not to sound condescending—when I was a student. I just haven't felt the need in recent years to read Dr. X's revelations on Milton. I'm much more interested in Milton than I am in what yet another academic has to say about it. Which is not to say that I don't think there are extraordinary clarifications that can still be made of passages in a writer as enormous as Milton or Shakespeare, and I'm always happy when I come across one, but I find that an increasingly rare pleasure, especially now that critics are attempting a kind of stellar status for themselves. But, alas, one of the first things they should do is to look at their sales figures and realize that nobody else thinks the criticism is very well worth reading.

JH: But doesn't poetry have similarly low sales figures?

RP: It does indeed.

JH: I guess one of the things that bothers me the most about academic criticism is the lingering tendency, and it's very much institutionalized in publications like *PMLA,* to make criticism into a kind of programmatic stultification of literature, a demonstration of how many references to previous works, to every previous commentary on the subject can be made. I guess I'm stubbornly naive but it surprises me to find that still maybe 90 percent of the academic community believes that criticism is not a really strong response to a text primarily, but rather a very boring academic exercise.

RP: A reshuffling of the marginalia one more time.

JH: Yes. And this is very much what the Modern Language Association seems to wish to stand for, to enforce.

RP: Well, it's a very ancient concept. It certainly goes back to Greek rhetoricians and Roman and medieval scholars. Scholars of that narrow historical sort have been indispensable keepers of all sorts of flames. A good deal of that kind of conservative, conservationist-type criticism is always necessary and always welcome. I think it's unfortunate that it has overwhelmed American academic study to the exclusion of other more exciting and fertile kinds. It's the thing which British critics and scholars continue to find most amusing and sad about American academic scholars and literary study.

JH: What's that?

RP: This drowning in the trivia of the past, the inability to choose between the opinions of Professor X and Professor Y in 1918 and 1943. They're all laid down cheek by jowl as though they're equally deserving of memory and study, when in fact in the history of Milton studies in America there are probably about four people who are really worth continuing to read, and they can be read in a matter of a week.

JH: Who're those people?

RP: I don't want to get into the living; but I would think, amongst the dead, you certainly have James Holly Hanford and William Riley Parker and Allan Gilbert, most any Miltonist would agree with those three names.

JH: What do you read on a day to day basis?

RP: Very little. I read voraciously as a child, an adolescent, a college and graduate student; but since I began in the late '50s spending an enormous amount of time writing myself, I find that my reading consists to a large extent of perusal of magazines and fairly short things. If I'm going to read anything substantial and time-consuming, it almost invariably tends to be history or biography, always my favorite kinds of reading. I read very little new fiction because there's not much in the new fiction I've encountered that really interests me. I think anybody, once they're past middle-age or their late thirties, has really acquired his or her own pantheon of great writers; and we, of necessity, have to begin to close down. If I read every deserving young writer who's been published in America in the last ten years, I simply would never have had time to keep my address book up to date, much less write any fiction of my own. I do know good writers like Anne Tyler and Jo Humphreys who seem to read everything that's published. I simply don't see how they do it.

JH: Do you read mystery novels?

RP: Not very much anymore. I went through a period in the '70s of reading mystery novels rather voraciously because I was looking to purify my own concept of narrative, and they seemed to me excellent exemplars of the lean and straightforward, rapid, compelling narrative. But they finally didn't turn out to be very nutritious over the long haul for me.

JH: What do you make of the phenomenon of the drugstore novel, the Harlequin Romance, these novels that appear to be mass-manufactured and which are consumed in vast numbers by, I think, a largely female audience.

RP: Shop girls on buses, as far as I can see. Oh, I think they're just an ancient phenomenon of popular fiction that was as present in the eighteenth century as it is today. I'm not alarmed by it at all except insofar as there's the occasional human being whose vision of life seems formed by that sort of simplistic stereotypical depiction of reality, to the later pain of that individual or that individual's husband or children. But it doesn't alarm me that Danielle Steele sells more books than Toni Morrison.

JH: It is alarming, though, to find reasonably intelligent people who seem to think that there is no difference between what Danielle Steele does and what Toni Morrison does, or who are not sure what the difference would be if there is one.

RP: Well, I wouldn't call those people "reasonably intelligent." The fact that those sorts of people are in the majority doesn't suggest that they are intelligent. Unintelligence is always the majority.

JH: Don't you think though that those novels, those popular novels, do really inflict damage in people's lives?

RP: I don't know. I couldn't say that I've ever really known anybody who was damaged that way. Emma Bovary is the only person I know who's ruined by bad reading.

JH: But Emma Bovary is a very believable instance.

RP: I think she's a believeable instance, and I can imagine that there are American housewives sixty years old today whose lives were made worse by a generation of soap opera watching or listening. We seem to be discussing women entirely. I can't think of any men who've been ruined by books, though Hitler probably was and others that are slipping my mind. But men have not tended to be the consumers of popular Harlequin-type fiction in any case. I think what men have tended to consume in a comparable way is pornography, and I'm not at all convinced of the badness of that. I think it's basically a dead-end masturbatory kind of indulgence which seldom affects the way men behave once they've left the lonely room that contains their pornography collection.

JH: Is writing in any sense erotic, do you think? This takes me back to the question about the numerous unattached older women who have become known as writers of serious fiction in America.

RP: Not for me. I've never needed to get my Eros out of a written page, thank God. The world has obliged me richly and amazingly. And I don't know of any serious writer who I feel gets that sort of reward in or from his work. Someone might come to mind if I really race through the files, but certainly for me and the writers I admire, I detect no such thing going on.

JH: You've said that your writing in general is much more influenced by experience than it is by other literature, but the style of any writer has to be something that is developed and acquired through many early years of imitation of examples. Your style has changed a lot over the years. Could you talk about why and how it's changed?

RP: I disagree with your premise. I don't think that one's style is necessarily made primarily out of works of literature. Don't forget, none of us begins to read until at least seven or eight years old, if not twelve or thirteen, so the world has already had a terrific inning at us before we ever even encounter books.

JH: So you think parental influence is significant in the evolution of style?

RP: I was tremendously influenced by my parents, both of whom were wonderful talkers, vivid users of the English language. They grew up in highly vocal families who had already learned to convert their vision of the world into interesting, well-made narrative expression—always oral, never written, except in an occasional letter, and their letters are pale reminders of the richness of their oral performance. So I think, before books ever began to influence me seriously, the basic "style" with which I began to write was a set of verbal responses that had been implanted in my brain by my parents, and friends, and relatives.

I think that certainly, as I began to write, there were times when a similarity of subject matter or of a situation in a given fictional work might tip me toward rhetoric in which I perhaps reminded a sophisticated reader of some other writer that he'd heard—Mark Twain, Hemingway, Sidney Lanier's *The Boy's King Arthur*—but my own quite sincere, and, I don't think simply self-defensive, reply to that has always been that I think a serious artist's language is made out of the artist's contact with *spoken* language, his or her relations with parents and siblings and family and out of the very earliest readings, which are almost never in what is called serious literature but almost always children's books.

I luckily had my father's sisters, who started giving me—long before I had any standards of my own—excellent books to read: *The Arabian Nights, Alice in Wonderland, The Boy's King Arthur, Treas-*

ure Island, Robinson Crusoe. My own earliest approaches to language were formed by my parents and my family and by those good books which my father's sisters had endowed me with for birthdays and Christmas up until that point in late childhood, early adolescence, when I began to develop some taste of my own.

By then that taste was guided by good teachers who would simply say, "Why don't you read *Anna Karenina?* Why don't you go read *Madame Bovary?*" Or by simple expedience, such as, when I was thirteen years old, joining the Book-of-the-Month Club and beginning to acquire a set of the Ten Greatest Novels of the World as selected by W. Somerset Maugham. When one's young, the making of that kind of list is always fascinating, "Hey, wow, these are the ten best novels ever written!" Well, they weren't of course. But they were certainly ten very fine novels, and I sat down and read those when I was thirteen and fourteen.

I think one lights one's way as best one can at any stage in life, and I'm sure that anyone who wished really to understand a writer's influences would not proceed as most academic critics do and book journalists do, by picking a line in X which sounds like an earlier line in Y but by really seriously investigating a given writer's biography and finding out what that writer was reading in the formative pre-literary stages of his career during which his imagination was being formed along with his unconscious sense of language and the possibilities of language. I think anything that comes later is very unlikely to make any sort of serious inroad. I never read anything substantial of Faulkner's until I was twenty-one years old, so I think the frequently diagnosed influence of Faulkner in my early work couldn't be less accurate. Faulkner and I sound alike occasionally because we're describing, in its native rhythms, the same civilization.

JH: Well, it's unquestionably true. I've had the same experience, that people from another culture, usually the North, are inclined to see people who grew up hearing a southern cadence of voice and who reflect that cadence in the way they write as having been influenced by this or that prior southern writer who also was influenced by that same cadence of voice.

RP: I know. It's just one more form of ignorance to which serious writers are subjected, and there's nothing we can do about it except wait for time to take care of fools.

JH: What impulse is reflected in that desire to pigeon-hole some-one? To classify a story or a novel as being in such-and-such a vein and then dismiss it without any effort at understanding? To say, "Oh, this is influenced by such and such?"

RP: Laziness and ignorance—nothing else.

JH: It's an extremely common impulse.

RP: Of course it is. It's found amongst chaired professorships at major universities, so why wouldn't it be found in lesser mortals?

JH: You mentioned the importance of a writer's auditory memo-ries a minute ago. Would you describe the process of writing, as some writers have, as the transcription of a "voice" that you hear almost dictating?

RP: Anne Tyler has always spoken of a voice that she hears just above her right or left ear, I've forgotten which it is. I don't think of myself as getting any sort of direct dictation. I do know that whenever I've written dialogue, I've always found that it comes to me far more rapidly than anything else because, again, I was taught to talk and to write by people who were marvelous talkers, so the one thing I always know about all my characters is exactly how they talk—which is one reason I think I can write plays rather rapidly. They're all people talking and, though they certainly don't talk in plays the way they talk in real life, there is a more than casual relationship between human speech and dramatic speech.

JH: To me *Love and Work* is one of the most fascinating novels that you've written. Maybe that's because I've read it within the last year, knowing that it was the only one of your novels that I had not read, so I went out and got it and read it knowing that we were going to do this interview. I found it very compelling, but one of the grimmest, bleakest novels I've read in a while. Both of the characters are fascinating, Eborn and his wife.

RP: I imagined them confronting a crisis in Eborn's life which is the death of his mother and the closing down of that whole parental world that is so important to middle-class Americans in our time. It doesn't happen to coincide with a particular crisis in his wife's life, but it does become a crisis in her life simply because she happens to be his wife at a time when he's going onto the emotional and spiritual rocks.

My agent, Diarmuid Russell, wrote to me when my mother died in

1965 when I was 33 years old, and he said—he then was in his own late fifties or early sixties—"Reynolds, I think you'll find it very strange when you have time to realize that now there's no backstop; the older generation is gone, you're *it,* and the clock is now counting for you." And it does become very strange, I think, for any child whose parents have been emotionally an important factor in his life, as has been the case with most middle-class Americans. The final vanishing of the parental generation is a very rocky passage. It certainly was for me, and *Love and Work* was the most immediate visible response to that passage in my own life.

JH: You seem to imply that being a writer as a vocation and life with another human being are not really compatible ends. Am I wrong to infer that?

RP: I don't think you're wrong. I think that the statement in the novel is made, as all statements are in my fiction, strictly within terms of particular characters in a particular human narrative context so I would not say that *Love and Work* is a guide, or meant to be a guide, to modern marriage or modern anything else. It's the story of Thomas and Jane Eborn in nineteen-sixty-whatever.

In fact a student of mine who was in great personal and marital difficulty phoned me shortly after *Love and Work* appeared, late at night, and said, "Do you really mean what you say in the novel?" And I—it was late and I was bored—said, "Oh, yes, of course, I do." And he committed suicide a few weeks later. Someone later told me, "What you said to Allen about *Love and Work* was very important to him late in his life." I wrote a poem about that which appeared in *Vital Provisions.*

It appalls me to think that I participated in any way in someone's own self-destructive impulses, but I think it is a great fault of readers everywhere in the world, not just in America, to believe that novels are guides to life. The Greeks thought that Homer was a guide to life but he wasn't—Homer was to a very large extent telling a good story to earn his supper. The same is true of me.

I do think, however, to try to face your question a little more candidly head on, that if one looks at the marital history of most distinguished American writers, one can't say very much for the hopes of emotional intimacy and contingency between an obsessed good writer and a mate who happens not to be that.

JH: Is that because of the obsessive way in which serious writers tend to work or think about work?

RP: I think it's partly because of that. It's partly because the literal scheduling of any creative work is inimical to normal human scheduling. The family, as we've invented it, is largely based upon the existence of a father who works from nine to five and is home and available the rest of the time. Writers very seldom operate that way, as performing artists also very seldom operate that way. I wouldn't say it is a difficulty of writers specifically, but of creative intellects of all sorts whose great, great obsession in life happens to be their work. That's very, very dangerous to emotional intimacy.

JH: Why?

RP: Because very few mates can, over a long term, deal with the fact that the other mate has something in his or her life which is more important than the mating, the matehood. That just happens to be the statement that is perpetually being made by an obsessive worker to his or her mate, "There's something that matters more to me than you do."

JH: Would you say then that writing has been the most important thing in your life?

RP: I'd say it's been the thing that's brought me the second most pleasure in my life.

JH: What's brought the most?

RP: The most pleasure's been brought to me by love, by the marvelous people that I've been intimately involved with for over thirty years now in my life. Writing's been the second best thing to that. I've never lived with a particular person for longer than four or five years in the last thirty, but that doesn't to me seem like any form of tragedy, and even now, when I'm faced with a life in which I depend upon help from other human beings, it doesn't seem to me at all a catastrophe that I didn't enlist, early in my life, someone who would later become a handservant—which is, alas, what a mate very often has to turn out to be in a long-term relationship.

I'd much rather purchase that kind of care in the world than to have it forced upon someone all unbeknownst but after years of loyalty. One of the nicest things I can say about my life is that I've loved a good many people, been loved by a good many people, and that in all these years of adult life, I'm still in close contact and in intimate friendship with all but two or three of the people I've ever loved. I'm not someone who's lost or broken off relations with people who've been dear to me, and that's been an enormous continuing source of pleasure. Work has been the more reliable pleasure certainly, and it's been a very great pleasure indeed. So love and work are for me the great pleasures of life in that order, far surpassing all other pleasures.

JH: Your teaching, is that something that's very important to you?

RP: I think, on balance, teaching has been very important to me, and I consider it part of my work—it's the second-most-important work that I've done. I've taught now steadily for twenty-eight years with leaves and sabbaticals. Since 1963, thereabouts, I've only taught for one semester a year, which has been very lucky for me as a writer. But it is very important to me as a single man with no children that I have at least a few months in each year in which I am brought into forced contact with younger people in my civilization.

I think now, paradoxically, that I, as a childless bachelor, have more of a continuing and mutually fertilizing relationship with young people than do most of my contemporaries who have had children but now have seen the children grow up and leave home and who basically have no close relation with anyone but their wives and their own fifty-year-old colleagues. I think I know much more about what's going on in youthful America now than all my fertile contemporaries.

JH: Is that because you have a distance that allows you to be intimate with those younger people who are *not* your children?

RP: I think that may well be the reason, but it is also simply that my awareness of young people has never been dependent upon the existence of lab examples under my own roof. I think I would have been very unwise to have done what William Blackburn and certain other great teachers that I know have done, which is to invest the center of my emotional energy in my students.

To do that is, alas, to be an ever-aging creature who's proceeding through a perpetually young population and who's relying for his emotional gratification and his professional judgement upon the very shaky standards of post-adolescence.

JH: The shaky standards of post-adolescence. How do you feel about the practice which has, I think, become pretty much universal, since the sixties, of having students evaluate their teachers?

RP: I think it's nice for the students themselves if they want to have a little book where they tell each other about their teachers and courses—a sort of consumer's guide to teachers. I must say that the ones I've read at Duke strike me only by their softheadedness. They seem to me much too kind to the really bad teachers who are, even in a place as good as Duke, littering the ground, and they're rather injudicious about the better sorts around.

I do very much object to a policy that Duke has, and that I've always refused to comply with, which is the solicitation from students of anonymous evaluations. I grew up in the era of Joseph McCarthy, and I refuse to ask my students to evaluate me anonymously. I have to evalute them; I have to sign my name to their grade card, so I'm not going to invite adult males and females in a republic to submit an anonymous evaluation of me which may turn out to be entirely zany and cannot be weighed because no one knows who it comes from. I invite my students to file a letter with the head of the department the day after I give them their grades, and they can say anything they like, provided their names are on it.

JH: Why has that procedure become so common? I think it's almost universal now, that students are allowed—*forced,* really—to turn in anonymous evaluations.

RP: I really don't know because any one of us who's worked in a serious research university knows that student opinion amounts to absolutely nothing in the real career advancement of a particular faculty member. The most popular teachers often turn out to be professionally the least respected teachers, and students almost never understand this. So I don't know why their advice is still solicited. Maybe it's part of the youth worship that's built into a certain kind of academic administrator's mind, ducking and bowing for student favor. I've thoroughly enjoyed my students and found many of them whom I could respect and admire and be friends with for life, but I really don't seriously value the personnel ratings of a bunch of eighteen to twenty-one year olds.

JH: My college at LSU has recently adopted a procedure which I think is really hilarious, of having students evaluate teachers not only anonymously, but on a numerical system.

RP: Oh, we have a numerical system too; rate Mr. X from 1 to 10 in the following six sub-headings!

JH: A friend of mine, a very prominent member of the English department, told me that he had observed a great many teachers in that department and that consistently the best teachers do not get the best evaluations.

RP: I must say through the years that I've been at Duke, nearly thirty, I have observed the tendency for teacher popularity to run toward very mediocre scholars and very mediocre critics.

JH: But there's got to be a reason for that.

RP: Sure, they're easier and some of them have a genuine flair for popularization. Don't forget they're talking to post-adolescents; they're not talking to highly mature, highly literate people. I've sometimes had to, as member of various evaluation committees, attend classes taught by teachers who were wildly popular by student enrollment figures, and I've almost always been professionally em-barrassed by the superficiality of their method and matter.

JH: If you could change anything you wanted to about the univer-sity as an institution, what would you change?

RP: I think the first thing I would change at Duke is this left-over nineteen-sixtyish sort of scout master truckling after student opinion and student approval. Students really don't care; they're here for only four years in a continuing and busy life—witness the fact that almost none of them ever reappears after the day they walk out of here with their diploma. They may send us a check twenty years later, bless their hearts, but they're not profoundly interested in the place, though they will probably realize by the time they're forty that they were profoundly influenced by the place. Many of them leave thinking that they wish to shake the dust off their feet forever. They find out that the dust won't come off, that it's permanent paint. Beyond that I would change a few little practices such as the inimical practice that we now have at Duke of having a university-wide committee which vetoes the opinions of a department about its own personnel.

Beyond that I have great admiration for the workings of Duke University and tremendous gratitude to the institution which has made it possible for me to live and work fruitfully in the same place in which I was myself an adolescent from 1951 to 1955.

JH: You and I had one teacher that we can remember in common.

His name is Harold Parker and he belongs to an older generation of teachers. I think he's still teaching.

RP: He's recently returned from retirement and has taught occasional courses.

JH: Yes. He was an extraordinary teacher when I knew him, and I can only assume he still is. Are there many teachers in the younger generation coming along who are going to have that kind of impact on students?

RP: There may well be. Of course one of the things you know, now that you're a teacher yourself, is that you never know what your colleagues are like as teachers because there's a sacred tradition of not invading the classroom space of a colleague, so I couldn't tell you the first thing about the teaching methods of most of my colleagues. I can hear student opinion, but I know how unreliable that is—though I have certain mature and intelligent students whose opinion I do respect. Harold Parker, whom you and I shared as a teacher of nineteenth and twentieth century intellectual history, was one of the two or three greatest teachers I've ever encountered in my life, and I have no doubt he still is. And I would say that afterwards when I went to graduate school in England I met only one other teacher who was in Harold Parker's league and that was Lord David Cecil at Oxford.

JH: What was it about Harold Parker and David Cecil that set them apart? Was there something about their sensibility that was radically different from teachers who are being formed now?

RP: Those two teachers were utterly different kinds of men. David Cecil came from one of the great intellectual political families in English history, a direct descendant of Queen Elizabeth and James I's Cecils and brother of the Marquis of Salisbury, who was a very important political figure in the Conservative Party in England in the latter half of the twentieth century. David Cecil had grown up at the heart of British culture and politics. He was a man of enormous personal intelligence. He'd read everything ever written and could comment on it with wonderful intelligence and linguistic grace and with a hilariously original personal wit. He remains one of the two or three funniest conversationalists I've ever known, with a sane but quite intense interest in communicating to his students. David Cecil was a happily married man with three fine children whom I also knew, and any tutorial with David always meant bumping into his wife Rachel and his children in the halls.

A visit to Harold Parker in the 1950s was the same thing as a visit to St. Thomas Aquinas in his cell in the thirteenth century. David Cecil effortlessly involved his favorite students in his own life in the Great World; Harold Parker had an almost frightening intensity of monastic focus. Like Blackburn, he was the sort of teacher who was perfectly capable of crying in class, in the presence of his students, about Napoleon as Blackburn might have cried about John Donne or Spenser. So I'd say that those two men were the really greatest teachers I have observed in action. Blackburn would come a little behind them. Several fine women: Florence Brinkley, who was the first teacher of Milton that I had; Helen Bevington, who taught me contemporary poetry at Duke; Helen Gardner, who was my thesis advisor at Oxford. They were perhaps what was necessary for women of their generation, more withdrawn, much less emotionally involved with their students than any of the three men I've mentioned, but they were nonetheless tremendously important influences in my formation.

JH: Changing the subject sort of radically, I wonder how you answer the charge—it's been made not only of you but of other southern writers, male white southern writers—of racism in your work, because for instance you talk about the way a certain black woman character smells. How do you answer that charge?

RP: I think it's just indescribably dumb. If any southern writer has ever gone dangerously close to sentimentalizing and making a hero of the black race, I think it might be me. Black characters in my books from the very beginning—from Mildred in *A Long and Happy Life* to Grainger in the Mayfield novels—are morally, by some length, the superior of all the white people contained in the books. So I can't imagine why one or two currently voguish black writers might think I was anti-black.

I think it's largely because there're certain black writers in America who just leap on anyone who doesn't match their particular short list of the best possible way to deal with blackness. One runs into, with some black writers, what one runs into with any kind of minority—black, gay, female, Jewish, yellow, red: a certain proprietary sense that no one who's not black, red, or green should be allowed to poach on these reservations.

JH: I wonder what you think of one black novelist who has recently become an object of controversy because of her depiction of black men. Alice Walker has been attacked in the press because of her depiction of black men, specifically in *The Color Purple,* and since the release of the movie by Stephen Spielberg, she has been attacked not only for her depiction of black men but of black women. I wonder what you think of this case in which the novel was written by a black woman, the film was made with heavy involvement by her and by a number of very prominent black actors and actresses?

RP: I've never read the novel, nor have I seen the film. I would like to read *The Color Purple*; I would like to see the film because I've admired many of Spielberg's films. I have no comment whatever on her treatment of black males, though I understand that not only have there been the objections you mentioned, but that very soon the *New York Times Book Review* is about to publish an essay by a black male novelist which attacks Alice Walker and some other black females for the same kind of denigration of black masculinity.

JH: Do you know why that happened, why there should have been an (alleged) denigration of black men by women and why there should be a clash between genders among black writers?

RP: I'm sure there are ancient enmities and warfares in existence here which I wouldn't want to comment on without a lot more thought. We know, because of the eminence of several black female writers in recent years, a fair amount more of what fortyish, fiftyish black women think about black men than we know of the reverse. And certainly recent reports on the continuing absence of the black father from the family unit again suggests that it was the black males who behaved in what white-middle-class Americans would only think of as irresponsible ways.

I have to believe, however, that there's something that remains to be said by black males themselves about the structure of black femininity which may have driven a good many of these men away. I absolutely refuse to believe that the abdication of an entire gender, or large parts of an entire gender, can be explained only by the majority's emasculation of black males. I think there has got to be something happening in black homes, half of which are female, that has at least contributed to the disappearance of so many of these men.

So I am interested in the attack which you report and will be very interested to see some of the male response. Maybe black male writers can be galvanized now to tell us a bit more than they have about black femininity. Certainly my own essay for the *Times* urges men and women of all sorts to tell us more about one another.

JH: Well, of course, there have been black male writers who have depicted—Ernest Gaines, for instance—black women, and there never has been this same sort of attack on their depiction of black women that there's been on the depiction of black men by black women writers like Alice Walker.

RP: Well, I think Jane Pittman is rightly portrayed as heroic; so who's going to attack a heroine?

JH: Exactly. I'm convinced that there has been a very important influence by blacks on southern writing in general, on whites and blacks. Do you agree with that?

RP: Of course.

JH: In many cases, some of the earliest voices that we heard and listened to were black voices.

RP: Enormously important in forming the southern white imagination, sexual morality, ethics, sense of humor, sense of music, sense of almost everything you can imagine—even bodily movement. Ralph Ellison has pointed out that if you go to Europe and you run across an American who may have already lived in Europe for five or six years and has European clothes and haircut and everything else, the one way that you can finally detect that he's American is by his movement. As Ellison points out, American blacks have greatly influenced the way Americans walk and move and certainly the way in which southerners walk and move.

I would certainly and gladly say that my life, literally from the moment of my birth at which a black midwife was in attendance, has been heavily contributed to and influenced by black women and men. Luckily I wasn't simply limited to the presence of black maids and nurses. I was also exposed quite early on to the presence of a very powerful and very loyal black man; so I grew up knowing black men who were as solid and faithful as any of the black women I knew, and I'm sure there are many such black men available today.

We just apparently are not being given lots of fictional pictures of them.

JH: I wonder if that influence of black culture on white southern-ers—an influence which many white southerners have denied for one reason or another, though I think writers in general have not denied it but willingly and gladly admitted it and its reflection in their work—I wonder if that influence is not dying out, is no longer an active force for most white southerners?

RP: I couldn't be sure, but I suspect that you're right. There're very few young southerners whom I teach now who have grown up with the kind of black presence in the home that you and I experi-enced. They are, however, growing up with intimate knowledge of their own black contemporaries through the public schools; south-ern schools have been integrated with a success and a completeness that's been unheard of in other more morally censorious parts of the country. Ann Arbor, Michigan, of all places, of all whited sepulchres, is only presently undergoing a great school busing hurrah.

I must say it gives a certain malicious pleasure to southerners to hear about these great bastions of northern superiority, like Boston and Ann Arbor, undergoing situations that we got settled about twenty years ago.

No, I think coeducation is a very different thing from experiencing adults, and it may not be so good a thing, but it's different at least. It's bound to have an effect on the writing of my nieces' generation, let's say, who will be beginning to write twenty years from now—fifteen or twenty years from now.

JH: You don't write *all* the time. What do you like to spend your time doing when you're not writing?

RP: Watching movies on my VCR. I've watched every movie made since *The Great Train Robbery* in the last three years, thank goodness. I've spent a great deal of time being with my numerous, blessedly numerous, friends. I have, in recent years, spent a good deal of time returning to one of my earliest obsessions as a very young child—a lot of drawing and painting.

I began that before I underwent this recent physical ordeal. But when I had undergone the ordeal and found it very difficult to return to writing, one of the methods that I attempted to use to jog myself back to work was to begin a series of drawings. And since my particular kind of ordeal had produced a strong period of spiritual searching for me, I found that one of the things I was doing was generating a series of sketch books that were filled with imaginary images of Jesus—a figure who's been both spiritually and aesthetically a figure of great fascination to me since I was a pre-literate child. I generated away with my icons of Christ for months before I was able to get back to work.

But in general, drawing has been something that I've turned to at various moments in my life, and it's been not only an aesthetic end in itself but another form of lovemaking in my life. I think I've very frequently drawn portraits of people who were extremely precious to me in the flesh, and I've continued to do so. Drawing is something that I've spent a lot of time doing—and photographs, again almost always of people. I'm generally bored by photographs of anything except other human beings. Photographs of trees and buildings and mountains leave me fairly cold, but I can consume endlessly photographs of people's faces.

JH: You did the cover illustration for *The Surface of Earth,* didn't you?

RP: I did the allegorical emblem which is on the cover.

JH: You haven't done any other illustrations for your books?

RP: No, I tried to think of one to do for *The Source of Light* and was unable to come up with a similar kind of emblem. I've participated in the design of a number of my jackets, as I did with the jacket for *Kate Vaiden* and the forthcoming jacket for *The Laws of Ice*, but I haven't actually designed any jacket but that one.

JH: Are there any other recurring sorts of drawings that you do, besides portraits of people who've been close to you and the drawings of Christ that you described, in that sketchbook?

RP: Those particular sketchbooks are essentially icons, drawings of sacred figures—both traditionally sacred figures, as in the drawings of Jesus, and figures that are sacred to me alone, who are people that I've loved and really emulated and wanted to study at close range in my own life. My house is full of photographs of people who've been very dear to me because I find something magical about their condensation into a two-dimensional form; and I share the basic primitive savage's belief that a picture of someone is in some sense a supernatural receptacle of that person's virtue, of that person's spirit.

JH: Your house is not only full of photographs and pictures of people that you know, but also full of paintings, icons, pictures, masks of people. What do these mean to you?

RP: They mean, first and foremost, my own lifelong curiosity about the reduction or the metamorphosis of the visible, audible, sensible world into two-dimensional visual form in works of painting and drawing and sculpture. Then beyond that, they have all sorts of other spiritual and personal vibrations for me that I wouldn't want to try to discuss.

I love to look at beautiful and interesting things. It does amaze me, I must say, that I've put together here this quite nice museum of good pictures, but I would have to say that about 80 percent of all people who enter my house leave without ever having really glanced at the walls. I notice that continually, to my amazement.

JH: That's astonishing, that anyone could come in *this* house without looking at the walls.

RP: Very, very few human beings have any visual sense. I've walked down the streets of New York and Washington and several other great American and European cities with very famous people and in some cases with very famous beauties and have noticed that no one ever sees them. People are just tucked under their own little belljars going their own little way.

JH: So even beautiful people in the flesh, and well-known people in the flesh, have to be framed and presented in a certain way, thrust forward before they're noticed.

RP: Framed and presented. I once walked through Times Square with Melina Mercouri when she was a very, very famous beautiful woman in the world press and absolutely no one recognized her.

JH: Why do you think that is?

RP: We're not trained to recognize in three dimensions those things which everyone knows in two dimensions, or magnified by thirty feet. Also because most people never see anything; they don't want to; they want only to see their own preoccupations.

JH: What does it mean to you to have lived in this same house, for how many years?

RP: Twenty-one exactly.

JH: What's it mean to your work and your sense of yourself in the world?

RP: I think it means an enormous amount. I've always been a very sedentary, certainly a very rooted person, primarily perhaps because as a child I was forced to move very frequently. My parents were tossed around North Carolina by the rigors of the Depression, in search of money. They were also tossed around the few towns that we spent several years in by my mother's own restlessness to find a particular better kind of house or apartment; so I've never counted up, but I must have lived in twenty houses by the time I was twenty years old.

I hated every single move so that once I was able to buy this house in 1965, I've really wanted to stay here and have basically done so with very short stints away—probably never for longer than two to three weeks at a time. It's a very important socket into the earth and into the sky for me. When it began to seem, some months ago, that this house might prove uninhabitable for me since I can no longer walk and since it's a house built on three floors, I was really so alarmed and unnerved by the apparent necessity of having to move, that I quickly designed a ground floor addition which would make it possible for me to continue to live in this place where I've been for twenty-one years.

One of the really important things about this house for me is that it's a house which my mother visited, in fact spent a few nights in before she died. I bought the house in January of 1965, and she died in May. It's nice for me that at least one of my parents has been in this space. I'm horrified by the awareness that something like one in three American families moves annually. No wonder we know so little about the effect of the passage of time upon human life; we never stay still long enough to develop a set of reliable landmarks.

JH: And there are apparently statistics that imply that every time you move, you actually cut off a number of years from your life-expectancy.

RP: Really?

JH: The stress involved is supposedly comparable to losing someone very close to you.

RP: Goodness, it strikes me that I've always known that. My mother repeated an old truism which was that "Three moves equals a fire."

JH: If you could speak now to yourself when you were, I don't know, twenty, twenty-two years old, is there anything that you would want to say to yourself, any advice you'd give yourself? What is there of use that you know now that you didn't know then, that would have been useful to you then? As a writer or a human being.

RP: I think I could summarize it best in a few lines from a poem of A. E. Houseman's. The poem is a very close translation, though a rhyming metrical one, of an Ode of Horace's, Book 4, No. 7; the title given in Houseman's collected poems is "Diffugere Nives," Horace's opening phrase. Towards the end of the poem, Horace and Houseman say,

> *Torquatus, If the gods in heaven shall add*
> *The morrow to the day, what tongue has told?*
> *Feast then thy heart, for what thy heart has had*
> *The fingers of no heir will ever hold.*

I think that my own recent brush with mortality has led me to want more than ever to feast my heart, and perhaps if I could look back at the young man I was when I left North Carolina to spend three years in England, I would just say, "Feast thy heart"; but then I think I did, I think I always have. For a person who to many observers has had what looks like almost a hermetic existence, I think I have emotionally a far more intense existence than many of my more apparently public colleagues.

But feasting the heart would certainly be advice that I would give to any talented and intelligent and disciplined young person. Feasting doesn't mean gorging; it doesn't mean destroying through excess, but it does mean seizing what in life and in art is intense and excellent. Keats says late in his life in an important letter, "The excellence of every art is its intensity," so I would wish upon myself as a young man more intensity and more seizure of what in life is more nourishing and most productive of happiness, of happy memory.

JH: Is there anything that you have published or been quoted as saying in print that you would like to change or take back?

RP: Oh, gosh, there must be. I would hate to be faced with a heavenly record of everything I've ever done or said, especially in interviews which are so frequently given when one's exhausted or angry or bored by the interviewer or appalled by one's own ignorance in the face of a given question so there must be numerous things. I can't think of any major thing.

There's certainly no story or essay or novel that I wish I could call back. There're certainly numerous stories and novels that I think I could make better today, but I don't ever believe in publishing revised versions of my works because I'm no longer the person who wrote them. It would be absolutely an act of forgery for me to attempt now to revise *A Long and Happy Life,* which was made by Reynolds Price when he was twenty-five to twenty-eight years old. Someone coming along thirty-odd years later should never attempt to pretend he is the same person. So I abhor the kind of disfiguring alterations that even as big a writer as Henry James or W. H. Auden made in his work late in his life.

JH: Anne Tyler says she can't bear to go back and read herself. Do you feel that way?

RP: I don't feel that I can't bear it. I just don't ever do it unless I read a few pages at a reading, though even there I find that the audience wants you to read, you know, Reynolds Price's greatest hits, those songs and sonnets which they've learned to love in the past but which you long since feel that you've bettered or at least gone beyond. For me to stand up now and read pages from *A Long and Happy Life* is about as exciting as reading you an excerpt from my high-school yearbook. I like the book but I certainly don't feel any longer like the man who wrote it; I don't have any specially proprietary sense about it. I'm always far more interested in what I'm doing now or have just done.

JH: You don't have the horror of what you've written that some writers have?

RP: I have no self-hatred. I hope I don't have preening self-love either because I don't ever go back and reread a story or book of mine unless I'm required to do so, as I said, by a reading or unless it's for some purely practical purpose such as the appearance of a new edition which I might need to proofread. Or in the case of a book like *The Source of Light,* I had to go back and reread *The Surface of Earth* to be sure that I had the story and the chronology straight before I began to write its continuation.

JH: What would you say to an intelligent student whom you thought had some potential, who came to you and said he or she just didn't believe that even great art was of much value in life?

RP: I would have to say, "Well, give it up. Don't attempt to pursue it because you're wasting your time, and you're certainly wasting art's time." I don't think that art is the most valuable thing in the world, by any means. I think charity and kindness and human understanding and love are, on the face of it, the most important things. If you don't want to learn, then don't expect me to come to your room and seduce you. I'm on display in such and such rooms at such and such hours doing my thing, which is lecturing on *Paradise Lost* or on the writing of the novella or in my office writing my own works. If you want to participate, you're welcome to sign on board, but I'm not going to come get you or do little toe dances in the street to try to bring you downstairs.

JH: How would you like to be remembered by posterity? A century or two centuries from now, assuming that the human race still exists?

RP: As an amusing and helpful friend to know, as a challenging adult teacher who wasn't going to beg or seduce people to learn but liked to be present while they were learning and to assist them in whatever adult ways I thought I could. And as the maker of a number of objects—novels, stories, poems, essays, plays—which have proven beautiful and durable.

Staying Power of Reynolds Price
Wendy Smith/1986

From the *Chicago Sun-Times,* 24 August 1986, 25. Reprinted by permission of Reynolds Price.

DURHAM, N.C.—With the exception of three years at Oxford, Reynolds Price has always lived within 60 miles of little Macon, N.C., where he and his parents were born. His fiction has been similarly rooted: from *A Long and Happy Life* in 1962 through *Kate Vaiden* this summer, his novels, short stories and plays (he also writes poetry) have chronicled life in a small portion of the rural South, often using his family's history as a springboard for an examination of the complex emotional bonds that link all human beings to the people they love.

In a universe he divides into leavers and stayers, Reynolds Price is emphatically a stayer. He has taught English at Duke University and lived in the same community just outside of Durham since 1958. Even a recent operation for spinal cancer, which left him unable to walk, couldn't dislodge him from his home of 21 years, a two-story house not best suited to the needs of the wheelchair-bound; a single-floor addition is being built so that he can again be self-sufficient.

The walls of this house—crammed with signed photographs of opera singers, drawings by Price and his friends, an assortment of masks and animal skulls—attest to its ownership by someone who has not moved often or easily.

Price, a gray-haired man of 53, has the ease of someone completely comfortable with his surroundings and the charm that seems to be a birthright of every Southerner. There is always a laugh lurking in his eyes and mouth, and like his characters he possesses not a trace of self-pity. His only complaint about the wheelchair is that it forces him to diet.

When discussing his work, he is candid about its roots in his continuing preoccupation with family.

"*Kate Vaiden* began because I had become fascinated with lots of questions about the life of my mother," he says. "I wanted to write about the way in which a woman from her part of the world would have the kind of life that in some ways my mother was qualified for. I think Mother would have loved to have a great deal more independence than she wound up having in her life.

"As I worked with the idea of that kind of woman, it just became inevitable that I was going to have to speak, or want to speak, in the first person, which was a form I had never used before in a novel. I gave Kate essentially my own generation, though, because I didn't want to do a lot of research into the social reality of my mother's early life. Once I knew when she was born and what her name was, it proceeded very smoothly. I simply had to do each day a quick metamorphosis into being another person of another gender.

"It was great fun; I was going through a lot of trouble with this spinal tumor, and it made it much easier for me each day to just go into a room and become somebody else for a good part of the day."

In one fundamental way, however, Kate is utterly different from both Price and his mother. "Kate's a leaver," he comments, "and my two parents, God knows, were the champion stayers of all time, people of enormous stability. But I always perceived as a child that Mother might have liked to run, and one of the great personal fears I've dealt with in my work is the fear of abandonment.

"I guess I've always been fascinated by leavers, very afraid that I was going to bump into them. America, after all, is a country of leavers. Everybody who's here except the Indians is here because they left somewhere else, and everyone except black Americans left of their own volition. So in a sense we are a nation of quitters."

There were a few leavers in Price's own family. "The character of Eva in *The Surface of Earth* [who leaves home to marry, with disastrous consequences for her family] is based at least in terms of action on my father's elder sister, who ran away with [and married] her high school teacher and came back several years later with no explanation, never went back and never saw her husband again," he says.

"I was fascinated by that as a child: there she was, a perfectly functional human being with a wonderful sense of humor, and I was trying to put together this old woman with the wild young girl back in the early years of the 20th century. But I didn't ask anyone in the family questions; I simply dived in and invented a story. Later I found out that Eva's story bore some resemblance to events in my aunt's life I hadn't known about."

His relatives never seemed to mind these raids on their personal history—"I think they were sophisticated enough, though none of them was really an inveterate reader, to separate what was imagined from what they knew was real," Price comments—and this understanding may have come from the fact that they were themselves tale-spinners.

"Both my parental families were terrific storytellers, my father's side especially," the author says. "I grew up in a constant marinade of narratives, most of which had comic endings that reflected on the narrator's intelligence, or resourcefulness, or courage. I was very impressed as a child by their toughness in being able to joke about themselves.

"I think very few of my characters are weak or self-pitying people, and that was very true of the older generations of my family. They seemed to be people who barely ever paused to think about themselves, much less wallow in self-pity. And I've tended to invent characters who are to a large extent buccaneers or adventurers; they simply go about doing what they want, and to hell with the consequences."

Yet, as Price shows in his fiction, the consequences were broken hearts and broken relationships, broken homes and abandoned children. "Don't you think that's a tremendous characteristic of family living? Insofar as their world becomes the extended family, as it was in both my parents' cases, they inflict the most awful sorts of punishment on one another. My father especially had been hurt by his own family, but he nonetheless remained very loyal. Most of the people in my work live very much within the framework of a familial society, but there are very few of them who don't have terrific reservations about it and many times try to flee it."

Price's characters often feel desperately alone in the midst of the crowd of relatives among whom they live. "I think it's a paradox that exists in that kind of old-time family, a small village with 10 or so people under the same roof, which was the basic condition of middle-class families in the South when my parents were growing up and in my own childhood," he says.

"You had to learn to deal with everyone there, but in the midst of it you felt tremendously alone with whatever objections you had to the society. My mother, especially in my childhood, impressed me as a person who had a great deal of solitary trouble going on inside herself. I would come home from school in the afternoons and know the minute I walked into the house whether she was going to be up and about making cookies in the kitchen or lying on the sofa 'feeling blue.' "

Price had his own objections to the familial society, some of them having to do with racial attitudes. "I never pretended to be a racist, but I sat silent in the presence of racists, some of whom were members of my own family, people whom I loved very much. One reason I did was because I wanted to continue being a spy; I wanted to be able to stay around everybody and learn about them without having declared a personal position which was so antithetical to theirs that they would shut up in my presence.

"I think that to a very large extent a writer has to be a spy, and this is one reason why novelists tend to be tremendously tolerant people. We're able to accept a great deal because we realize that we are spies and take on protective colorations in the hope of getting material for our work: 'I'm just here listening. Keep talking to me.' If someone on the bus—and people are always doing this to me—starts telling you their wildest personal confessions and you say, 'How awful! How could you have done that?' they're just going to change their seat fast! People always tell me their stories. It's probably one of the born traits of writers: we are the people to whom people talk."

The talk in his own family was beautiful in its eloquence, but often brutal in its content.

"My father's family were into really rough confrontational language, all delivered with icy reserve. Mother's family were much more Italian and operatic: everyone would have great storms, then cry and make it all up and be happy for another week.

"Father's family would plot these long punishments and confrontations; they were verbally much more precise and memorable than my mother's family. So they were not as much fun to be around when you were a child, but much more interesting once you were an adult.

"As a child, I watched all this with fascination, but definitely chose at a very early age not to secrete a family around myself. I didn't want that sort of thing, and when I went away to graduate school [at Oxford] at the age of 23 I thought: Whew! I can shut that door for awhile."

Yet he stayed away only three years. "Duke out of the blue offered me a job," he explains, "so I thought I'd take it and then decide where else I wanted to go. Then I gradually began to realize that if this was going to be my subject matter it might as well be where I stayed. Everything that comes to me comes out of the worlds I've watched very closely, the worlds of my family and friends. These are the places I've inhabited."

Reynolds Price
Daphne Athas/1987

From *Listen* (magazine of WUNC radio, Chapel Hill, NC), April 1987, 4–8. Reprinted by permission of Reynolds Price.

I hadn't seen Reynolds Price for three years, though we had intermittently been in touch. And now, after cancer, recovery and two new books, the very successful *Kate Vaiden,* a novel, and his new book of poems, *The Laws of Ice,* he was greeting me in his large study. Seated in a wheelchair, he dominated the room. The trees standing in silence outside the window, the hardwood floor, the heavy wooden crucifix to one side of the great bed, the ramp—everything gave off an aura of wood. As in Russia, in the forest, where wood listens.

In fact the December day was cold and misty and a Russian icon stood next to the computer with haunted eyes. This sense of listening was multiplied by pictures everywhere, on walls, on desks, pictures of writers looking out of frames. There was Milton, Emily Dickinson, mysteriously formal but vulnerable, Hemingway, Emily Brontë, Arthur Rimbaud, Christopher Isherwood, impossibly young, Auden, Tolstoy.

In real life writers are always saying silly things, behaving less than nobly, and these pictures of them in their vulnerability, even inconsequence gave a feeling of comfortable familiarity. The cosmos behind great accomplishment. When Reynolds spoke, his mouth was both sensitive and pugnacious. His hair was peppered with silver, his black eyes snapped. His words were measured, gentle, and happily outrageous. The late Jessie Rehder, who taught Creative Writing at Chapel Hill, used to say that Reynolds was either a North Carolina oaf or an Oxford elegant. Nothing in between.

He had recently done interviews on National Public Radio's "All Things Considered" and "Morning Edition."

"You know you have a wonderful voice? Did you ever study music?"

"I was a famous local boy soprano in Asheboro and Warrenton. I was always singing solos in church and getting dollar bills thrust at me by local moneybags gents. When I was a senior in high school I had a lot of throat problems, constantly getting what I thought were throat infections. So I finally came to McPherson's Hospital, in Durham, and Dr. Ferguson there said: "You don't have throat infections at all. You're speaking incorrectly like most Americans. You're speaking with your throat muscles and not from your diaphragm." And he said "Can you take singing lessons this summer?" I said: "Oh sure," and so every morning of that summer of 1951 I drove over to Durham and took lessons with a very fine teacher called George Moore and gradually my voice deepened and I wound up with whatever voice I presently have. It has helped me a lot as a teacher to be audible. It's sad that in America most people have been taught to ignore the voice as a means of narration and that most people do everything they can to be inaudible, to the point of stuffing their fists in their mouths. Some of our greatest poets like Robert Penn Warren—I've seen auditoriums empty themselves within ten minutes after Mr. Warren began his invariably inaudible reading. I was far more influenced by music than by writers. Everyone thinks that everybody born in the South is created by Faulkner. I never even liked Faulkner very much and still don't. I'm far more influenced by baroque poetry, especially Milton. Baroque poetry and baroque music."

He grew up in Eastern North Carolina, reading his way, he said, through all the municipal libraries in the towns he'd lived in, getting into the adult section by second grade with special permission from the librarians "who'd let me bring home scandalous books like *Gone with the Wind* and *The Grapes of Wrath,* which, you recall, were the bilious pornography of the time."

I wondered if Eastern North Carolina people were unique, different from Piedmont people, and whether they had changed.

"They're very Tidewater. Farmers. You have to remember that. And 70 percent black in my childhood. Warrenton was a real architectural gem, along with Edenton and New Bern, and now it's this sad, still lovely town, abandoned by young people. Warren County has always had this official policy of wanting to industrialize but as soon as someone comes in and builds a little underwear factory, the people take a sort of unofficial line against it and the factory packs up and leaves five years later. I remember once standing with my aunt out on Main St. Warrenton on a Saturday and three or four strangers rode by in cars and a friend of my aunt's looked at us and said: "Look at all these strangers in here, just wearing our streets out."

After he graduated from Duke he spent 3 years at Oxford, then came back and taught at Duke for 3 more years. He planned to go back to Oxford for a doctorate, but the novel he'd been working on, *A Long and Happy Life,* was published with extreme success, so he decided not to get the doctorate but went back to Oxford for the 4th year anyhow.

"When I came back in 1962 I realized for good that this is where I was going to live. I just realized that I loved it very much and didn't want to leave. And I have always been proud of those of us who stayed in the South through the bleak and difficult years when everybody was saying, 'Get your A— out of the sticks and come on up here to the East Side.' "

We switched to the subject of reading.

"I don't now read a whole lot of serious fiction. I write more or less all the time. I used to read a lot of poetry primarily because I have a lot of poetry-writing friends and want to keep up with them. But poems tend to be short, and you can read a poem while you're waiting for the bus."

"Do you ever read trash?"

"*People Magazine.* They do it very well. But I get a lot of my trash on TV."

"Falcon Crest? Dynasty?"

"The thing I watch vividly is 'The Young and the Restless' which a friend of mine calls 'The Hung and the Breastless.' I'd refuse lunch with the Queen if I had to miss that. I used to read a lot of detective fiction, but that's not trash."

"The characters in your novels seem to me so wholly self-contained. They accept their destiny."

"I think it's very much a result of the kinds of people I told you I grew up with in Eastern North Carolina. Paradoxical in that they were tribal but familial. The only things they had to talk about were food and family, because they hadn't read books, they hadn't seen movies, they hadn't been to plays. They were familial yet self-dependent, yearning to be individuals to the point of nearly driving themselves crazy. Virtually every male in my mother and father's generation was a serious alcoholic. My brother and I are the first two men in the family not to be major drinkers. Virtually every woman desired to be an escapee. Two or three of the women in my family had serious nervous breakdowns exacerbated by powerfully warring attitudes, both loving and hating all the family stuff, the children and husband stuff. That's why I say Kate Vaiden at one level is very much a fantasy about my mother's life. Mother thought of herself as an orphan. Kate is a fantasy on a certain kind of wildness that was implicit in my mother and that I picked up on as a young child. I adored her and was both tremendously in love with her and also very afraid of her because I knew she had this wild frightened-deer in her who was liable to bolt at any moment. She never did, really, for more than a day at a time, though she might just suddenly truck out one morning after breakfast and no one would know where she was until supper. That would be sheer terror for me, because I would think she was never coming back."

"She wanted to escape?"

"She didn't want to make all these commitments that she was hour-by-hour required to make. Still, no one was a more loyal mother nor family member. I've always thought there must be secrets of my mother and father's lives that would shock the hell out of me if I knew them, yet now that I'm heading into what amounts to age, I think I would be fascinated to know them. There were times—even up to my mother's death when I was 33—when there were questions I was afraid to ask her because I thought she would tell me the truth. And I wasn't ready for it. But now I would really love to sit in a room with my mother and just ask her anything and know that I was going to get a candid answer, because my mother was very candid with her children. So I would love to know all of that. I would love to know everything about everybody. Don't you think one of the greatest fears of childhood is that you're going to wake up one day and your parents are going to turn out to be somebody completely different? I mean, not that somebody else is going to walk in the house and say 'I'm your real mother.' But that suddenly your mother is going to tear off what you thought was her face and reveal this awful thing underneath? And all the rest was some horrible charade to deceive you, her little child."

"Your poem, 'The Laws of Ice' in your new book has this feeling to me. Do the laws of ice mean something about being trapped by forms? What do the laws of ice mean?"

"I don't think I could answer in any way that would make sense. This isn't writer's coyness. I certainly couldn't state the laws of ice. The little poem called that comes nearer to it than anything, and really that's based on my recent illness, in which over a period of six weeks I just lost my legs apparently forever. I think the laws of ice are those things which, at some point in all our lives, early or late, freeze us in a sudden random position—moral, physical, whatever. And we wind up being inexorably what we're going to be from then on. The Laws of Ice are the Laws of Death. They're the laws that are implicit in all of our physical and spiritual natures. They are the realities that the whole of American life is dedicated to concealing from us. We are the only country in the history of the world that gets guaranteed happiness in its constitution. The right to pursue it anyhow. How much time and energy has been wasted in this country pursuing happiness! You asked about eastern North Carolinians, what distinguishes them. Well, one of the things is that feature of farmers everywhere on the globe: 'Scratch a farmer and find the tragic sense of life.' You can't convince a farmer that life is just one big Coors beer bash. They're closer to the Laws of Ice. They live according to the laws of sun, ice, and water. They know. I think one of the urgent things that I've wanted to do as a writer was to preserve a sense of what it felt like—well, not what it felt like to be alive at certain moments in American history—but what it felt like to be Reynolds Price at certain moments. I've tried hard to do that."

Reynolds Price on the South, Literature, and Himself
S. D. Williams/1987

From *Leader Magazine*, 4 June 1987, 4–6. Reprinted by permission of Steven D. Williams and Reynolds Price.

Reynolds Price hasn't changed. He is sitting in the relatively new wheelchair in his country house outside of Durham, speaking in the rich voice that is like a worldly Episcopalian priest's. The voice predates the wheelchair by three decades. It found and formed itself in the 1950s, and on this day it is speaking about the changes in Price's worlds.

The wheelchair sits on a peninsula of pine floor between desks and bookcase. Price is surrounded by his writer's icons: busts of Homer, Byron, Shakespeare, Schiller and Dickens; photographs or prints of Eudora Welty, Hemingway, Rimbaud, Milton; Christian art and crosses above the IBM computer and Savin copier. He says guests have come into his home and never noticed the multitude of things on his walls. He notices and remembers everything, from the habits of his childhood schoolmates to the faces of students at Duke University 20 years ago, including those he never taught.

Within the compact space of hours, the voice will say at one point, "I write for myself and God," and at another, lamenting the lame topics of recent student fiction, "Christ, can't somebody bugger their grandmother or something?"

Price lost the use of his legs to a malignant spinal tumor in 1984, at the age of 51. The cancer, in return, has tied him to his desk, where he has been productive. He has written more in the last three years than during any previous six-year period: a novel and a half, three plays, essays and poems. He is more out of shape than he was before cancer, but he says he rarely exercised anyway. His hair had been turning gray for a decade. Eighty-seven-year-old Crichton Davis, the woman who taught him the eighth grade at John Graham High School in Warrenton, says Price the man is still the logical extension of Price the boy. He saw into everyone, she says, and usually forgave them.

Price's career has a neat pair of bookends. His first novel, A Long and Happy Life, received the William Faulkner award as the best first novel of the year in 1961. Kate Vaiden, his latest, won the National Book Critics Circle Award last year. With Kate, Price returned to the kind of rural North Carolina people about whom he'd written in the first novel. These are his most commercially successful books. Next spring, the bookend Kate will move toward the chronological center of his oeuvre when a new novel, Good Hearts, is published.

Price's characters struggle with a universal theme, the price of love, but most have roots in the geography and traditions of the South. Price has watched and tried to understand his culture since at least the age of 5, when he realized he was different.

"I don't know any of my Northern, liberal friends who grew up having complicated human relationships with black people," he says. "My childhood was filled with that, although every single member of my family was a card-carrying racist.

"The basic cultural superstructure of Eastern North Carolina had remained virtually unchanged from Reconstruction, 1865, until 1945. I am only 54 now, but when I was born in 1933 there were several people alive in my family who had clear memories of the Civil War. My grandmother had met General Lee when she was a little girl. I really grew up in an intellectual and emotional atmosphere which was in no serious way different from 1865.

"The Second World War produced an extraordinary set of changes, in the country and in the South. Lots of working class white boys and black men went off and saw France and Germany, England, met other kinds of women and men, and had what now look like tiny amounts of money from their mustering-out pay but were then big pieces of money. They bought cars; they came back and bought pieces of land in families that had never owned land before. They could go out and buy a little trailer and not have to live in the kind of shanty they would have lived in previously, where the snakes could slither in and out of the living room. So very quickly the shape of things began changing.

"The racial situation didn't really begin altering until the mid- and late-1960s. When I went through high school in Warrenton in the 1940s, the last thing that crossed anyone's mind was that a black student might go to John Graham High School. Twenty years ago I wouldn't have given you 10 cents for the possibility of the legal situation and the employment situation having altered as dramatically as it has.

"We no longer have black maids and janitors around the house, so middle-class white kids are no longer reared by black women and gents, thereby getting a lot of intimate knowledge of black culture and black thought patterns and folkways. That's regrettable. I'm glad I got it. It's helped me enormously in my writing and I think in my tolerance for other human beings. But I certainly wouldn't want to go back to the old system just to award me that, or award other middle-class white boys that.

"What is still extremely powerful in the South, as it is in Iowa and California and Oregon and Connecticut, is the country club-Rotary Club set where the upper-middle class and wealthy males of the community run everything. That is I think as powerful as it's ever been: the community cabal of bankers and doctors and lawyers who have always run America and still do and always will as long as you and I are alive, unless there's a nuclear holocaust to interrupt it.

"I don't easily get angry about social injustice. My basic temperament has always been much more of a calmly watchful attitude than of someone who took quick glances at things and got angry and maybe wanted to have a fight about them. I've always wanted to be a kind of spy who rather invisibly moved through the world and collected evidence which he then used in benevolent ways.

"I've just gone on trying to watch the way my world works, the way my world is constructed, and to try to offer in my fiction and in my poetry the clearest reports on that that I can give. Not that I see that as the primary thing that I'm doing. I don't think of myself first and foremost as a social analyst. What I do think is that if someone were interested in trying to understand the structure of the Upper South, say from 1900 to 1987, then my novels could offer him a good deal of quite reliable social information; social, cultural, religious, linguistic, you name it.

"I'm very aware that Durham, Raleigh, and Chapel Hill are being profoundly altered in appearance and accent and cooking and

what you can buy in restaurants and Fowler's gourmet store as
opposed to the old country corner store. Yet I'm also aware that I can
wheel a hundred yards down Cornwallis Road and go and visit the
James Rigsbee household and talk to people who have lived on that
land for 200 years, and who've owned it and worked it and worked
in the Durham tobacco mills, and whose standards and language are
very old traditional Southern standards.

"I think one of the things that investigative journalists are very bad
at realizing is that for all the rise of Fowler's fancy food stores all
over the landscape, there's still a tremendous number of James
Rigsbees living around who don't get interviewed and who don't turn
up on talk shows and don't run for the city council, but those people,
quiet and silent as they are, are still out here seasoning the air and
the landscape, and to that extent a great deal of what we mean by
the Old South is still very much present, because not only is there
Mr. Rigsbee, who's in his 70s, but Mr. Rigsbee's got children and
grandchildren living within a hundred yards of his own house. I think
we can still say that for all the influx of IBM and Telecom employees,
you can go in Kroger's or you can go in the Record Bar and know in
10 seconds if you're at all sensitive that you're not in New Jersey or
Michigan. The old culture isn't going to vanish any time soon.

"When I came to Duke as a student in 1951, there was a stronger
component of Southern students. Economically speaking, they
were not nearly so well-heeled as they are now. They were therefore
intellectually and socially much more varied and much more interesting than the student body we have now. I'm awfully oppressed and
depressed by the kind of sameness of the student population we
have at Duke these days. For my tastes, it's too much of a wealthy,
spoiled, upper-class crowd.

"I've been very disappointed with the results of my recent prose
classes. I know everyone is very bored with hearing how television is
destroying the world, but in fact it has done a number of bad things,
and one of the really bad things it's done to young people in America
now is the destruction of the individual imagination. You almost
never get the sort of wonderfully independent and outrageous stories
I would have gotten from students of the '60s and '70s. You get
much more of a sort of pablumized, Sunday Night Movie family
entertainment stuff. If they're going to get independent at all, their

idea of what's interesting is one more story about coke dealing
on campus, which I find pretty depressing.

"My earliest students in the late '50s, although no paragons of
preparation, were better read. They tended to be much more imaginative in the sense of a personal vision of the world than kids now,
who largely have had their visions of reality constructed for them by
television series writers and rock musicians. It isn't just a veneer. It's
very very profound.

"I don't acknowledge any responsibility to my culture at all. My
responsibilities are to myself and God, who gave me the ability and
no doubt expects me to farm it the best I can. Which means that I
take extremely seriously the use of my own faculties. That implies
that I hope and believe that my work will ultimately have benevolent
results upon its readers. But I don't sit down and ask, 'What is my
responsibility to my readers?'

"I would correct that to one extent. I have always felt a responsibility to be as clear and communicative as I could possibly be. I never
wanted to be a difficult or obscure writer. I think part of that is the
result of the place that I come from and the kinds of people I grew up
with. These were not highly educated, supremely literate people, and
yet I wanted to be understood by them. So I realized that I couldn't
be T. S. Eliot or Ezra Pound or Henry James.

"I write because it's the only thing that I'm really very good at in
the whole world. And I've got to stay busy to stay out of trouble, to
keep from going crazy, dying of depression. So I continue to do the
one thing in the world that I feel very very good at. I get an
enormous amount of pleasure out of it. It's the kind of pleasure that a
great athlete gets out of slam dunking a basketball. It's showing off at
a pretty high level.

"I'm very into imitating reality. I'm trying to get it straight in my
own mind and my own sight. It's a way of understanding and it's a
way of making things better than they are in reality; making things
come out right, come out right in a more formally interesting and
beautiful way than they do ever in life. When Lear comes out with
Cordelia dead in his arms and his whole life ruined and his kingdom
lost, he says that very desolate line, 'Never, never, never, never,
never.' But if you listen at the line carefully, it's a line of regular
trochaic pentameter. It's not a line of someone saying, "Baa ooh ska,

tragedy oy vey!' So you know that it's coming out in an orderly controlled way out of the mind of a genius. It's not coming in some catastrophic way out of the mouth of Satan, or someone screaming in the middle of a Beirut bomb site.

"Literature is not a slice of life, and it shouldn't be. Life is horrendous enough, far too horrendous. Literature shows us life in a far more organized and controlled way, so that we can begin to attempt to understand it in a way that we can't hope to understand the chaos of the world that just comes at us raw all day long like a hawk flying at our eyes.

"I had my first surgery the first week of June 1984. Within no time they realized something neurological was wrong and immediately sacked me into the hospital. I entered Duke Hospital on May 31, 1984 on the day of the total eclipse of the sun. Certainly no ancient Roman would have gone in under such terrible omens.

"Within a couple of days they had discovered this 10-ich tumor in my spine, and at that point they were basically unable to operate. They didn't have the tools to poke around in the spinal column with any degree of safety. So they did a very long scouting biopsy initially, and then shut me back up and gave me five and one half weeks of radiation, and about midway through the radiation I very rapidly began to lose my legs. So that by September of 1984 I basically couldn't walk.

"The radiation arrested the tumor for a couple of years until technology produced a new scalpel, an ultrasonic scalpel with which in May and November of 1986 they were able to go back and remove what was left of the tumor in there. We just did some scans six weeks ago, and there's no sign whatever of any tumor growth in there now.

"Death has been something that I have lived on very close terms with since I was 21, when my father died in my arms. In my hands anyway. I was holding his hand when he died. Most Americans have never laid eyes on a person in the instant in which he passes from life to death. Believe me, in my father's case at least, and in many others I'm told, it's not an easy moment in which people shut their eyes. It was a horrible moment of great physical struggle and reflexive reaction.

"So I'm somebody who's thought a lot about death for more than

half of my life. The challenge to me now is to learn to live with
steady, tremendous, 24-hour-a-day pain and greatly diminished
physical scope. It hasn't affected my writing except to make it better
and faster. It's a very difficult and complex ongoing challenge, but so
far it's not a situation that has silenced me."

The *Booklist* Interview:
Reynolds Price
Brad Hooper/1989

From *Booklist* (August 1989), 1944–45. Reproduced with permission of the American Library Association and Reynolds Price. Copyright © 1989 ALA.

Reynolds Price was born (in 1933) and raised in North Carolina. As a Rhodes scholar, he spent four years in England. Shortly after his return to the U.S., he began teaching at Duke University, where he now holds the James B. Duke Professorship of English. His first novel, *A Long and Happy Life*, was published in 1962 to loud applause from critics and fellow writers. Each subsequent novel, as well as his poetry, essays, drama, and now his recently released autobiography, *Clear Pictures* [BKL Ap 1 89], has added more shimmer to Price's reputation as a writer of superior dimensions.

With the publication of your memoir, you have now demonstrated proficiency in all literary forms. I would guess, though, that you find expression in the novel form to be more to your satisfaction. Am I right?

I wouldn't say it is more satisfying. I don't really feel I have special preference for any particular form. But in fact, the memoir went, for its length, more rapidly than anything I've ever written.

Your poetry is narrative. What impels you to render a certain idea into poetry rather than prose?

It's hard to say. The impulses just tend to arrive in the form in which I'm going to write them. I don't remember having begun something in prose and converted it into poetry. The idea comes already packaged. Most of my poems are indeed narrative poems, and they arrive as fairly brief pieces of narrative. If there would be any question, it would be whether to do it as a poem or as a short story. I think, indeed, they share the closest relationship of the literary genres. And I have very often written short stories that are in many ways intensely poetic, not so much in language but in concentration of narrative.

You hear a lot about a short story renaissance these days. Do you believe there truly is a current flowering of the short story in the U.S.?

There is indeed. I went on record in the New York Times Book Review six or eight years ago saying that I thought the short story was awfully exhausted. I think I was speaking accurately then, but shortly thereafter, and certainly in no relation to my saying so, there has been an exciting revival of the short story. I myself have recently been writing short stories for the first time in 20 years.

Any ideas why we are undergoing such a revival?

I couldn't begin to guess, because the number of magazines with national circulation that publish stories continues to shrink, so that the possibilities of publishing any individual short story are worse than they ever were.

Perhaps it has something to do with the growing number of creative writing programs.

But there have been writing courses since the 1920s and MFA programs for the past 40 years, so I'm not certain at all that that is one of the reasons. An avalanche situation develops when there are x number of people writing good stories. They begin to collect more and more people as they roll downhill, and more and more people get excited by the prospect. You reach a kind of point of critical mass when you have a number of good people writing and more good people say, "Gee, I can be doing that, too."

So it's fashionable again to write short stories?

Probably not so much fashionable as it looks possible again.

And, also, perhaps people can concentrate on the short story these days without fear of not being taken as true fiction writers?

Yes. I must say, though, that anyone with the hope of making any money better forget story writing.

Do you ever get criticized for working in different genres? We seem to be in an age of specialization, so do people expect you to work only in one area and leave the others alone?

The only time I run into that is when I do plays. And then I find a
lot of drama critics saying, "Well, Mr. Price is, of course, a novelist.
There are complicated subplots and people speak in an elevated
fashion." As though they'd never heard of Shakespeare or Chekhov
or anyone before the current minimalist writers.

*Getting back to the question of writing programs—Do you believe
there are simply too many of them?*
I agree with that. I think that in the 1960s and 1970s, as English
graduate programs came more and more under fire, a lot of English
departments invented themselves an MFA program in the hope of
getting more students. And the programs turned out to be popular.
And there are certain ones which are excellent. If a person is temper-
amentally able to keep up with that kind of schedule and work
within a group of people who are doing the same thing, they can
have fun with all that. I don't think that any of the programs would
claim to take a modestly talented person and make anything very
special out of him or her. I know people who have benefited a
lot from writing programs; I have also known a great many others
who gave up writing when they came out of writing schools and
became lawyers. Writing programs offer no magic formulas for
succeeding in life.

*From a student's point of view, what would you say were the
benefits and drawbacks of learning about writing in a classroom
setting?*
The benefits are that the students are required to write. I think the
drawbacks are that writing courses put people into unreal competi-
tion with other members of the class. In the real world, writers do not
line up and a bell goes off and they all run for the prize. And
programs often give very young writers a false sense of professional-
ism before they've really earned their professional spurs. In MFA
programs, there generally are a lot of people sitting around in bars
telling you how great they are or they are going to be great in a good
10 years down the road.

*Any comments on so-called minimalism? Or do you agree there is
a minimalist movement today?*
If I were to identify minimalists today, I would say the prime

flagbearer, as defined back in the early 1980s, would be Raymond Carver. I admire his work immensely. In general, I suppose I am not a minimalist. I don't know what the opposite is—a maximalist? I would much rather be a maximalist.

Do you think that the popularity of minimalism stems from creative writing programs? That Raymond Carver has been set up as a god for story writers?
Some programs are perfectly capable of getting people launched into a kind of couturier status. What writer is "in" this decade and who is "out." Like whether hems are short this season or hems are high.

It seems that for every southern writer there are the inevitable comparisons to Faulkner. Do you find the label "southern" writer restrictive or, in fact, do you think it energizing?
I've given up complaining, because it is unavoidable. Like the color of one's eyes. My first novel was published the year Faulkner died; it won the Faulkner Prize, and I came in for a lot of "Oh, well, he's the poor man's Faulkner." I spent so much time denying that in my early years, but the suggestion never arises anymore. In my case, it is perfectly clear that I am as different a kind of writer from Faulkner as could be imagined. I think Faulkner was an extraordinary writer, and it was understandable that for 20 years after his death reviewers and critics focused on him, so everybody after him was considered an imitation. I think that the very persistent arrival of new southern writers in every decade for the past 20 or 30 years has been quite amazing and gratifying and basically has nothing whatsoever to do with the life and work of William Faulkner.

I wonder why it is we seem so quick to label southern writers as such.
We do occasionally speak of Jewish novelists, but you never hear anymore of a "Chicago" novelist or a "New England" novelist. I think it represents a symptom of an ancient love-hate affair the rest of the nation has with the South. It is thought of as being in many ways another country. But certainly in the last 20 years, with the technocracy and interstate highways entering the South, it is becoming more like the rest of the country.

Speaking as a northerner, I would say that the term "southern writer" implies "naturally good writer."

I've begun to realize that. Especially in the 1960s and early 1970s when the South was behaving so badly with integration, there was sort of an insult involved in being labeled southern: those "yahoos" down there who can't speak proper English. But I think you're quite right, the term has less opprobrium attached to it than it did even 20 years ago. Part of it, too, is just reviewers whistling in the dark trying to think of things to say—so they talk about Mr. Price being southern for 50 words and then they have only 250 more to make up.

But you must admit it's pretty lofty company you keep.

Yes, it's an awfully lofty company; I'm delighted to know it's there, and I certainly never wanted to put any distance between the reality of the American South and myself. Besides the four years living in England I've lived here my entire life, and I live here because I love it.

Memory is certainly a vein you mine heavily in your writing, and your fiction is imbued with a sense of having been derived from stories families tell about themselves. How much do you feel a writer should abide by the old axiom that says writers should write about what they know?

I would go a step behind "Write what you know about" to a step I always try to take with my writing students, which is "Write about what you're passionately interested in." Probably 85 to 95 percent of the time that turns out to be a kind of emotional situation that springs out of the writer's own experience. On the other hand, I wouldn't say that if you are passionately interested in warfare in ancient Japan you shouldn't write a samurai novel. I don't tell students to write autobiographically but to try to find forces which are powerful or fascinating or terrifying and try to write at that level.

Flannery O'Connor said that anyone who has lived to the age of 14 has enough to write about for the rest of their life.

Various people give various ages. If you've been an alert child, certainly by the time you're into puberty you've been given most of your basic angles for watching the world. One of the definitions of greatness in art is that the greater the artist, the more that person is capable of accessing new areas of the world. Americans have tended to glorify the writer who drinks or goes crazy or in some other way silences himself or herself. To me the great heroes of art are people like Michelangelo who was still working at 89, or Verdi who was writing his greatest operas in his 80s, or writers who are capable of going on working into the grave.

Whom would you count among your literary masters?

At the beginning of my career, when it's most important, were Tolstoy and Flaubert. I was received very warmly in England by some extraordinary writers there—people like W. H. Auden and Stephen Spender, who greatly encouraged me and gave me a sense of what a writing career would be like. And Eudora Welty had encouraged me when I was a senior in college, and her work has remained a kind of touchstone of quality for me. I've been tremendously lucky in the dead and the living writers that I've known.

Do you believe writers have a certain nobility over the rest of humankind, that they exist in a closer state of grace, are more chosen?

I don't think it's more chosen, it's just the thing that I've got and I think it's a very good thing and I'd rather have it than a great many other talents that God seems to be in the business of giving out. Certainly it's a talent that has served me virtually all my life.

What, may I ask, are you working on now?

I've been writing a lot of short stories lately. I made a deal with myself when I began teaching a short-story writing class last January that I would try to write along with the students, and we discussed my stories in class right along with theirs. It was interesting for them and for me. I wound up with a lot of short stories as a result.

Are these going to be going out in a collection soon?

I hope so. And I have another novel finished, which will probably be the next book.

What is the novel about?

It is set in a boys' summer camp in the 1950s in the mountains of North Carolina, and it's really about an event told in the voice of one of the counselors, about a particularly gifted boy whom he comes to know in the course of that summer and whom he comes to encourage and about whom he discovers some of the awful tragic mysteries in the boy's life.

Do you think that something clicks when writers find the subject matter or theme or time period that for whatever reasons seems to be their destiny to write about?

I certainly do. There are things that I have tried to do that I couldn't get off page one. A friend of mine once said, "If I tried to write a historical novel set in Constantinople in the third century I would try to write the first line, 'The sun rose and the birds sang,' and I would wonder if they had birds in Constantinople and I would have to go study the ornithology of ancient Byzantium.' I would feel the same way. I'm such a stickler for authenticity that I'm pretty positive I could not write any fiction set any earlier than the mid-nineteenth century.

Any words of encouragement for those of our readers who yearn to have a career in writing??

I try very hard not to mislead young writers or even older people who are hoping to make a career of writing. It's a very difficult, complex, solitary job, and you shouldn't do it if you can help it. If you can quit, do. The world just doesn't need any more mediocre writers. We're quite well stocked, thank you very much. But if you feel compelled to do it and think you've got the goods, then by all means go to it, and I'll be rooting for you.

Index